T0330438

The Literary Text in the Digital Age

Editorial Theory and Literary Criticism

George Bornstein, Series Editor

Palimpsest: Editorial Theory in the Humanities, edited by George Bornstein and Ralph G. Williams

Contemporary German Editorial Theory, edited by Hans Walter Gabler, George Bornstein, and Gillian Borland Pierce

The Hall of Mirrors: Drafts & Fragments *and the End of Ezra Pound's* Cantos, by Peter Stoicheff

Textualterity: Art, Theory, and Textual Criticism, by Joseph Grigely

Emily Dickinson's Open Folios: Scenes of Reading, Surfaces of Writing, by Marta Werner

Editing D. H. Lawrence: New Versions of a Modern Author, edited by Charles L. Ross and Dennis Jackson

Scholarly Editing in the Computer Age: Theory and Practice, Third Edition, by Peter L. Shillingsburg

The Literary Text in the Digital Age, edited by Richard J. Finneran

The Literary Text in the Digital Age

Edited by Richard J. Finneran

Ann Arbor

THE UNIVERSITY OF MICHIGAN PRESS

Published in the United States of America by
The University of Michigan Press
Manufactured in the United States of America
∞ Printed on acid-free paper

1999 1998 1997 1996 4 3 2 1

A CIP catalog record for this book is available from the British Library.

Library of Congress Cataloging-in-Publication Data

The literary text in the digital age / edited by Richard J. Finneran.
p. cm. — (Editorial theory and literary criticism)
"Most of the essays in this collection were first delivered at scholarly conferences, particularly the 1993 meeting of the Association for Documentary Editing and the 1993 and 1994 meetings of the Modern Language Association"—Acknowledgments.
ISBN 0-472-10690-2 (alk. paper)
1. English literature—Criticism, Textual—Data processing. 2. English literature—Publishing—Data processing. 3. Manuscripts, English—Editing—Data processing. 4. Textual criticism—Data processing. 5. Text processing (Computer science) 6. Editing—Data processing. 7. Electronic publishing. I. Finneran, Richard J. II. Series.
PR21.L59 1996
820.9'000285'5—dc20 96-9951
CIP

Contents

Acknowledgments

Most of the essays in this collection were first delivered at scholarly conferences, particularly the 1993 meeting of the Association for Documentary Editing and the 1993 and 1994 meetings of the Modern Language Association. I am grateful to George Bornstein for his interest in publishing this volume in the University of Michigan Press series on Editorial Theory and Literary Criticism; and to Susan B. Whitlock and Kevin M. Rennells for their assistance in seeing the volume through to publication.

As a traditional Yeats scholar becoming involved with digital technology, I am especially indebted to the advice and assistance received at an early stage from Paul Kahn, George P. Landow, James Noblitt, William H. O'Donnell, Peter Robinson, and Peter Shillingsburg. Particular thanks also are due to Susan Hockey and the staff and participants in the 1993 Summer Seminar of the Princeton/Rutgers Center for Electronic Texts in the Humanities. Indeed, the welcome that the electronic scholarly community offered to an uninformed neophyte has been a rewarding experience of no small measure.

Preface

This collection of essays is based on the assumption that the development of digital technology and its widespread availability on the desktop computer is bringing about not simply a modification or an improvement in the ways in which literary texts are created, preserved, disseminated, and studied, but a revolution, a fundamental paradigm shift. As George P. Landow has argued in *Hypertext: The Convergence of Contemporary Critical Theory and Technology,*

> Electronic text processing marks the next major shift in information technology after the development of the printed book. It promises (or threatens) to produce effects on our culture, particularly on our literature, education, criticism, and scholarship, just as radical as those produced by Gutenberg's movable type.[1]

Or, as Richard A. Lanham suggested in a lecture later incorporated in *The Electronic Word: Democracy, Technology, and the Arts,* "the fundamental 'operating system' for the humanities is changing from the book to the digital multimedia computer screen."[2]

We live, in other words, in the twilight of the Age of the Printed Book. It is at least arguable that many of today's children, and most if not all of their children, will come to think of the printed book as a quaint device from another era—useful in many ways, to be sure, and no doubt never to altogether disappear; but fixed, linear, noninteractive, and, most restrictive of all, essentially confined to a single medium. Indeed, many of those aspects of the printed book responsible for its hegemony over the last several centuries are precisely those that are now seen as crucial shortcomings, yet another instance of a process well described by W. B. Yeats: "every movement, in feeling or in thought, prepares in the dark by its own increasing clarity and confidence its own executioner."[3]

Before proceeding, let me say that I do not dispute the principle that any revolution not only creates a new order but also destroys an old one. There are certain aspects of the printed book that digital technology will doubtless never fully replicate or replace, and among those are some that many of the contributors to, and readers of, this volume have come to cherish. But there is no use in denying the future, considerable loss in the attempt, and, as *The Literary Text in the Digital Age* hopes to demonstrate, significant gain to be had by embracing the new technology.

In what may be either a historical accident or a stroke of luck—Yeats's Thirteenth Cone intervening for once on our side—the availability of hypermedia technology for the personal computer has coincided with a fundamental shift in textual theory, away from the notion of a single-text "definitive edition" and toward a recognition of both the integrity of discrete versions of a work and the importance of nonverbal elements, particularly the "bibliographical codes" described by Jerome McGann and the "contextual codes" noted by George Bornstein, among others.[4] A traditional printed edition is able to accommodate this new thinking in textual theory either awkwardly or not at all; in contrast, digital technology is its necessary and inevitable realization.

Thus, although many of the first attempts by literary scholars and editors to employ digital technology resulted in "electronic books" (more evidence for the truism that significant new developments often begin by attempting to replicate what in fact they will replace), the present challenge is to discover the full potential of the new medium, to produce editions—or, if you prefer, "archives"—that transcend the inherent limitations of the printed book and that present the literary text in a form now understood to be the norm.

The Literary Text in the Digital Age opens with a survey by Susan Hockey of past developments and the present state of electronic editions. Peter Shillingsburg outlines the *desiderata* for such projects. In complementary essays, C. M. Sperberg-McQueen and John Lavagnino address the crucial question of text encoding. There follows a series of essays that discuss particular projects while also addressing theoretical issues: Hoyt Duggan on *Piers Plowman;* Peter Robinson on the *Canterbury Tales;* Ian Lancashire on English Renaissance texts; Jerome McGann on the poems and paintings of Dante Gabriel Rossetti; Simon Gatrell on Thomas Hardy; and William H. O'Donnell and Emily A. Thrush on Yeats. Phillip E. Doss and Charles L. Ross relate the question of electronic editing to some of the central issues in contemporary critical theory. John Unsworth concludes by placing the developments in digital technology in a wide cultural context. In the afterword, A. Walton Litz reflects on the essays in *The Literary Text in the Digital Age* from the perspective of one of the senior scholars of modern literature.

My remarks in this preface, as well as some in the essays that follow, underscore the possibilities of electronic texts while suggesting the limitations of printed editions, including some to which many of us have devoted (and indeed continue to devote) considerable effort. Arguably, we have not been immune from the inherent human characteristic of always believing that the present moment is one of transition, if not of revolution, and that a new and better dispensation is just around the corner, as near as that elusive green light across the bay in *The Great Gatsby*. And yet, and yet. . . . "All's changed, changed utterly." Scholars like Landow and Lanham are right: we *are* at the beginning of a time of profound change, one that will forever alter our notions of "literature." Thus, it is clear that if the achievement that we have come to value is to remain a viable part of our cultural inheritance, it needs to be made accessible to future generations in the form that they will understand as the standard way of interacting with "monuments of magnificence." *The Literary Text in the Digital Age* is a gesture in that direction.

NOTES

1. *Hypertext: The Convergence of Contemporary Critical Theory and Technology* (Baltimore: Johns Hopkins University Press, 1992), 19.
2. "The Implications of Electronic Information for the Sociology of Knowledge," available by anonymous ftp from cni.org, in the directory cni/documents/tech.schol.human/papers; *The Electronic Word: Democracy, Technology, and the Arts* (Chicago: University of Chicago Press, 1993).
3. *Per Amica Silentia Lunae* (1917), in *Later Essays,* ed. William H. O'Donnell (New York: Charles Scribner's Sons, 1994), 14.
4. See McGann, "What Is Critical Editing?" *Text* 5 (1991): 15–29; George Bornstein, "What Is the Text of a Poem by Yeats?" in *Palimpsest: Editorial Theory in the Humanities,* ed. George Bornstein and Ralph G. Williams (Ann Arbor: University of Michigan Press, 1993), 167–93. Taken together, these codes encompass

those aspects of a text apart from the "linguistic codes," or the words themselves. Put in another way, textual scholars have largely moved away from the position enunciated in the opening lyric of Yeats's *Collected Poems*—"Words alone are certain good"—and toward a recognition of the importance of what he described in the closing poem of that volume as "the figured page." *The Poems,* rev. ed., ed. Richard J. Finneran (New York: Macmillan, 1989), 7, 448.

Creating and Using Electronic Editions

Susan Hockey

The term *electronic edition* is now in fairly widespread use, but there seems to be no clear specification of its meaning. Rather than attempt to define the differences between electronic archives, scholarly editions, critical editions, diplomatic editions, documentary editions, or whatever, in this essay I discuss various methods of creating and using electronic representations of humanities primary-source material. The emphasis is on how to make those representations available to the scholarly community in such a way that the potential of the electronic medium for new forms of publication and research is fully exploited while still maintaining the integrity and authority we associate with the traditional printed edition.

USING COMPUTERS TO PREPARE EDITIONS: A HISTORICAL SUMMARY

Computers have been used in literary scholarship ever since 1949, when Father Busa began work on his monumental *Index Thomisticus*. Early work concentrated on the preparation of concordances and indexes for publication,[1] but even in the 1960s, a number of groups recognized the possibilities afforded by the computer for the compiler of an edition. Attempts to write collation programs date back to the early 1960s, the most notable examples being OCCULT[2] and the programs written by Vinton Dearing.[3] Other projects began to develop mathematical models of stemmata; often the interest lay as much in the mathematics as in the texts being studied. In the early 1970s Penny Gilbert developed a set of programs intended to provide a comprehensive set of tools for the textual editor.[4] Not only did they collate multiple manuscripts, but they also stored the variant readings in the computer for further processing and analysis. In Tübingen under the direction of Wilhelm Ott, work was also well advanced on TUSTEP, which consists of a set of text analysis tools oriented toward the compiler of an edition.[5] Of these programs, only TUSTEP is still in use. Hans Gabler's edition of *Ulysses* is one of its most notable products,[6] although TUSTEP can provide material in other formats as well. Also in the 1970s, David Chesnutt pioneered the use of computers in the documentary-editing community.[7]

By the early 1980s computers were used by a good many compilers of editions.[8] A fairly typical methodology was to perform any collation by hand and then to create an electronic representation of one manuscript, perhaps with some variant readings. A concordance of the electronic text was then generated by programs such as the Oxford Concordance Program. The editor could then use the concordance as a tool when deciding on particular readings or preparing a commentary or glossary. For a glossary the entries would normally be lemmatized manually, usually by editing the file on a word processor. Sometimes an analysis of the variant readings was also carried out, using cluster analysis or other mathematical models of the stemmata. Among the early proponents of these tools for the analysis of variants were Gian Piero Zarri[9] and particularly John Griffith, who was probably the first to use cluster analysis techniques to study manuscript traditions.[10] Electronic copy could then also be used as input to a typesetting or desktop publishing system for the final printed version. In 1978 a conference in Paris brought together scholars from different disciplines who were using computers for textual editing, and the published proceedings of that meeting give a good overview of the state of the art at that time.[11] It was these methodologies that Peter Robinson studied as he began work on Collate and the series of programs that derived from its use. Peter Shillingsburg's CASE (Computer-Assisted Scholarly Editing) system employs similar methods.

These early methodologies use computer programs to simulate the traditional model of the edition. The final product is in print form and is thus constrained by the format of the printed page. Discussion about the use of computers has concentrated as much on achieving the final appearance of the print product as it has on tools for the processes that precede page makeup of the final text. Editors have looked for programs that can handle multilevel footnotes or print various nonstandard characters, and the word processing program Nota Bene was created with the needs of this community foremost. Those who prepared camera-ready copy have had to become experts in typesetting and book design.[12] Prose text in particular could create a lot of extra work if it was reformatted several times using different line lengths and type sizes that cause the lineation to change. More often than not, the editors of prose texts have had to spend time rekeying the entries in a glossary to correspond with a new pagination generated by their publishers' typesetting program—after they had created a glossary keyed to their word processors' pagination.

The electronic medium frees us from the format of the printed page, but we need to think about what is taking the place of the page. Even though he or she can interact with an electronic edition in many different ways, the user still sees the material on a rectangular shape, a screen, which in the current state of technology is not as easy to read as print. It is likely that print will continue to exist as a reading medium of choice for some time. Developments for the electronic medium should concentrate on those functions that cannot easily be replicated in print. These functions are not yet well understood and much research still needs to be done on what scholars may want to do with electronic resources. It is unlikely that there will ever be a definitive set of functions, but at the present stage of our understanding we can make a start in the right direction.

CREATING AN ELECTRONIC TEXT

By *electronic text* we mean a transcription of the text, as opposed to a digital image. (Digital images are discussed below.) Most electronic texts in the humanities have been created by keyboarding from the original, and this is still the recommended method of input for most projects. Many hopes have been pinned on optical character recognition (OCR), but this technology is still at a fairly rudimentary stage. A typical OCR system consists of a scanner and a desktop computer that drives the scanner and runs the recognition software. The normal process is for a bit-mapped image of the page of text to be created first. This is then analyzed by the recognition software, which converts the data into ASCII text. OCR is most successful with modern printed text. Most OCR systems use a dictionary to help in recognizing words in which one or two letters are doubtful. These dictionaries are rather like spell-checkers in a word processor. They may work only for the English language and thus be unsuitable for material in other languages or multilingual text. Even with this type of material a rate of no more than 99.5 percent accuracy can be achieved and it is often less than that. Accuracy of 99.9 percent would mean one mistake per one thousand characters, or about one mistake per ten lines. Common misreads can be *h* and *b*, *c* and *e*, *rn* and *mm*, and the letter *l* and number *1*.

The list of material that is unsuitable for OCR may sound familiar to readers of this volume. It includes old printed books in which the baseline is uneven; manuscripts in which the letters are either joined together or are inconsistent in shape; handwriting, which can be even more inconsistent than manuscripts; newspapers in which the inking is blurred; and microfilm and microfiche prints, in which the image can be blurred.[13] Even if the text can be read by an OCR system, much more work needs to be done on it. OCR yields a typographic representation of the text. It shows page numbers, line numbers, footnotes, and so on exactly where they appear on the page but does not indicate what they are. As we understand more about electronic text, we see that a typographic representation on its own is not enough for electronic manipulation. (See the third section, below, for a further discussion of this point in the context of markup.)

The levels of accuracy reached by the current generation of OCR software on most types of texts are not high enough for scholarly applications, particularly in editions where the actual text itself is under close scrutiny. Fine detail is very important in this application. Even if the OCR system can recognize the letters, it may not fare so well on the punctuation, which may be just as important. Commas and periods are often confused, and extraneous material can be seen as apostrophes. Sometimes a space is inserted between a word and the punctuation that follows it.

Those OCR programs that perform better tend to be more difficult to use. They can be trained to recognize specific typefaces.[14] In this training process the machine is shown sample bits of text and an operator identifies letters whose shapes the machine then "remembers." Ligatures and accented characters can be included in this training phase. This means that the machine can be fine-tuned to the peculiarities of specific typefaces. This approach is therefore more suitable if a large amount of material of a similar appearance is to be scanned. It is not so cost-effective for many different small items.

Most substantial textual data entry projects in the humanities do not use OCR. The material is keyboarded, either offshore, where costs can be kept down, or by personnel hired locally. Much better accuracy can be achieved in this way, even when keyboarders are not familiar with the material. It has been said that keyboarders who cannot read the language create the most accurate text because they do not subconsciously correct "errors" in the original or regularize spelling.

A detailed discussion of text entry methods may seem unnecessary in the context of this essay, but I have included it because creating the electronic text is the major cost of any electronic edition. A clear idea of what is feasible may prevent wasted time and effort, and an assumption from the beginning that OCR may be unfeasible may provide a more realistic perspective on the task of data entry. It is perhaps worthy to also be aware that projects making use of volunteer labor to input texts have often found it created extra work. With the best will in the world, volunteers may want to do things their own way and may not follow instructions as carefully as they might.

MARKUP AND THE RELEVANCE OF THE TEXT ENCODING INITIATIVE FOR EDITIONS

An electronic text is much more useful when it contains markup to encode specific features. Markup makes explicit for computer processing features that are implicit for the human reader. Other essays in this volume address markup in much more detail, but a few remarks here on the history of markup schemes will help to clarify why good markup is so important for the electronic edition.

Until recently two different types of markup schemes developed in parallel. One was typographic and is most readily seen now in word processors in which functions, such as Reveal Codes in WordPerfect, show the codes that drive the printing or display of the text. Earlier manifestations included many proprietary typesetting programs as well as document formatters and typesetting software mainly used in the academic world, such as TROFF, Scribe, and TEX. Such programs are driven by codes embedded in the text, for example, to center the next line or move down two blank lines. The function of typography is to reinforce the text and help the (human) reader to follow and understand it. However, typographic markup on its own is not rich enough for a computer program to "understand" the text well enough to do anything with it other than print it or search for typographic features. A simple example shows the problem. A word in italics may be part of a title, may be emphasized, or may be foreign. These functions need to be distinguished for a program to search all the titles embedded in the text or to make an index of foreign words. Even if all the foreign words have been found, the index needs to show their locations within the text. This means that referencing information must be embedded in the text in such a way that it can be recognized as such and not treated as if it was part of the text. Many different referencing schemes exist for humanities texts, and a markup scheme should be flexible enough to handle all of them and to allow for multiple parallel referencing systems, which are not uncommon. Typographic representation is not enough to indicate references. For example, act and scene numbers in a play may appear as *Act I* or *Scene I* in a printed text, but there is no easy way to distinguish them from the words *Act, Scene,* and *I*. Folio or line numbers may appear in the margin, difficult to distinguish from numbers that are part of the text.

Almost all early attempts to encode electronic texts for analysis devised markup schemes that were predominantly typographic, because that was all that the compilers knew. Most also used a different syntax for encoding references than for encoding other features of interest. It was some time before enough was understood about encoding and computer analysis of texts to see that a richer markup scheme was needed. Incompatibility of existing schemes was by then also becoming more of a problem. The typical project created an electronic text in a markup scheme that could not be used by other programs. The scheme was often capable of encoding only one theoretical orientation and was not well documented, so that persons other than the compiler were not sure what they had got when they tried to use the text.

All this led to the development of the Standard Generalized Markup Language (SGML), which became an international standard in 1986.[15] SGML provides a way of encoding electronic texts that is independent of any particular computer hardware or software. It consists of plain ASCII files with markup tags embedded in the text that are themselves ASCII characters. The principle of SGML is descriptive, not prescriptive. SGML views a text as a collection of objects that are interrelated. Normally this relationship is hierarchic, but objects can override the hierarchy. Multiple hierarchies are possible in SGML, but they are somewhat clumsy to deal with. The markup indicates what a particular component within a text is, not what a program is to do with that object. This means that different programs can perform different functions on the same object, for example to print all titles in italics, to search all titles, or to make all titles "hot text" in a hypertext.

SGML has several more advantages for the compiler of an electronic edition. An SGML text can easily be moved from one platform to another. It is not locked into any particular hardware or software. Given the expense of creating a good electronic text, it is essential that the text will last for a long time. Although problems of hardware incompatibility such as disk formats are largely overcome now, those of data and file formats remain. A plain ASCII file and one that can be reduced to the seven-bit character set that is transmissible across all networks ensures longevity. SGML is much richer and more flexible than any other markup scheme. Almost anything can be defined as an element or object within an SGML-encoded text. The encoding can be incremental, in that different people can add new encodings to the text within the same overall syntax. The encoding can also include analytic and interpretive material as well as objects that are directly visible within the text. SGML also contains mechanisms for cross-referencing that define pointers to other elements or places within the text.

The Text Encoding Initiative (TEI) has provided an SGML tag set suitable for use with scholarly texts in the humanities.[16] It includes some four hundred elements that have been defined as a result of a detailed analysis of the features that occur in humanities texts. Several aspects of the TEI address the needs of compilers of electronic editions. Nonstandard characters can be dealt with by entity references or by a writing-system declaration that allows the encoder to define his or her own transliteration scheme. A tag set for the transcription of primary sources includes ways of encoding abbreviations and expansions, corrections and conjectures, additions and deletions, substitutions, cancellation of deletions and other markings, text omitted from or supplied in the transcription, as well as nonlinguistic phenomena such as document hands, damage, illegibility, supplied text, and ways of representing space or lines. The tag set for a critical apparatus provides several different methods for encoding the apparatus and linking it to the text. Another set of tags includes techniques for indicating certainty and responsibility and can be used to provide additional information if a reading is not clear.

These tag sets are simply a start in defining ways of encoding source material. They may satisfy the needs of some projects, while others will need to encode features not defined within the TEI scheme. However, this is not an argument against using the TEI. Methods for extending the tag sets are well defined, and sufficient information is provided in the TEI guidelines about modification of the Document Type Definitions (DTDs) that give the formal specifications of the SGML elements permissible in a text. Much work is still to be done in the area of encoding the transcription of sources, but the TEI scheme provides a much better foundation on which to build than any other existing scheme. SGML is often described as a markup scheme that emphasizes the structure of the text, but there is no reason why it should not be used to encode the physical appearance of the source. The TEI has not yet concentrated as much on this area as it has on others, but it is not difficult to add tags that encode more information about the physical appearance of the source, if that is of interest.

The TEI contains some other tag sets that will become increasingly important for the compiler of an electronic edition. One of these tag sets is concerned with linking, segmentation, and alignment. It provides SGML mechanisms to link sections of text and, more generally, to point to other text. In effect these are hypertext links or cross-referencing mechanisms. SGML includes a mechanism for cross-referencing within a document, and the TEI has extended it to provide cross-referencing to other documents and to images. The cross-reference can point anywhere within the document, not just to the beginning (often what happens with the Hypertext Markup Language [HTML]). The destination of the cross-reference can be identified by the SGML elements within which it occurs or by the occurrence of strings of characters or (for images) coordinates of a location within the image. The destination of the cross-reference may be a single point or an area of text. An example in the TEI guidelines shows how these mechanisms may be used to encode a modern commentary on an older text and associate passages of text and notes with individuals mentioned, ancient authors imitated, or thematic content. The TEI also includes ways of linking disparate elements in a single document or different documents and of representing correspondence or alignment among groups of text elements. The correspondence tags could be used, for example, for parallel texts or translations.

Another set of tags provides ways of encoding analytic and interpretive information. This can be done simply by notes attached to a point in, or span of, the text, or by feature structures. A feature structure is a general-purpose data structure that can represent many different types of information. Within the TEI scheme they are intended mostly for encoding analytic and interpretive information. A feature structure can be related to any point in the text or with any span of text. In fact, more than one feature structure can be related to the same section of text, thus allowing multiple and possibly conflicting interpretations to be associated with the same text. It is also possible to indicate who is responsible for each interpretation. So far these have been mostly used for linguistic analysis, but there is no reason they should not be used for literary and historical interpretation. The guidelines do in fact contain one example for historical data. Anyone looking at the chapter on feature structures in the guidelines will see that in the raw SGML form these are complex and somewhat intimidating. The SGML is needed for a machine-independent representation of them, but users should not need to see it. It is expected that SGML of this complexity will be generated by programs from another format and that it will be transformed to a more readable form for display. One can imagine a simple point-and-click or drag-and-drop operation to associate interpretations with sections of text.

The TEI header is also very important for the compiler of the electronic edition. The header provides documentation for the electronic text. The first major section within it is the file description, which includes elements that map more or less directly on to fields in a Machine Readable Cataloging (MARC) record and can thus be used as a chief source for catalogers.[17] But more than bibliographic information is needed to document an electronic text. The encoding description documents the editorial principles that governed the transcription of the text from its source. This is where the encoder defines how, for example, quotation marks and hyphenation are treated and specifies under what circumstances any corrections and normalization has been made to the text. The profile description brings together information characterizing various descriptive aspects of the text, for example, language usage and classificatory information. The fourth section is a revision history in which changes to the text are noted with an indication of who made them and when they were made.

The TEI header represents the first systematic attempt to document an electronic text file. It is designed for use by catalogers and software developers as well as the end users of the text. For many of the features in the header, one chooses between describing the information in prose text and using a subset of elements that gives more granularity to the information. The latter format is more suitable for computer processing, but users have so far tended to prefer the prose format, as it is simpler for them. Software to encourage the use of the nonprose format would be helpful.

Nontextual Data

So far this essay has concentrated on handling textual data, but the electronic edition is going to contain digital images, sound, video, and so forth. The technology for dealing with these and our understanding of how they might best be used in an electronic environment are far behind our knowledge of handling text. Digital images, sound, and video are of course much more recent, but we can learn a lot from the history of working with texts. First, since the cost of creation of an electronic resource is so high, it makes sense to do it as well as possible. This means high-resolution images and high-quality sound and video. At present these take up large amounts of storage space, but this will be less of a worry in the future as hardware costs come down and the capacity of disk drives increases.

An image is not sufficient on its own. It needs the kind of information in the TEI header to make it usable. There is scope for extending the header to describe images. The file description would need to have some information about the type of image file. One can imagine extensions to the encoding description that document whether the image was enhanced or otherwise manipulated as it was being digitized. Many of the functions of the profile description and revision history would stay the same. Similar methods would be needed for sound. The TEI guidelines already include a chapter on encoding spoken texts. The profile description includes elements that describe the participants in a conversation and the linking mechanisms allow for links to audio. Digital video is only just beginning, but there is no reason why this kind of approach should not be extended to video as well.

DELIVERING THE ELECTRONIC EDITION

With SGML and the TEI we now have a much better understanding of how to create a good electronic text. Effort must now turn to making that text usable as an operational electronic edition. SGML allows us to separate data from the delivery vehicle that presents data to users. This is very important, but it is often difficult to grasp until someone has worked with computers for some time. All too often, projects begin by choosing software after an examination of what exists within the right price range. The choice is often determined by features of software that are primarily visual, for example, the display of high-quality images or the ability to handle nonstandard characters. Functionality often takes second place, but it is functionality that determines what the program can be used for. If the functionality is poor, the scope of the research that can be performed on that data is also poor. It takes a lot longer to grasp the scope of the functionality of a program than it does to see what is on the screen, and it is inevitable that sales and marketing efforts concentrate on immediate reactions to the visual.

Once software is chosen, new projects often start to prepare data for it, either by using data entry forms within the software or by preparing material according to its required input format. Two or three years later, the project may have a good deal of data locked into one software product that may not still be supported. In five years' time, better software will probably be available, and much effort may then be spent converting the data from one program to another. Not only does this conversion take time, it may also result in loss of information if the different programs have different underlying data models. The advantages of SGML for an archival format of the data are very clear here. Since it is richer, it enables the user to create his or her own data model with very few constraints. The model can easily be modified if new material comes up that does not fit into the existing structure. A program can convert from the SGML format to almost any other format. This may result in some loss of information, but the richness is still there in the archival format.

New projects often also focus too much on the mode of delivery. They want to make a CD-ROM, but are less clear about what software will be used for accessing that CD-ROM. CD-ROM is still the medium of choice for many electronic publications, largely because it is easier for publishers and librarians to handle. It fits in better with procedures for handling books and in some ways can be seen as an extension of them. However, for the long term CD-ROM has serious limitations. There has been much discussion about the longevity of CD-ROMs. Since the medium has been around only a short time, no one knows whether they will be physically readable after a long period. Even if it is readable, the format of the files stored on it will most likely not be. CD-ROMs are also too small. They cannot hold sufficient data, especially when images and other nontextual media are used. Even with text only, six hundred megabytes is not enough for a lot of text indexed in different ways. Multiple CD-ROMs are awkward to handle, even on a CD-ROM tower or jukebox.

Since the user cannot write to it, the CD-ROM presents a closed system. The information can be used only in ways that have been predetermined, largely by how the data are indexed. More often than not, the software developers build the indexes, and they may have little understanding of the detailed needs of scholars. At present a variety of CD-ROMs are appearing that contain humanities primary-source material. Each provider or publisher is using different software, with a bewildering variety of user interfaces.[18] For the individual scholar who may purchase only one or two of these, learning how to use them may not be such a problem. For the library that purchases most of them, the support costs can be very expensive.

THE NETWORK AND NETWORK NAVIGATION TOOLS

The network holds out much more promise for the electronic edition of the future. *Network* is here taken to mean remote distribution and access of data, that is, the means to use data stored in many different places. We are at the very beginnings of the potential for networked information. At present the Internet seems to be synonymous with the current generation of network navigation tools. These are reasonably adequate for the kind of information service now in common use, but they are limited in scope and cannot deal with the complexities of much scholarly material. File Transfer Protocol (FTP) provides fast transfer of a file from one place to another, but no other tools to operate on that file. Gopher presents a simple set of hierarchic menus and is best suited for the purpose for which it was originally developed, that is, a campuswide information service. It provides limited search facilities, but no other tools for analysis of the text. WAIS (Wide Area Information Server) provides a more sophisticated way of searching texts that is based on latent semantic indexing. This approach is suitable for scientific or technical material where the search is for all documents about a specific topic. For humanities primary-source material, the search may be for almost anything, including function words, rare words, punctuation, and codicological features. A WAIS server is unlikely to provide access to any of these, and it would also be unable to cope well with foreign words.

At the time of writing this essay the World Wide Web is seen by many as the future for network navigation, particularly through the Netscape interface. Netscape's appeal is visual, and it can be very attractive to new users, particularly when images are displayed. It also incorporates some hypertext facilities. However, the underlying data format is limited, and the hypertext linking is primitive. The World Wide Web uses a simple SGML application called Hypertext Markup Language. Its current implementation includes about fifty elements. They are more suitable for prose text and are oriented toward the display of that text on a screen (or in print). HTML includes a tag <*title*> but very little else for documenting the electronic text. The hypertext links in it are built on a system of Uniform Resource Locators (URLs) that provides a unique location identifier for each document on the Web. But these links are also very simple in nature. Whenever a Web user accesses a document remotely, the entire document is transferred to the user's machine—hardly sensible if the user requires just a few lines from a long text. In order to get around this problem, documents on the World Wide Web are being broken up into small pieces, with each piece stored in a separate file. It would make far more sense for the linking mechanism to use the SGML structure to access parts of the document. The TEI's hypertext mechanisms contain the structures needed to do this. Another annoying feature of the Web is that backtracking usually takes the user back to the beginning of a document, even though the link began somewhere in the middle of it. The World Wide Web is therefore giving us a taste of what is possible, but its limitations are now beginning to be felt.[19] It is most useful as a front-end interface and display mechanism for a more sophisticated retrieval-and-analysis system.

Another problem with existing Internet tools and resources is the absence of any kind of authentication of the material. There is no way of knowing whether a document is accurate other than to read it and check it. Documents are copied from one system to another, often also going through various reformatting programs that may not work perfectly, particularly if they have been written by amateur enthusiasts. There is no way of knowing the source or provenance of a document. Unless the provider of the document inserts this information somewhere, there is often not much more than an electronic mail header to go by. Anyone can put anything on the Internet, and it is then entirely up to the user of the information to determine whether it has any value. Maintenance of Internet information is also becoming a serious issue. Those who put information on the network are sometimes less enthusiastic about ensuring that it is up-to-date and that the links it provides to other material still work. Backup, testing, and updating of software on host machines all need to be done, but individuals are in general less likely than institutions to deal with these on a long-term basis.

BUILDING THE ELECTRONIC EDITION OF THE FUTURE

What then would be the components of a network-based system for supporting electronic editions? Such a system would need to satisfy many different and possibly conflicting scholarly concerns and also be manageable from the point of view of librarians, who will increasingly take over the maintenance of electronic resources. The core of the system would be one or several linked host sites where master copies of the editions would reside. Ideally the master copies would consist of transcriptions of the text and digital images of the source material. There may be one or many versions of each text. The archival versions of the text would be encoded in SGML, and at present only the TEI's implementation of SGML comes anywhere near being able to handle this kind of material. There would be a standard format for the archival form of the images that would be at the highest resolution possible. A minimum set of TEI elements would be required, and many texts would have more than the minimum encoding. This archival form of the texts would be the one that is guaranteed to be available for the future.

Each text and image would be accompanied by header information. This would require some enhancement of the TEI header, particularly to deal with images and so that the mapping to a MARC record could be done automatically. The archival format would also include detailed levels of granularity rather than prose text to make the header more amenable to computer processing. There would be a central repository of this common descriptive information. The repository of descriptive information could be accessed directly, or through the World Wide Web or an OPAC (on-line public-access catalog). It would form the major entry point for people who want to use the electronic-edition system.

Software to access the edition archive would provide a range of options for the user. The functionality of this software is very important. It should be capable of handling detailed and specific requirements as well as more general-purpose and easy-to-use options. To date, not much research has been done on the user requirements for humanities software applications. Most of the knowledge we have is based on the long tradition of concordance and retrieval software in humanities computing. It is worth noting that the two most successful programs here (Textual Analysis Computing Tools [TACT] from the University of Toronto[20] and the Oxford Concordance Program [OCP][21] from Oxford University) were both developed within humanities computing centers that had a lot of experience of user requirements. For OCP a specification was developed, widely circulated for comment, and discussed at various conferences before the program was written. Retrieval software for the electronic-edition archive will need to draw on some of the special features of OCP and TACT. Both programs allow many different alphabets and character sets to be handled, giving the user much flexibility in the way they are defined. They allow indexes on the ends as well as the beginnings of words, which is important for languages that inflect heavily or for some kinds of verse. The user can search for punctuation and other features that are not strictly part of the text. There are also options to search for words by frequency, for example to find all the once-occurring words. Collocation and phrase searches are also provided. Various options for displaying or printing the results of a search or analysis allow individual usages to be studied in detail. TACT uses UNIX-style regular expressions as part of its query language. Neither TACT nor OCP uses SGML.

Building the functions of TACT and OCP (and more) into a retrieval system based on an SGML application like the TEI would make a very powerful tool for humanities research and teaching. However, retrieval techniques have not developed much since they were first used in the 1960s.[22] String searches with Boolean logic are a very crude way of examining text. As more and more text becomes available in electronic form, string searches will be less and less successful. There need to be ways of separating the different meanings of homographs and for lemmatization (putting words under their dictionary headings). Morphological and syntactic analysis would also help. Current research in computational linguistics is focusing on looking at text beyond the level of the graphic word and on developing and testing some of these methodologies. These efforts are concentrated mainly on scientific and technical material. Humanities texts, particularly editions, are much more complex, and the things that users want to do with them are more varied. Applying these methodologies to humanities texts would be a major challenge, but one that we know how to tackle now much more than we did a few years ago.

Language engineering research is now concentrating on the development of electronic linguistic resources, such as lexical databases.[23] The retrieval program uses the database to derive a lot more information about the search term before it searches the text. The normal procedure for building a lexical database is to convert a print dictionary into electronic form and then restructure the material into semantic hierarchies. For each word the database would also contain the lemma, morphological analysis, possibly the metrical analysis, and some indication of the semantic field. The latter can be specified by common collocates and references to items above and below it in the semantic hierarchy. The lexical database can be treated as a dynamic resource that is constantly being enhanced with new material as new texts are processed. Different databases would be necessary for each natural language, but they can be linked in some ways. Having such a tool on the network and linked to the electronic-edition archive would open up many more possibilities for research on the editions and make them more useful also for teaching purposes.

There is now a reasonable body of expertise in retrieval methodologies, but the network and the electronic edition are making other techniques and functions possible. Our understanding of these is much less complete, and there is a need for much more research on what scholars want to do with electronic editions. However, with what we know now it is possible to define some functions that would be useful. The electronic environment provides scope for multiple versions of material. It should be possible to model the development of a text from its early state to later ones and to create all intermediate states (either existing or hypothetical), if sufficient tagging is embedded in the text to reflect all these possibilities. The question would then arise of how to document these different versions of the text—whether a TEI header would be needed for each of them and whether much of this header can be created automatically. In the traditional view of an edition, the apparatus for any word or section of text can be inspected at the click of a mouse button as a hypertext link, either showing all the witnesses or just a selection of them.

Annotation is another process that the electronic environment can facilitate. It is technically possible to have a text on the network that can be accessed and annotated by many different people.[24] Whether this is desirable or not is a different matter, not a technical issue, and is not addressed here. One can envisage this kind of annotation best operating in some kind of controlled environment where specific users are given privileges to make annotations much in the same way as multiaccess database software has access privileges for certain users. When the annotations are made, the software would add to each annotation information about who made it, when, and so on. It should be possible to store the annotations internally in the TEI's feature structures, although the user would never need to see them in this format. Multiple and possibly conflicting annotations could be associated with the same section of text. The annotation management software would control who makes the annotations and present a kind of menu of annotations to users, who would use this to decide which annotations they wanted to look at.

When text is properly marked up, the electronic environment facilitates using only part of a document. The ability to access small units of information from many different places on the network can be exploited in many areas of humanities scholarship. For this to work effectively there will need to be an underlying markup scheme that can be processed universally. But fragmenting the information into small pieces for storage is cumbersome to manage, and so the linking mechanisms from one document to another need to be flexible. Ideally they could be to absolute positions within a document or to positions that would be computed on the fly. We are barely beginning to understand how this might operate, but one can speculate that scholarly interpretation of the future might consist, not of written prose, but of links between already existing material, with annotation on the links indicating why that link has been made.

The electronic-edition archive would also have software for handling images. Image manipulation software typically provides enhancement, rotation, zooming, or superimposing one image on another, all of which can help in the study of certain manuscript features. Descriptive information about the images would also be provided in a modified form of the TEI header. However, the strength of this system is for images of the source material for the electronic edition to be linked to full SGML-encoded transcripts of the material. When a word is retrieved from the text, it should be possible either to display the image of the page where that word occurs or to display the transcript of the text. But ideally the linking of the text to image should be at the word or even character level. Since making these links manually is extremely time-consuming, research is now concentrating on automating at least part of this process.[25] Linking at this level will make possible a number of functions that should be very attractive to researchers. When a word is retrieved from the transcript, the display of the image can highlight exactly where it occurs. The user should also be able to outline a word or codicological feature on an image with the cursor and then go to all (or selected) other places in the text where that word or feature occurs. Alternatively, he or she can outline some text on an image and add an annotation to that text. All the other text-retrieval and annotation functions will also be available.

Authentication mechanisms also need to be provided for the electronic-edition archive. Users will want to have some assurance that the material they are using has not been corrupted in any way. Some technical developments are now making this possible. Time-stamping applies a complex hashing algorithm to give a unique number to each document or image.[26] The numbers are stored on a server that acts as a validation point on the network. Users who wish to verify the authentication of the document apply the algorithm to the document and check the result against the number stored on the server. If it is different, the document has been corrupted somewhere. However, we need to find a way of using authentication mechanisms while still exploiting the potential of the electronic medium to change things and move them around. It would be possible to apply the time-stamp only to certain SGML elements, which would form the core of the electronic edition, or possibly to have different time-stamps on different elements within a document. There could be a place in the TEI header to store the time-stamp and indicate to which SGML elements it was applied.

Further research and experimentation is also needed on the economics of the electronic-edition archive. Costs will be involved in maintaining the system, keeping it up to date, and creating backup copies. The prevailing view today about much of the information on the Internet is that it should be free and readily available to everyone. However, at present much of the freely available material is maintained by volunteer labor, which is not very satisfactory for the long term. Enthusiasm for the project may wane, or the volunteer could take another job or have too many things that take priority. A properly maintained system requires some institutional support and commitment for the future. The institution would then be able to guarantee the availability of the material for some time and to ensure that it is supported. It would also be in a much better position to manage updates in a controlled fashion, so that adequate notification of them is always provided. Monitoring of usage is another advantage of a properly maintained system. It should be possible to determine those aspects of the system that are used most often and concentrate optimization and development efforts in these areas.

Charging procedures for CD-ROMS are either one-off payments or a license fee. For those products on a license fee, usually the old disk has to be returned before a new one is provided. Charging for facilities on the network is more complicated, and various models are being proposed. They range from pay-per-view to monthly or annual subscriptions. The library cataloging cooperatives have various charging mechanisms that give credit in some way to those who contribute to the databases, and in more and more institutions it is the library that is taking on subscriptions to text databases. It is not the place here to discuss these models in detail, but it must be stressed that there are costs involved in providing electronic information, and these will have to be paid somehow. This is one of several research areas in the National Science Foundation's Research in Digital Libraries Initiative. From the point of view of the humanities scholar, annual subscriptions paid by the institution would seem best, but it is important that whatever mechanism is established fits in with charging procedures in other discipline areas.

The route toward an electronic archive as outlined here is a collaborative process. It will involve scholars, librarians, and computer scientists. It will entail much research to examine the needs of different groups and to identify those requirements that are common to several groups and can thus be satisfied by the same computer code. Flexibility and a path to enhancement are essential. The system must provide texts that are recognized scholarly resources and provide sufficient functionality in the software to exploit those texts in many different ways. The development of such a system is also an iterative approach. It is usually easier for people to comment on the functionality of software when they have used it for some time and become fully aware of its features and limitations. Development in stages over a period of time will help to satisfy as many needs as possible and to bring together different viewpoints. In our view this is an essential component if the system is to last well into the next century.

NOTES

This essay draws on ideas from many sources, but I would particularly like to acknowledge the work of Peter Robinson, John Lavagnino, the Electronic Peirce Consortium, and the draft Modern Language Association proposals for electronic editions circulated by Peter Shillingsburg.

1. For a survey of early concordance projects see the series of articles by Dolores Burton in *Computers and the Humanities:* "Concordance-Making: Fifties," *Computers and the Humanities* 15 (1981): 1–14; "Concordance-Making: Early Sixties," *Computers and the Humanities* 15 (1981): 83–100; "Concordance-Making: Programs and Products," *Computers and the Humanities* 15 (1981): 139–54; "Concordance-Making: Machine Decisions and Editorial Revisions," *Computers and the Humanities* 16 (1982): 195–218.
2. See George R. Petty and William M. Gibson, *Project OCCULT: The Ordered Computer Collation of Unprepared Literary Text* (New York: New York University Press, 1970) for a description of OCCULT including a listing of the SNOBOL source code.
3. Vinton Dearing, "Computer Aids to Editing the Text of Dryden," in *Art and Error: Modern Textual Editing*, ed. Ronald Gottesman and Scott Bennett (Bloomington: Indiana University Press, 1970), 254–78.
4. Penny Gilbert, "Automatic Collation: A Technique for Medieval Texts," *Computers and the Humanities* 7 (1973): 139–47.
5. See Wilhelm Ott, "Computer Applications in Textual Criticism," in *The Computer and Literary Studies,* ed. A. J. Aitken, R. W. Bailey, and N. Hamilton-Smith (Edinburgh: Edinburgh University Press, 1973), 199–223 for an overview of some of the tools in TUSTEP. Recent PC-based versions of the program incorporate very similar methodologies.

6. See Hans Walter Gabler, "Computer-Aided Critical Edition of *Ulysses*," *ALLC Bulletin* 8 (1980): 232–48 for an explanation of some of the TUSTEP programs applied to *Ulysses*.
7. For a description of some of the early methodologies employed by Chesnutt and his team, see David Chesnutt, "Twentieth-Century Technology and Eighteenth-Century Letters: A Case Study of the Papers of Henry Laurens," in *Sixth International Conference on Computers and the Humanities,* ed. Sarah K. Burton and Douglas D. Short (Rockville, Md.: Computer Science Press, 1983), 94–103.
8. See chapter 7 of my *Guide to Computer Applications in the Humanities* (London: Duckworth; Baltimore: Johns Hopkins University Press, 1980) for an overview of these approaches.
9. G. P. Zarri, "Algorithms, *Stemmata Codicum,* and the Theories of Dom H. Quentin," in Aitken, Bailey, and Hamilton-Smith, *Computer and Literary Studies,* 225–37.
10. See J. G. Griffith, "A Taxonomic Study of the Manuscript Tradition of Juvenal," *Museum Helveticum* 25 (1968): 101–38, and also J. G. Griffith, "Numerical Taxonomy and Some Primary Manuscripts of the Gospels," *Journal of Theological Studies* 20 (1969): 389–406. Griffith used a program developed specially for his project, but cluster analysis modules are now available in most statistical-analysis programs.
11. J. Irigoin and G. P. Zarri, eds. *La pratique des ordinateurs dans la critique des textes* (Paris: Centre National de la Recherche Scientifique, 1979).
12. Words of caution on do-it-yourself typesetting are expressed by Wilhelm Ott in "Textual Editing and Publishing in Literary and Linguistic Research," *ALLC Bulletin* 10 (1982): 35–39.
13. See *Optical Character Recognition in the Historical Discipline: Proceedings of an International Workgroup Organized by Netherlands Historical Data Archive and Nijmegen Institute for Cognition and Information* (Göttingen: Max-Planck-Institut für Geschichte, 1993) for a recent collection on optical character recognition. Mark Olsen's paper in this volume, "Scanning, Keyboarding, and Data Verification: Factors in Selecting Data Collection Technologies," is a useful examination of data entry methods for ARTFL (American Research on the Treasury of the French Language). Olsen concludes that "there are many instances where OCR is not cost-effective, since the technology is still prone to making numerous errors" (112).
14. Omnipage Professional has been found to be one of the better trainable programs available on desktop machines. The various machines sold by the Kurzweil company and Makrolog's Optopus are used by some scholarly projects. My "OCR: The Kurzweil Data Entry Machine," *Literary and Linguistic Computing* 1 (1986): 63–67 describes the earliest Kurzweil machine in some detail. The functionality of later Kurzweil systems has been found to be somewhat less suitable for scholarly projects.
15. A good introduction to SGML is Eric van Herwijnen, *Practical SGML,* 2d ed. (Dordrecht: Kluwer, 1994). The first edition of this book is also available as a DynaText electronic book from Electronic Book Technologies, Providence,

Rhode Island. Chapter 2, "A Gentle Introduction to SGML," of the Text Encoding Initiative's *Guidelines for the Encoding and Interchange of Electronic Texts,* ed. C. M. Sperberg-McQueen and Lou Burnard (Chicago: Association for Computers and the Humanities, Association for Computational Linguistics, Association for Literacy and Linguistic Computing, 1994) is also a good starting point.

16. Sperberg-McQueen and Burnard, *Guidelines.*
17. For a discussion of the relationship between the TEI header and the MARC record, see Lisa Horowitz, *CETH Workshop on Documenting Electronic Texts,* Technical Report 2 (Center for Electronic Texts in the Humanities, Rutgers and Princeton Universities, 1994).
18. Among these products are the *CETEDOC Library of Early Christian Fathers, Global Jewish Database, WordCruncher CDROM* (mostly American Literature), *Perseus, St Thomas Aquinas CDROM.*
19. For a discussion of the limitations of the World Wide Web see John Price-Wilkin, "Using the World-Wide Web to Deliver Complex Electronic Documents: Implications for Libraries," *Public Access Computer Systems Review* 5 (1994): 5–21.
20. See *A TACT Exemplar,* ed. T. Russon Wooldridge (Toronto: Centre for Computing in the Humanities, University of Toronto, 1991) for an overview of TACT and its applications. A manual for the latest version of TACT is to be published by the MLA in 1995.
21. A description of OCP can be found in Susan Hockey and Jeremy Martin, "The Oxford Concordance Program Version 2," *Literary and Linguistic Computing* 2 (1987): 125–31. The user's manual for Micro-OCP (for the IBM PC) is published by Oxford University Press.
22. This is lamented by Father Busa in "Half a Century of Literary Computing: Towards a 'New' Philology," Reports of Colloquia at Tübingen, *Literary and Linguistic Computing* 7 (1992): 69–73.
23. See particularly Nicoletta Calzolari and Antonio Zampolli, "Lexical Databases and Textual Corpora: A Trend of Convergence between Computational Linguistics and Literary and Linguistic Computing," in *Research in Humanities Computing 1,* ed. Susan Hockey and Nancy Ide, guest ed. Ian Lancashire (Oxford: Oxford University Press, 1991), 273–307, for the relevance of these techniques for the humanities.
24. The Electronic Peirce Consortium was one of the first projects to propose the use of the "collaboratory" for multiple interpretation of texts on the network. See "The Pilot Project of the Electronic Peirce Consortium," a panel presentation by Michael Neuman, Mary Keeler, Christian Kloesel, Joseph Ransdell, and Allen Renear, ALLC-ACH92 Conference Abstracts and Program, 6–9 April 1992, 25–27.
25. Andrea Bozzi and Antonio Sapuppo of Pisa presented preliminary results of their research in this area for the Bibliothèque de France at the ALLC-ACH conference in Paris in April 1994.
26. Stuart Haber and W. Scott Stornetta, "How to Time-Stamp a Digital Document," *Journal of Cryptology* 3 (1991): 99–111.

Principles for Electronic Archives, Scholarly Editions, and Tutorials

Peter Shillingsburg

A scholarly edition is a thick book (five hundred to a thousand pages) printed on acid-free paper guaranteed for 350 years, in sturdy bindings, with a list of ten to twenty editors and advisory editors, published by a reputable academic press and costing a minimum of fifty dollars, but more often over one hundred. It contains a Pure Virgin Text or, unironically, a Fully Restored one. Already a thick tome because of the historical and textual introductions and textual apparatus, scholarly editions frequently exclude explanatory annotations because the space they require would add unduly to the cost (already out of the reach of ordinary mortals and nearly out of reach for the ordinary research library).

Sophisticated users of scholarly editions also know that the textual record ordinarily omits accidentals from the historical collation, except those falling into that marvelous category, semisubstantives, and that frequently the records of manuscript alterations—or for that matter, manuscript readings except for the most significant ones—are also truncated.

It is true that many readers and even students do not miss the omitted materials, but the fact that most literary criticism fails to cite available scholarly editions and, further, fails to find textual criticism central to its concerns, suggests that print scholarly editions have failed to impress their importance upon the academic establishment. The dissatisfaction with scholarly editions evinced in the actions of critics indifferent to the consequences of textual criticism, while a serious concern, is not as impressive or thought-provoking as the dissatisfaction of textual critics themselves. Scholarly editions were once fiercely touted as definitive, but if a print scholarly edition actually contained all that scholars might be interested in relative to a text, why, it would be an archive, a library, and it would cost a mint.

That scholarly editions have not revolutionized literary criticism and that they do not fulfill the needs or desires of the cognoscente are very good reasons for thinking that textual critics on the cutting edge must abandon the printed scholarly edition as the primary or final repository of their work. Printed editions are handy in ways I seriously doubt electronic editions will be in our lifetime: they can be read by the unassisted naked eye. But to be realistic, not many unassisted naked eyes have actually read the scholarly edition of Charles Brockden Brown's *Ormond* or William Dean Howells's *Our Silver Wedding Anniversary* or William Makepeace Thackeray's *The History of Pendennis* or William Gilmore Simms's *Voltmeier; or, The Mountain Men*. How many unassisted naked eyes should read them? What tale would be told if one could ask all those who read this if they always check to see if a scholarly edition is available of a work they are about to read. The last time you read *Moby-Dick* or *Middlemarch,* was it with a Northwestern-Newberry or a Clarendon edition? Or did you read the Norton Critical Edition or the Oxford World Classics? Or the Dell, Signet, or Wordsworth paperback?

When critics cite paperbacks, is it because the scholarly edition is too expensive, too difficult to find, too heavy, too hard to use for what it is supposed to do? Is it because when it comes to practice they do not actually believe that ignorance about small textual matters is important in what they do? One reason in recent days might be because in the electronic age we have seen new things we want to do with texts that print scholarly editions don't let us do—such as having a concordance of the work or, what amounts to about the same thing, being able to search for all occurrences of some name or word or phrase; such as being able to see reproductions of the covers and title pages and facsimiles of the texts of significant historical editions; such as having textual notes in more than one level of "verbosity" (either with or without accidentals); such as having the explanatory notes with the possibility of several levels of detail and pictures to go with descriptions of buildings, people, and places.

This vision of an electronic scholarly edition begins to resemble an archive of editions with annotations, contexts, parallel texts, reviews, criticism, and bibliographies of reception and criticism. In effect it is really a library we want. A William Faulkner library with all the texts in all the versions and pictures of Yocknapatawpha—or at least of Lafayette County, and maps. And the visionary won't stop there. How about movies? How about Faulkner reading his own works? How about someone else, Richard Burton or Shelby Foote reading them?

In the digital age, if we follow out, in the way of texts broadly defined, what we would like to have as scholars and critics and readers of literary texts, we very soon outstrip the printed scholarly edition's capacity to accommodate us. Scholars from small underfunded states with small underfunded libraries are hungry for archives. The electronic scholarly edition dangles tantalizingly in the not too distant future, and we want it now.

And for every textual visionary there is an electronic guru who says, "The future is now. You can have these things. But first we need to know what kind of platform you operate. We need to know if you have a CD drive, and how much RAM and ROM you have, and how big is your hard drive? If you want to enter the kingdom of electronic editions you must go and sell all your goods and purchase a super VGA 486 cpu running 66 megahertz with a 580 meg hard drive, preferably with four on the floor and glasspack mufflers—unless, of course, you are a Mac person or a UNIX person to whom we can only talk about the uses of the lower swing swivel, which in your case you have not got."

Sense must prevail somewhere. I have two generalizations to make. First, electronic scholarly editions can do for us things that printed scholarly editions cannot; and, second, they can do them in cheaper end-products. It costs more to be able to read a CD or networked archive than it does to read a scholarly print edition because you have to have a machine to do it with. But eventually it will cost less to produce and therefore, one assumes, to purchase a compact disk than it cost to produce and purchase Hans Gabler's edition of *Ulysses*.

Keeping potential users of electronic editions firmly in mind, it behooves potential editors and producers to think about industry standards for what we are doing, for we do not each want to reinvent the wheel, and readers cannot be asked to buy a different machine or different software for each of our editions in order to get the full use of our labors. Nor do they want to learn a new set of conventions for each edition they wish to use. In addressing the possibilities for "industry standards" for electronic editions, I see two general principles: the first addresses the potential of electronic editions to be something more and something different from printed editions: electronic editions should be designed for multipurpose, multimedia presentation, effectively breaking down barriers between the concepts: archives, editions, and course materials or tutorials (i.e., not just books on a screen). The second principle addresses accessibility: electronic editions should involve software systems chosen or developed in a way that confronts the difficulties of transport and communication between competing hardware platforms, so that the results of any scholarly editing project will not be restricted to use by Macintosh users, PC users, or UNIX users.

There are other issues of great importance, entailed by these two major concerns, such as the capabilities for sound, pictures (both still and moving), and text, such as accuracy in transcriptions and annotations, such as quality control in facsimile reproductions, and such as the extent and types of linkings or webbings of texts and contexts to provide. But these two major issues (the concept of the electronic edition as something that spans the notions of archive, edition, and course material, and the concept of multiplatform and Internet accessibility) are my central concerns in addressing the problem of emerging standards for our discipline.

I'd like to begin by quoting a jeremiad circulated on a book-history electronic mail list by Michael Cohen, who works for the Voyager Company. His job has been to help develop the interface, and he is producing an edition of *Macbeth*. Cohen writes:

> I would recommend that interested parties would profit by actually taking a look at some electronic texts in addition to reading the observations of those cited in previous posts [on the e-mail list]. The field is moving very swiftly: the conventional wisdom of two years ago is already out of date. Electronic text has moved from a theoretical discussion to a commercial product, and the marketplace has a way of ignoring theoretical considerations (and by marketplace I include not only for-sale products but freely available works accessible from various networks).
>
> Things to look at and ponder:
>
> —Voyager's Expanded Books (of course)
>
> —Borderbund's children's books on CD (e.g., *Arthur's Teacher Trouble*)
>
> —Project Gutenberg (lots of free text available through the Internet)
>
> —Some of the free HyperCard-based texts (e.g., *A Study in Scarlet, War of the Worlds*), available via the sumex-aim Macintosh archives.

> What you will discover is that there are all sorts of ways of presenting and distributing text digitally, and the idea of what a book is is becoming very broad and ill-defined . . . and may very well continue in that direction as a multiplicity of digital technologies intersect with textual technology.
>
> In other words, don't just get a book or two about electronic text—get some electronic text itself. And stay alert: the nature of electronic text is in great flux, and most of the "truths" about it are evanescent at this stage of development.

It is important at the outset to distinguish Mr. Cohen's community of interest from that of scholarly editing. We cannot concern ourselves with setting standards for his community; he cannot interfere with our concerns. The community of scholarly editing is relatively small. Its interests are intense and common. There is a yawning chasm separating scholarly editing from the Gutenberg Project, which is a hyperactive accumulation of, and distribution project for, electronic texts that are required to meet only one standard: Can it be distributed electronically?

The community of scholarly editing is almost completely represented by the members of the Association for Documentary Editing and the Society for Textual Scholarship. The mailing lists of the MLA's Committee on Scholarly Editions, the Canadian Early English Texts project, and the Australian Academy Editions project probably includes 90 percent or more of our community. Anyone not covered by these organizations is probably a member of the Scholarly Editing (SEDIT) or Electronic Text Centers (ETEXCEN) e-mail lists run by Susan Hockey and the National Center for Electronic Books. The point is that scholarly editors form a small, committed, intense, and in a sense manageable group. If it sets the standards for its own community, then Gutenberg and Chadwyck-Healey, Voyager Books, and Borderbunds Children's Books can do what they like—they will anyway—but scholarly editing will have a system that works: a system that improves on the printed scholarly editions in ways that we determine. That attitude underlies what follows as a tentative outline of our ideal goals.

In general what is imagined is

A. an archive of materials in textual, visual, and aural forms: documents in virtual image (color pictures of documents for accuracy and for iconic or bibliographic look) and searchable text form (straight ASCII and formatted [in Standard Generalized Markup Language]), pictures, videos, and sound tracks. The compilation of such an archive would be the work of the traditional literary-textual scholar with the skills and resources of an acquisitions librarian, but the goals of the collection would be altered to include the concept of archiving not only accurate ASCII transcriptions of texts or of standardized coding of such texts, but accurate virtual images of texts and of related objects and icons. Editors who once worked from microfilms and checked their printouts against original manuscripts would now need high-resolution reproductions of the manuscripts and permission to distribute them. Where they used to machine-collate variant texts and record only the differences, they would now need a full accurate transcription and full digital image of each source edition. Because so much more can be done with electronic texts than was done with print texts, we should think of recording and passing on that much more data.

B. Once an archive is collected, we need a webbing or networking of cross-references connecting variant texts, explanatory notes, contextual materials, and parallel texts. One should remember that computers are dumb and do only what they are told to do. The work of scholarly editing has never been easy or straightforward. The advent of computers gave us machines to do idiot work, but it did not cause formerly long-eared editors to become Housmans or Bowerses. But for the arduous labor of intelligent editors, hypertext environments seem the natural way to present the radiating access routes they discover to all parts of an archive. Traditionally, students read a novel, a poem, an essay, a treaty, or any other historical document linearly, from beginning to end. But traditionally they have not studied novels or treaties in that fashion. They want to be able to search texts from stem to stern electronically. They want to move directly from one passage in a work to its corresponding passages in other versions or from a text to its sources or contexts. They want, for any passage being scrutinized, to have annotations, textual variants, variorum critical commentaries, dramatizations, and movie versions available from the archive at the click of a "hot spot" in the text before them. Of course, they have never had that; but they have always wanted that whether they were conscious of the desire or not!

C. In order to have a webbing of materials and in order to move quickly to significant places in an archive, students/scholars need a navigational system. There are several separate problems here: the first is archival. How are texts encoded? When you wish to share a text with someone who does not have the same machine and software you use, a translation must take place, and in most cases something is lost—size and style of fonts, length of line and line breaks, indentations, italics, boldface, underlining, footnotes, side notes, logos. In the case of scholarly editions none of these things is trivial. If we lock the format and pass the material, it is rather like offering a fax, missing out the flexibility of computer capability. The most promising solution seems to be SGML, which codes all these matters and more in ASCII form, so that the file uploaded from the originator's hard- and software environment is duplicated when the material is downloaded into a different hard- and software environment and so that information about the origin, structure, and appearance of the source text is preserved—along with the capacity to search, display, and quote. Parsers (software to automate the uploading and downloading) are proliferating. There are other less promising solutions, and there will very likely be new ones before long. But sharing texts that carry more than letters and punctuation—that carry the full complement of textual signifiers—is only the beginning.

D. A second navigational problem begins with the question: How are texts linked to one another? Navigational systems are specific pieces of software, each in some way different from other software that might be used. And most navigational systems are platform specific, each software system designed to work with a specific operating system—such as Macintosh, Windows, or UNIX. One of the most successful systems currently available that attempts to overcome both of these problems is an Internet solution known as World Wide Web using Mosaic, a hypertext system. It employs HTML (HyperText Markup Language) coding for its texts, and it has reader software such that persons at any of the three major platforms (Macintosh, Windows, or UNIX, provided they have a fast enough processor, a sufficiently high resolution screen, a large enough hard disk, the right reader's software, and a sufficiently sophisticated printer) can access an archive or data bank on the Internet and read the texts, display the digital images, and activate the links that form the hypertext web, and copy significant portions to the hard disk or printer. The limitations of HTML are often repeated, but many active scholarly editors employ World Wide Web because it is fully operational.

E. Of course, if we ever get a fully webbed and fully navigable archive, we will not be content to see it work or find wonderful things in it. We will want to copy parts and react to parts, and to reconfigure parts, and to leave our two cents' worth in the margins for the benefit of posterity. We want interactivity with the archive, a commenting system, and downloading or copying features—none of which, however, should compromise the integrity of the archive.

If you had access to a computer that could read a CD of the *Moby-Dick* archive, or the *Vanity Fair* archive or the *For the Term of His Natural Life* archive, would you pay twenty-five dollars for the CD? Would you pay fifty dollars? And would you use it, or are you hooked forever on inexpensive paperbacks? What follows here represents an ideal to strive for and a set of problems to consider in designing scholarly electronic editions.[1]

GENERAL PRINCIPLES FOR ELECTRONIC SCHOLARLY EDITIONS

1. Usability: The ideal standard of usability should be that the archive be as easily available as possible to all potential users who have a sufficiently sophisticated computer system to take advantage of electronic scholarly editions. We do not want to make this difficult.

At first I thought that meant that the electronic edition should be packaged and sold or distributed in multiple forms: on floppy disks, tapes, CDs, and laser discs, and with separate forms for Macs, Windows, and UNIX. And in the short haul, that is already the case. It seemed clear that the archive and navigation system as a whole should be designed to take advantage of all the capabilities of desktop computers in their most advanced configuration; but I thought, as well, that the archive should be "available" in some of its basic forms to the least well equipped user. I suppose that idea results from the democratic principle and the hope that the work of the editor will be available to the greatest number of people. We all know that in the print world, few of us have been able to afford the full-scale scholarly edition of all the works we study. Even our libraries have trouble supplying a whole intellectual community with all the full-scale scholarly editions they should have purchased. So it seemed good to aim for wide distribution of electronic editions.

Reflection suggests that there are serious problems with the idea of distributing electronic editions on disks, CDs, and so forth—or at least with the idea of making that the primary mode of distribution—the one determining the standards of data capture and storage.

The first problem with it is the need to create multiple forms for different platforms and different levels of computer power and auxiliary drives. That means duplication of effort for every archive that is created.

The second is that, once distributed, any further improvements to the archive would either be foregone by previous purchasers or new editions would need to be distributed.

A third is that the multiple stand-alone concept requires that each user's computer be big enough to house sophisticated multimedia software *and* the whole archive in order to have maximum utility.

So, at the moment, the First Standard of Electronic Scholarly Editions appears to be: that electronic scholarly editions be databases attached to a network. That is, that other forms be considered subsidiary or temporary, or occasional products designed for limited or targeted markets. There are a number of distinct advantages to network access to the primary edition.

a. There will be one location for the archive where current updates will be made and will be simultaneously available to all users.
b. The integrity of the archive will be protected by its single location.
c. Each user will need the navigation software for his or her own machine but will not have to have room for the whole archive.
d. Each user, having the resident network access software, will be able to access all standardized electronic scholarly edition archives, no matter where in the world the archive is maintained. With standardization of network access, users will not have to buy new software every time a new archive is created.
e. Archives can be made available at any location on the networks and be maintained and updated locally by the editor. There will be no need for a centralized library, though there can be one or more if they are wanted.

Of course, archives could be made available whole to users capable of handling them, and spin-offs in the form of disks, CDs, and even printed texts could be produced as publishers or purchasers saw the need or opportunity.

2. Transportability: The largest problem for the concept of electronic editions when approached from the tradition of print editions—each user with a single final copy of the work—is that nothing, at the moment, that can be handled, owned, and sold, is platform-independent: if it works on UNIX, it won't work on DOS or Windows or Macintosh. The software system and the archival materials for electronic scholarly editions should be platform independent.

At the moment network access seems to be the most feasible long-term way to achieve platform independence. I say long term because the networks are currently unable to carry "real time" video, but that will change before long. In addition, we should be looking at progress in the handshaking department between IBM and Macintosh that would make it possible to use a single machine in either mode. That may be another solution, but it would be available only to persons with the right kind of machine, and that is a concept I would nudge us away from.

The question can be seen as an alternative between developing an edition that is available in a different form for each platform, or of developing access to the edition from many platforms. The latter seems more promising.

Because HyperCard for Macintosh and ToolBook for DOS and VNS (Virtual Notebook System [Rice University]) or Mosaic (University of Illinois) for UNIX and other hypertext- and multimedia-authoring systems have been developing, as they must, for specific platforms, it has been natural to think of developing an archive with one of these software and hardware configurations in mind. DynaText has recently been touted as a viable alternative, for it has a different version for each of the three main operating systems. But it is currently proprietary (expensive) and lacks some of the graphic capabilities of other systems. No system to date incorporates collation capabilities with graphics. But the standard we aim for must in some sense be universal. And it may be that access to the editions rather than the editions themselves is what needs to be platform independent. Once we find or develop the adequate authoring software and navigational software—adequate in the sense that it lets us do all the things that users of scholarly electronic editions want to do—then the archive version of the software and the user versions of the software can be linked. Users will have software resident at their personal workstations, the network will connect them to the individual archives, and the database version of the software will make use of the archive available regardless of the platform (hardware) the user happens to have.

3. Archive specifications: The design of the system and the storage specifications for the archived materials should anticipate the desires of the community of textual critics and scholarly edition users:

a. The electronic edition should be multimedia: able to integrate text (virtual and textual), images (still, animated, film/video), sound, and color.
b. The software design should incorporate the ideal that interaction with the material is desirable. Display of materials to a passive observer is not the only goal. The user must have liberty to navigate the materials at will. The user should have the option of entering parts of the program that are "tutorial" and that prompt the user to react to challenges and suggestions.
c. User commentary should be attachable to the archive, making a growing bulletin board that is indexed to the archive. A user with something to add to the archive or commentary to make on it should have space to make those contributions. User-added materials should be available to other users. If possible the users' additions should be accessible from particular places in the edition (through links), and they should be searchable separately as well. But the integrity of the base archive should not be compromised by users and their added commentaries.
d. The system must give users the capability of marking texts and quoting from any part of the archive for their own use. User commentary and the archive itself must be printable. (This idea raises questions of copyright, for which there are several opposing positions. The "capability" of printing and quoting from the archives and commentary should be separate from questions of charging for access or for quotations. In this system, each archive developer would have the right to establish access rules or subscription rates as they see fit.)
e. Linkings: A web or network of cross-referencing should be created. Collation, with programs like CASE (Computer-Assisted Scholarly Editing) and Collate, should link variant texts so that one can move immediately from a specific point in one version of a text

to its corresponding point in another (a feature that is already available in the Mac HyperCard version of CASE). Variant texts should be available in simultaneous multiple windows. Simultaneous scrolling of variant texts should be an available option. Links (through "hot spots" or menus) to annotations, glossary items, pictures, maps, and texts should be available in small, movable, quotable windows.

f. Intertextuality—linking parallel texts and countertexts. Parallel texts, annotations, visual contexts, and adaptations should all be linked and available in windows. Responses, sequels, adaptations for stage, radio, film and video (including screenplays), and parodies in any form should be ideal parts of archives and should be linked at least partially. It is very difficult to determine what to include and how to link. This part of the concept is very much dependent on the talent, interests, and resources of the archive compiler.

g. Contextuality and interpretations: archival materials should be linked to related materials in other media: Critical commentary (textual and video), interviews, letters, journals, histories, reviews.

4. Security and order: A system for protecting the original archive from user alteration should be combined with an orderly system for identifying user-created copies of any parts of the archive. The original materials should maintain integrity, but users must be free to create alternative versions. New versions should be automatically and permanently identified as new versions, not original.

5. Integrity: Archival materials must be linked to specific material sources. Provisions should be made to maintain and enhance a source copy of each scholarly edition. It seems ideal that each archive remain in process, but that the maintenance and improvement of each archive be centralized.

6. Expandability: The archive must be expandable: by the archive owner or compiler as new materials and new links seem appropriate; and by users in a parallel commentary field or bulletin board.

7. Printability: Hard-copy capability should be available for "on-demand" publishing. (The question of whether a user should pay for the privilege is separate from the question of whether the capability should be there.) This relates to the current debate about the future of hard-copy scholarly editions. The need for printed texts will continue, but an ideal electronic scholarly edition may make the printed scholarly edition obso-

lete. A printed text would come to be thought of as one possible version of the work more fully represented by the electronic archive.

8. User friendly: The "navigation" system should provide a set of options and indications of the availability of the links described in section 3. It should enable a user to retrace a session's use of the archive. It must provide a way to "get back" after chasing a particular line of inquiry through several levels of the hypertext. Likewise, it should be designed to keep the user easily aware of "where" the local viewing scene is in relation to the archive as a whole. In a printed book, one always knows how far one is from the beginning or end of the book. In electronic environments the size of the whole and one's place in the whole should also be readily knowable. Further, in a printed book one can leaf forward or backward or skip forward or backward, while in the electronic environment one can move anywhere and it appear that one has moved only one screen away. There are other ways to imagine the feeling of lostness one can get in the electronic environment; this merely points to the problem.

NOTE

1. The following outline of ideals for electronic scholarly editions is based on extensive informal talks with Graham Barwell and Paul Eggert, of the University of Wollongong and the Australian Defence Force Academy, respectively, and by helpful comments, particularly by Richard Finneran, Charles Faulhaber, and participants in the Electronic Scholarly Editing E-mail Discussion Group (ESE@ra.msstate.edu).

Textual Criticism and the Text Encoding Initiative

C. M. Sperberg-McQueen

In his essay "Das Kunstwerk im Zeitalter seiner technischen Reproduzierbarkeit," Walter Benjamin describes how art is affected by the development of new technologies of reproduction, which both allow existing artworks to be copied and widely distributed and also create new forms of art dependent on mechanical reproduction, notably photography and film. In the essay, Benjamin identifies the characteristic difference between original artworks and reproductions as the loss of what he calls the here-and-now, or the *aura,* of the original. Reproductions are not limited to a single here-and-now; they do not share the historical vicissitudes of their originals; they lack the original's chemical and physical reality; and therefore the concepts of *authenticity* and *historical authority* both become irrelevant and inapplicable to reproductions.

In the course of his essay, Benjamin makes a suggestive error. In brief, Benjamin believes that for any medium of technological reproduction, a copy is a copy is a copy. In a well-known observation, he writes: "Von der photographischen Platte zum Beispiel ist eine Vielfalt von Abzügen möglich; die Frage nach dem echten Abzug hat keinen Sinn."[1] This claim is of particular interest first of all because unlike many in our field, it is empirically testable, and second because it proves false: some prints do appear to be, or at least are treated as, more authentic than others: the price of a print from Ansel Adams's studio, for example, is many times the price of a print from the same negative prepared by commercial remarketers. Contrary to Benjamin's expectation, all prints are not created equal.

Three points are worth noting in this connection. First, aura is not an absolute, but a variable quantity. Second, aura can exist even in a mechanical reproduction because *even mechanical reproductions can vary.* Third, what differentiates a print prepared by Adams's own studio from a mass-reproduced copy is not the art of the photographic exposure (after all, the two prints share the same negative) but that of the photographic print-maker and touch-up artist. Two prints from the same negative can have unequal value because *reproducible arts separate the creation of the matrix (negative) from the creation of the reproduction (print)*.

All three of these points illuminate the condition of literature. In his essay, Benjamin mentions literature only in passing, and he stops just short of expressing overtly a commonly held view: namely, that the technological reproducibility of literature was accomplished with the introduction of printing. He writes: "Die ungeheuren Veränderungen, die der Druck, die technische Reproduzierbarkeit der Schrift, in der Literatur hervorgerufen hat, sind bekannt."[2] But despite the enormous changes introduced by printing, the technology which made literature reproducible was not printing, but the introduction of writing for literary texts. Oral literature has many of the characteristics Benjamin associates with the nonreproducible in art, though for obvious reasons it lacks those which apply only to physical artifacts. The characteristics associated by Benjamin with the technological reproducibility of art, by contrast, especially the detachment from the here-and-now of the original, are remarkably similar to some of those associated with the introduction of writing by, for example, Florian Coulmas, notably the *distancing function* and the *reifying function*.[3]

For my current purposes it suffices to observe that the variability even of mechanical reproduction ensures that books and other written matter, whether printed or manuscript, retain some measure of uniqueness and thus of aura. This in turn has a number of implications for the study of texts, whether literary or not. Like other arts subject to technological reproduction, literature is transmitted by, and thus dependent on, but nevertheless logically distinct from, its physical carriers. Because those physical carriers inevitably vary among themselves, the question of authenticity does arise for literary works, despite Benjamin's claim that authenticity is not an issue when dealing with reproductions. Those who address the question of authenticity we call textual critics. They, along with those scholars who study the reception and dissemination of a work, will necessarily be concerned with the individual histories of individual copies of the work, what Benjamin refers to as the "die Geschichte, der es [d.i. das Kunstwerk] im Laufe seines Bestehens unterworfen gewesen ist."[4]

At the same time, logical clarity requires a firm distinction between the creation of a text and the creation of a physical carrier for that text. Both may be part of the same social activity we call literature, but they may be performed at different times by different parties, and the same text may be preserved under wildly differing extratextual conditions. The task of the author and those of the printer, papermaker, and bookbinder must be kept distinct, if we wish to have any clear understanding of literature as a social activity.

Benjamin, of course, is by no means alone in passing over in silence the uncomfortable fact that mechanical reproductions can vary, nor is it hard to find others who confuse an abstract art with its concrete means of transmission. His illusions or evasions about the stability of mechanical processes and the uniformity of their products are shared by the vast majority of our colleagues, who are, painful though it is to say it, made nervous by the basic facts of (textual) reproduction and the variation it brings about, and who consistently ignore or evade evidence of textual variation in order to speak about texts as if they were singular, unchanging objects, stable artifacts whose details are not open to question.

In this essay I want to discuss some of the more obvious issues raised by efforts to create electronic texts, and in particular electronic versions of scholarly editions. Benjamin's essay is particularly suggestive here, in the context of efforts to make literary (and nonliterary) texts reproducible by new technological methods. I begin by making explicit some of my assumptions about the goals and requirements of electronic scholarly editions; in the second section I explain why my list of requirements says nothing about the choice of software for the preparation and use of scholarly editions. The third section will describe the work and results of the Text Encoding Initiative (TEI), a cooperative international project to develop and disseminate guidelines for the creation and interchange of electronic texts, and show how they relate to the requirements for electronic scholarly editions. In the concluding section, I will outline some of the implications of the TEI for electronic and printed scholarly editions, and some essential requirements for any future consensus on how to go about creating useful electronic scholarly editions.

REQUIREMENTS FOR ELECTRONIC EDITIONS

I begin by stating explicitly some assumptions I am making. Arguments could probably be made for some of these propositions, but I won't argue for them, lest I seem to belabor the obvious.

> Electronic scholarly editions are worth having. And therefore it is worth thinking about the form they should take. If present trends

continue, we will have, within a decade or so, enough editions available in electronic form to constitute a virtual or digital library. If we want that digital library to be a usable one, now is the time to think about how it should be built.

Electronic scholarly editions should be accessible to the broadest audience possible. They should not require a particular type of computer, or a particular piece of software: unnecessary technical barriers to their use should be avoided.

Electronic scholarly editions should have relatively long lives: at least as long as printed editions. They should not become technically obsolete before they are intellectually obsolete.

Printed scholarly editions have developed their current forms in order to meet both intellectual requirements and to adapt to the characteristics of print publication. Electronic editions must meet the same intellectual needs. There is no reason to abandon traditional intellectual requirements merely because we are using a different medium to publish them.

On the other hand, many conventions or requirements of traditional print editions reflect not the demands of readers or scholarship, but the difficulties of conveying complex information on printed pages without confusing or fatiguing the reader, or the financial exigencies of modern scholarly publishing.[5] Such requirements need not be taken over at all, and must not be taken over thoughtlessly, into electronic editions.

Electronic publications can, if suitably encoded and suitably supported by software, present the same text in many forms: as clear text, as diplomatic transcript of one witness or another, as critical reconstruction of an authorial text, with or without critical apparatus of variants, and with or without annotations aimed at the textual scholar, the historian, the literary scholar, the linguist, the graduate student, or the undergraduate. They can provide many more types of index than printed editions typically do. And so electronic editions can, in principle, address a larger audience than single print editions. In this respect, they may face even higher intellectual requirements than print editions, which typically need not attempt to provide annotations for such diverse readers.

Print editions without apparatus, without documentation of editorial principles, and without decent typesetting are not acceptable substi-

> tutes for scholarly editions. Electronic editions without apparatus, without documentation of editorial principles, and without decent provision for suitable display are equally unacceptable for serious scholarly work.
>
> As a consequence, we must reject out of hand proposals to create electronic scholarly editions in the style of Project Gutenberg, which objects in principle to the provision of apparatus and almost never indicates the sources, let alone the principles which have governed the transcription, of its texts.[6]

In sum: I believe electronic scholarly editions must meet three fundamental requirements: accessibility without needless technical barriers to use; longevity; and intellectual integrity.

In the case of text-critically aware scholarly editions, intellectual integrity demands at least that the edition meet the standard demands of textual criticism. It must at least contain a good or intellectually defensible text. The definition of *good* in this context varies with the editor, of course, and an appalling amount of ink continues to be spilt, at least in Anglo-American text criticism, in vain attempts to prove once and for all that there is only one plausible answer to the question *What kind of text is good, what kind of edition should we produce?*

The edition must also record text-critically relevant variants, so that specialists can evaluate the text and the work done in establishing it; the apparatus of variants must indicate in some way the degree of reliability with which the manuscript transmission allows the archetype of the text to be reconstructed. The entire transmission of the text must be surveyed and, where possible, explained. The French classicist Louis Havet puts these extended demands neatly:

> Le fond de la méthode critique, ce n'est pas une appréciation immédiate des leçons connues; c'est une reconstitution historique de la transmission du texte, depuis les plus anciens manuscrits.
>
> Tant qu'une faute reste inexpliquée, la bonne leçon demeure entachée d'un reste d'incertitude.[7]

The German medievalist Georg Steer poses a similar requirement:

> Der Herausgeber eines Textes hat über die gesamte erhaltene Textüberlieferung, noch schärfer formuliert: über jede Variante Rechenschaft zu geben.[8]

At the same time, some selection from the wealth of material must usually be made, at least in printed editions. An absolutely complete apparatus, warns Steer, will produce "giant compost heaps of variants of highly disparate quality" [Riesenkomposthaufen von Lesarten unterschiedlichster Qualität]. In order to avoid overburdening the apparatus with variants irrelevant for the reliability of the reconstructed text, many editors include in the apparatus only "text-critically relevant" variants: that is, variants which, given the relationships thought to hold among the manuscripts, might conceivably derive from the archetype (the latest common ancestor of all extant manuscripts). Text-critical books and essays, even of the most abstruse theoretical type, devote incredible amounts of critical acumen to the task of selecting which variants to include in the apparatus and to making the apparatus more compact, easier to typeset, or easier to omit from a photomechanical reproduction.

Not all editions are selective in their apparatus, however; some include every nonorthographic variant reading of every witness, including variants clearly useless for the reconstruction of an archetypal text. This gives a clearer picture of the forms under which the text actually circulated and is particularly useful to those tracing the reception of a work. Some editions, notably for relatively recent printed books, include orthographic variants as well. Graphetic variants (distinctions among different letterforms) are sometimes made in electronic editions for philological work, but I have never seen such distinctions in a printed edition of any work in any European language.

Beyond recording the variations in the text found in different sources, scholarly editions must indicate any disturbance in the normal physical character of the source (be it printed book, manuscript, or something else), as it can materially affect the reliability of the transcription offered in the edition. Many editions also indicate that some portions of the text are less reliable than others, sometimes using four or more levels of certainty.

Let us make this discussion more concrete. A survey of various sets of rules for the construction of critical apparatus and for the use of special signs in critical texts reveals that scholars have found the following features of texts significant enough to merit mention in the apparatus, or (in some cases) special signs in the text itself. An intellectually sound electronic text will need methods of indicating the occurrence of these phenomena.[9]

The word or passage marked has variant(s).

At the point indicated, other manuscripts insert additional material.

The word or passage marked is omitted in some variants.

The passage marked occurs in some variants with a different word order (transposition).

The material marked is not present in the source and has been supplied conjecturally by the editor or transcriber, although the source in question has no physical gap in the text.

The passage marked is a conjectural addition, to fill a physical lacuna in the source (space left by the scribe, damage to the page, etc.).

The passage marked is transcribed from another witness to the text, to fill a physical lacuna in the source.

The material marked appears in the source, but is thought by the editor to be superfluous (e.g., words written twice) or inauthentic (an interpolation).

The passage is a crux: it is unintelligible or otherwise apparently corrupt and the editor can make no conjectural emendation to solve the crux.

The editor has altered the reading of the passage marked, against the source.

The letters marked are doubtful (either damaged or illegibly written).

The letters marked are certain, despite being damaged, unclearly written, or unexpected.

A certain (or approximate) number of characters in the source cannot be read.

The source has a lacuna of a precisely (or approximately) measurable size.

The source has a lacuna of a nonmeasurable size.

Text is (or is not) supplied for a lacuna; it is certain or uncertain.

An abbreviation has been resolved.

The material marked was erased or canceled by the scribe (or by a later reviser, or by some other hand).

The material marked was erased or canceled but restored (the cancellation was canceled).

The material marked is an interlinear addition to the text.

Beyond this, some editions use distinct symbols in the text to signal variants occurring in different families of manuscripts, or variants whose claim to authenticity is very strong, strong, weak, or very weak.

In addition to recording in some detail any disturbance in the normal physical characteristics of the source (such as damage or illegibility), the nondisturbed characteristics of the witness also need to be described: the writing material (paper, parchment, papyrus, etc.), its normal preparation (for manuscripts, the pattern of prickings and rules, and which side of the sheet is the flesh side and which the hair side; for printed books the nature of the imposition, the font and leading used, etc.).

It is emphatically not sufficient to provide the full text of each witness to the text, without providing collations and information on their interrelationships. For this reason, if no other, it is not sufficient to represent witnesses to a text by means of page images. Such page images are very useful but cannot by themselves provide insight into basic text-critical questions. How often does manuscript A differ from manuscript C in containing a markedly archaic word, where C has a less archaic near-synonym? How often and where do A and B agree against C? B and C against A? A and C against B? Page images provide no help at all answering questions of this kind.

SOFTWARE IS NOT THE ANSWER

Not included in my list of requirements for a successful electronic scholarly edition is a satisfactory choice of software for its preparation and use. Far more important than choice of software is the use of standard software-independent notations for the edition (such as those defined by the TEI), which help ensure that the edition is not irrevocably tied to any particular piece of software. Standard notations, like the TEI's encoding scheme, provide a notation independent of specific hardware and software platforms, in terms of which the intellectual content of an edition can be formulated.

Of course, it is not logically necessary for an electronic edition to be formulated in a notation like that of the TEI. It might be conceived in terms of some particular piece of software, and released in a form designed to allow it to be used with that piece of software. Some electronic texts are now being published in WordCruncher format, to allow them to be used with the popular interactive concordance program; others are released in Folio Views form, or for use with some other software. Other materials, like the Beowulf Workstation developed by Pat Conner of West Virginia, are released in the form of HyperCard stacks.[10] Just as traditional printed editions are conceived in terms of a particular technology—that of printing—so these new editions are conceived in terms of the technology represented by the programs they use. Such editions have the advantage of being self-contained: they can be consulted at once, right out of the box, because they come with software for consulting them.

Like traditional printed editions, however, such software-centered editions have the disadvantage that, being conceived in terms of a particular technology, their use is limited to those with access to that technology. Print technology, for example, is inaccessible to the print handicapped. Software technology is inaccessible to potential readers who use computers of the wrong make or model: Macintosh users cannot run UNIX programs, and vice versa.

We should not try to build our digital library of scholarly editions around any particular piece of software, for at least three reasons. Software is

never equally palatable to all users,

never adequate to absolutely all uses,

too short-lived.

Software never appeals equally to all users. Computers provide tools for thought; we work with them intimately. Naturally, we conceive a liking, or a disliking, for this or that piece of software for intimate reasons we may not even grasp ourselves. If a digital library is to serve all readers, we need to leave the readers some leeway to choose software they are comfortable with; we should not impose one piece of software on them all. The cultural heritage represented by editions should not be restricted to users of Macintoshes, or users of PCs, or users of UNIX machines, still less to users of some one particular program on those machines. It should be accessible to all.

Perhaps more important, *software is never adequate to all uses.* Software is designed to enable users to accomplish a certain set of tasks; good software can accomplish a wide array of tasks, many of them not apparent in detail even to the designer and builder of the program. But it is expecting too much of a program to say that it must meet the needs, for today, tomorrow, and the infinite future, of every scholar who will ever need to study a scholarly edition. Different types of research require different types of software; if a digital library of scholarly editions—or even a single scholarly edition—is to be useful to a wide range of potential readers, it cannot be tied to the capabilities of a single piece of software.

Most important of all, *software is short-lived.* This is, of course, a relative statement. Computer software has a longer lifetime, by and large, than computer hardware. But compared to books—in particular, compared to scholarly editions—software lives out its life in but the twinkling of an eye.

As a student of Germanic philology, I spent my academic career reading texts seven hundred years old, and older. Even for the most important texts, scholarly editions are not very frequently undertaken, and if an edition of a standard Middle High German text is less than forty or fifty years old, it is tolerably new. For many important authors, such as Wolfram von Eschenbach, the standard texts are still those edited by Karl Lachmann a century and a half ago. Later editions have appeared but have not dislodged the work of Lachmann. For documentary materials, the editions of the nineteenth century have not been superseded because the materials have generally not been re-edited.

In other fields, the material being studied may be more recent, but scholarly editions are still expected to last a few decades before being superseded—indeed, in many cases documentary editions take more than a few decades to be completed. Only in unusual circumstances does anyone have the energy to begin a replacement edition before another few decades have passed.[11]

In short, our libraries are full of current editions twenty-five, fifty, or one hundred years old, and of editions even older which continue to be consulted although no longer current.

Our computers, by contrast, rarely run any software which is even five or ten years old, and to find older software one must seek out some old-fashioned mainframe computer center, which may be running some antique program like the Computer-Assisted Scholarly Editing toolkit, or the Oxford Concordance Program, which even in its second release presumably retains some code from the first edition, released an astonishing sixteen years ago. It is just imaginable that some troglodyte in the air-conditioned basement of a bank somewhere is still running COBOL programs written in the 1960s, on an unaltered version of the operating system OS/360, released in 1964. But programs more than thirty years old have only historical interest and run, if at all, only as curiosities: the square-root extraction routines sketched out for ENIAC by John von Neumann on train rides between Philadelphia and Aberdeen, or the programs written by Ada Lovelace for Charles Babbage's Analytical Engine, which might conceivably be running on simulators in computer science departments somewhere. A Macintosh-based simulation of OS/360 is, I believe, the only way it is now possible to run the landmark hypertext system FRESS, developed at Brown University by Andries van Dam in the early 1970s.

There are editorial projects currently under way that had published their first volume before FRESS was a gleam in Andries van Dam's eye, and which will probably not publish their final index volume until sometime after the last programmer has lost track of where that OS/360 simulator program went, and FRESS is nothing more than a gleam in the shining eyes of hypertext enthusiasts with long memories and a love of history.

Software is short-lived. If we want the first volume of a major scholarly edition to remain usable at least until the final volume of the edition is completed, then we must ensure that that first volume does not depend on some specific piece of software. No software available when we begin a major project is likely to survive, let alone remain the best available choice, even for as short a time as twenty or thirty years.

Software is necessary for electronic editions to be successful, but any electronic edition conceived and formulated in terms of one specific piece of software will necessarily appeal only to those who like that particular program; it will be useful only to those whose research falls comfortably within the paradigm supported by that program; and it will die when that program, or the hardware it is designed for, also dies. So we should not try to build scholarly editions around a particular piece of software.

It is not necessary, however, to abandon the notion of making electronic texts easy to use, by distributing them with software which most users will find useful. The materials created by the Perseus Project at Harvard University (a large collection of textual and graphical materials for the study of Hellenic civilization) were published in HyperCard form. The TEI guidelines themselves are being released on CD-ROM with a browser called DynaText. That means that, like the software-specific editions I mentioned earlier, they can be consulted, right out of the box, using the software that comes with them.

The Perseus materials, however, and the TEI guidelines themselves, differ from the products I mentioned earlier because they are not conceived primarily in terms of a specific piece of software. In each case, they are conceived in abstract terms, as a particular network of textual and other materials, which can be presented in a variety of ways. The Perseus materials are archived in SGML (the Standard Generalized Markup Language), and the distributed HyperCard-based materials are derived from the archival form by mechanical software-driven transformations. The TEI guidelines are available in their native SGML (TEI-encoded) electronic form; they are also distributed in derivative forms: print, electronic form formatted for convenient viewing onscreen (much like a book from Project Gutenberg), and as a DynaText book. Independently of the TEI, others have used the original form of the guidelines to create still other forms: a Toronto vendor of SGML software has included the guidelines on a CD-ROM of SGML materials, where they can be consulted using a general-purpose SGML browser included with the CD-ROM. The library at the University of Virginia has put up a network server to allow searches of the guidelines in their native form, and to deliver the results in the HyperText Markup Language (HTML) tag set used on the World Wide Web.

Because Perseus and the TEI guidelines are not conceived in terms of a particular technology of delivering the text, they will not become unreadable when HyperCard, or Netscape, or DynaText are no longer current software. Software and hardware independence means they will survive the death of the software and hardware on which they were created. For scholarly editions, such longevity is essential. And that is why I say that the development and use of software-independent markup schemes like SGML and the TEI guidelines will prove more important, in the long run, to the success of electronic scholarly editions, and to a digital library of such editions, than any single piece of software can.

THE TEI GUIDELINES

In the previous section, I outlined some demands placed upon any serious representation of a text with a complex textual history. In the next, I will describe how the TEI guidelines attempt to meet those demands, for representations of such texts in electronic form. First, however, I need to describe briefly the goals and background of the TEI encoding scheme. The TEI has been described in some detail at conferences over the past several years; I will limit myself here to noting just a few salient points.

The TEI has adopted, as the basis for its encoding scheme, a formal language called the Standard Generalized Markup Language.[12] Formally, the TEI scheme is expressed as a *document-type definition* defined in SGML notation, which defines a large number of *tags* for marking up electronic documents. In practice, tags are used to control the processing of TEI documents, or their translation into other electronic formats.

The TEI groups its tags into *tag sets,* each containing tags needed for one particular type of text or one particular type of textual work, so users of the scheme can select the tags needed and exclude the rest from view. Very few tags in the TEI encoding scheme are unconditionally required; a slightly larger number are recommended; the vast majority of tags mark strictly optional features that may be marked up or left unmarked at the option of the creator of the electronic text.

Tags of very wide relevance, which will be needed by virtually all users, are included in the "core" tag sets. These include tags for identifying the electronic text, its creators, and its sources, and for common textual phenomena like paragraphs, italicized phrases, names, editorial corrections, notes, and passages of verse or drama. Other tag sets handle particular types of text (prose, verse, drama, spoken material, dictionaries, term banks)—these are the *base tag sets;* in general, every text encoded with the TEI scheme will use one base tag set. Still other tag sets support specialized types of text processing or areas of research (hypertext linking, analysis and interpretation of the text, manuscript transcription, special documentation for language corpora, etc.); these *additional tag sets* may be used in any combination, and with any base tag set.

The TEI guidelines do not represent the first concerted attempt since the invention of computers to develop a general-purpose scheme for representing texts in electronic form for purposes of research—but they do represent the first such attempt

> which was not limited to a single institution, but attempted instead to register the consensus of the entire community of interested researchers;
>
> which attempted to cover all types of text, in all languages and scripts, from all periods;
>
> which attempted to support all types of research rather than being limited to specific disciplines; and
>
> which actually came to fruition instead of perishing somewhere along the way.

That the TEI did come to fruition is a testament to the urgency of the need felt by the research community for some such mechanism for the sharing and preservation of their electronic texts, and to the tenacious work of the scores of volunteers who served on TEI work groups and committees.

A reference manual for the TEI encoding scheme was published in 1994 under the title *Guidelines for Electronic Text Encoding and Interchange.*[13] The TEI guidelines encompass some thirteen hundred pages of information, available in print and electronically. Introductory user manuals, tutorials, and similar ancillary materials are now being prepared, but for the immediate future it seems fair to predict that the TEI scheme will be adopted more commonly by large projects which need a systematic research-oriented encoding scheme and can invest time learning to use it, than by individual users who may not feel quite so much pressure to ensure the longevity of their work, and who may feel intimidated, rather than reassured, by the amount of detail contained in the reference manual.

Because the TEI scheme is an application of SGML, TEI markup can be used with any software which conforms to the SGML standard and which has sufficiently large capacity to handle the TEI document-type definitions. The document-type definitions (DTDs) themselves, like the full text of the reference manual, are freely available over the network. This means that the TEI encoding scheme can be used in the creation, dissemination, and study of electronic texts immediately, without the TEI itself having had to expend any time or effort on software development. SGML editors (from the public-domain SGML mode for the popular UNIX editor "Emacs" to state-of-the-art graphical interfaces for Macintosh and Windows users) can be used to create and edit TEI-conformant documents; SGML processing tools (from the public-domain parser "sgmls" to high-end fourth-generation language tools marketed commercially) can be used to process TEI-encoded material; SGML layout and composition tools can typeset TEI documents; SGML delivery tools and browsers can be used to disseminate TEI-conformant text in electronic form. Because SGML represents a major step forward for text processing, the number, quality, and variety of programs supporting SGML will continue to grow for the foreseeable future. The quality and variety of programs already available constitute one of the most persuasive demonstrations that the TEI made the right choice in selecting SGML as the basis for the TEI encoding scheme, and in concentrating on the definition of the encoding scheme itself, rather than on the development of software.

TEI AND TEXTUAL CRITICISM

I said above that the three overarching goals for serious electronic editions are accessibility, longevity, and intellectual integrity. The TEI encoding scheme secures accessibility and longevity by providing a software- and hardware-independent notation for the creation of electronic texts of all kinds. Electronic resources created in TEI form will by definition be usable on any platform, with a wide variety of software; they will not become technologically obsolete when the software and hardware used to create them do.

The intellectual integrity of materials encoded with the TEI encoding scheme is harder to guarantee. With the TEI, as without it, integrity remains inescapably the responsibility of the creator of an edition; all that the TEI can do is to provide the mechanisms needed to allow textual critics to create intellectually serious electronic editions using the TEI encoding scheme. It is not possible, within the scope of this essay, to describe SGML markup and the TEI encoding scheme in any detail, but it may be useful to provide a short overview of the TEI tag sets for text-critical apparatus of variants and transcription of primary sources, and describe briefly some other relevant parts of the TEI scheme.

Where possible, the TEI based its recommendations on existing practice in the creation of electronic texts. In this area, however, there was not much to work from. A number of programs have been developed for collation of witnesses and for typesetting an apparatus criticus. Most general-purpose schemes for the encoding of literary or historical texts, however, make no provision for text-critical variation or for recording physical characteristics of the source.[14]

The TEI provides tags for a variety of problems arising in textual criticism, most critically the encoding of an apparatus criticus, the registration of alterations and physical damage to the source, the indication of uncertain readings, and the association of arbitrarily complex annotation with any passage of text:

> A group of tags for apparatus entries (*app, lem, rdg, wit,* and *witDetail,* for apparatus entries, the lemma and variant readings, the lists of witnesses attesting each reading, and further notes on each witness, as needed) allows readings to be transcribed, attributed to different groups of witnesses, and classified according to any typology deemed useful; this would allow an apparatus of variants to be rendered properly by a display or page-composition program.

A group of tags for editorial or other intervention in the text allows material to be marked as added above the line or in the margin (the *add* tag), canceled or erased (the *del* tag), canceled and then restored *(restored)*, not canceled but extraneous *(del)*, or supplied by a modern editor or transcriber *(supplied)*; the creator of the electronic text may associate with any of these tags information about the hand responsible for the deletion, addition, and so forth.

Other editorial tags may be used to mark correction (the *corr* and *sic* tags) or normalization *(reg* and *orig)* of the text in the source, whether by the transcriber or by some other party.

The *space* tag may be used to indicate blank space left by the scribe (or compositor) in a source.

An *unclear* tag may be used to mark text which is hard to read, whether because of damage or because it was written illegibly in the first place.

A tag for marking *damage* to the source may be used to indicate lacunae or other problems in the source, and their exact or approximate size; if the *unclear* tag does not also occur, the implication is that the material is clearly legible despite being damaged.

If material is omitted because illegible, its absence and extent may be indicated using the *gap* tag.

A separate tag *(certain)* may be used to mark uncertainty of many kinds regarding the transcribed text or its markup.

The *abbr* and *expan* tags may be used to mark abbreviations in the source, whether they have been resolved or left unresolved.

Several methods are provided for annotating a text with structured or free-form annotation, ranging from free-text notes *(note)*, to simple or complex mechanisms for identifying any feature or characteristic of interest to the encoder and associating it with any portion of the text (the *span* tag for simple associations of a span of text with some interpretive construct, and a more complex set of tags for interpretations with strong internal structures, expressed as *feature structures*); cruxes can conveniently be marked with these tags.

For historical reasons, the current version of the TEI encoding scheme is slightly better developed with regard to manuscript materials than with regard to printed matter; a number of manuscript specialists participated actively in the project, but we were unsuccessful in attempts to form a work group for analytical bibliography. As a result, the current version of the guidelines limits itself, as regards the transcription of printed materials, to some fairly obvious basic requirements. Catchwords, signatures, page numbers, running heads and footers, and other material that does not fit into the ongoing stream of the text are often omitted from transcriptions but are often crucial for text-critical work with an edition; the current TEI encoding scheme provides a single catchall tag for these, called *fw* (for "forme work"). Gatherings may be recorded using the general-purpose *milestone* tag to mark the boundaries of the gatherings. No specific provision is currently made for imposition information; it is not clear what form such information needs to take when it is recorded.

Page layout and typographic features of the source may be described at any level of detail desired, using the global *rend* (rendition) attribute, but the TEI currently provides no formal language for the description.[15] This omission has a number of reasons. First, different portions of the community have very different requirements in this area: many creators of electronic text have no interest whatever in the typographic characterization of the source; others would like merely to record shifts into italics or bold fonts, without actually identifying the fonts used; still others will need or desire an extremely detailed description of the font and leading (or hand and size), and the layout of the page. The simplest way to serve all these different requirements is to provide a location for recording information on these matters, without restricting the form in which the information is to be recorded. This is what the TEI has done. The advantage of this approach is that it allows text critics and analytic bibliographers to record whatever information they wish about the typography of any printed or manuscript document; the disadvantage is that it provides no guidance to those trying to decide what features of the text are worth recording, and no way to standardize such information, even among people who are recording the same characteristics of the source.

A second reason for the sparse treatment of typography and layout in the TEI guidelines is political: the marketplace of text-processing software is currently dominated by WYSIWYG (what-you-see-is-what-you-get) word processing systems which are singularly ill suited to the needs of scholars transcribing original source materials, precisely because they focus exclusively on the appearance of the printed page. In order to distinguish the TEI clearly from such word processing systems, the original development laid great stress on developing an approach to text which stressesits linguistic and literary structure, instead of its appearance on the page.

A third reason typography receives no formal treatment in the guidelines is the most serious, at the moment. It is not at all obvious how best to describe the layout of a page in an electronic transcription of that page. For all their convenience and sophistication, conventional word processing systems limit themselves to trying to get a printer to recreate the page itself; they do a very poor job at expressing the fundamental rules governing a page. Further work requires a much deeper understanding of historical page design and typography than most word processor developers can be expected to acquire.

Despite a tradition of book design going back centuries, and despite the efforts of many devoted critics, no one could claim that there is a consensus on how to describe a printed page in detail. Some critics speak of the "bibliographic codes" that form part of the publication of any work. But the term is, for now, still more a metaphor than a sober description. The characteristic of any *code* is that it is made up of a finite set of *signs,* which as Saussure teaches us are arbitrary linkages of *signifier* and *signified.* For artificial languages, the sets of signifiers and their meanings are given by the creator of the artificial language. For natural languages, dictionaries attempt to catalog the signifiers and their significance; grammars attempt to explain the rules for combining signs into utterances. We have nothing equivalent for the physical appearance of texts in books. Any serious attempt to record the bibliographic codes built into the book design and typography of a literary work must begin by specifying the set of signs to be distinguished. Is 24-point type different from 10-point type as a bibliographic code? In most circumstances, yes. Is 10-point type from one type foundry different from 10-point type in the same face, produced by a different foundry? In most circumstances, no. What about 10- and 11-point type? Ten and 12? To specify a formal language for expressing significant differences of typographic treatment, we need to reach some agreement about what constitutes a significant difference—what the minimal pairs are.[16]

The natural constituencies for such work include text critics and analytical bibliographers; it is to be hoped that the TEI will be able, at some point in the near future, to charter a work group to explore the relevant issues and make recommendations for extending the TEI tag sets to handle relevant information better.

CONCLUSION

It remains to describe briefly some implications, for scholarly editors, of standards like SGML and the TEI guidelines, and some basic requirements for our future work in creating electronic scholarly editions.

First, it is only fair to point out that the TEI guidelines, like any standard notation, may prove dangerous. Like any notation, the TEI guidelines inevitably make it easy to express certain kinds of ideas, and concomitantly harder to express other kinds of ideas, about the texts we encode in electronic form. Any notation carries with it the danger that it must favor certain habits of thought—in the TEI's case, certain approaches to text—at the expense of others. No one should use TEI markup without being aware of this danger—any more than we should use the English language, or any other, without realizing that it favors the expression of certain kinds of ideas, and discourages the expression, and even the conception, of other ideas.

Such dangers cannot be evaded by any means short of eliminating the use of all notations or symbolic systems from thought—which in turn would appear to mean they cannot be evaded by any method short of ceasing to think at all. The danger can be mitigated, or minimized, by facing it clearly and attempting to provide mechanisms for modifying, or extending, a notation to allow it to express new concepts conveniently. In the TEI's case, several steps have been taken to minimize the danger that the TEI guidelines will have the baleful effect of standardizing the way scholars think:

> The formal requirements of the TEI guidelines are very small: TEI-conformant electronic texts must be in SGML and must bear a title identifying the text; the title in turn must be distinguishable from the text itself. The overwhelming mass of the guidelines consists of optional methods of marking items of interest.
>
> As far as possible, TEI work groups have endeavored to express the consensus of scholarship, rather than attempting to impose tag sets which reflect the views only of one or the other school of thought. The TEI tags for linguistic annotation, for example, do not require that the encoder subscribe to transformational grammar, phrase-structure grammar, dependency grammar, or any other current school; instead, they are formulated so as to make it possible for

> adherents of any of these schools, or of any other linguistic approach, to express their analysis of a text in a natural way.
>
> Several tags are provided which allow encoders of electronic text to mark items of interest for which no special tags are provided in the guidelines. These tags allow the defined *semantics* of the tag set to be extended, without requiring the defined *syntax* of the tag set to be changed in any way.
>
> New tags can be added to the tag sets, provided that certain rules are followed, which have the effect of ensuring that future users of the electronic text can find out what the new tags are intended to mean.
>
> Tags now defined in the TEI scheme can be suppressed, renamed, or modified, provided the changes are properly documented.

Such methods mean the TEI scheme makes far more explicit provision for the views of dissenting scholars than any other method of creating electronic text ever formulated. They do not eliminate entirely the dangers which any notation poses for those who use it, but they do go far to ensure that the TEI guidelines can be used by scholars of widely varying views as to the proper interpretation or study of the text.

On the positive side, standardization of notation does mean that it will be possible to develop software to handle a wider variety of text types and scholarly needs than can easily be handled without such standardization. Since the TEI encoding scheme is not specific to any one piece of software, many TEI-aware programs can be written, and the same TEI-encoded data can be used with any such program. TEI-aware software, in turn, should in principle be usable with any TEI-conformant text. Both text and software should thus be reusable in wider contexts than is the case without standard notations like SGML.

The highly structured nature of SGML markup makes it feasible to verify the structural soundness of markup mechanically, by means of software to parse and validate the SGML data. Such mechanical validation can detect a wide variety of typographic and conceptual errors in the input. Application programs can rely more confidently on the quality of their input data, which means they can be simpler and less expensive to write.

Equally important, the structure of SGML markup makes it possible for markup to become much more elaborate and subtle, without overwhelming the ability of either software or users to deal with the complexity. It will become feasible, as it has never been before, for the same textual material to be annotated in many different ways: a legal document might have a detailed diplomatic transcription of the text, linked to a scanned image of the original manuscript, with an analysis of the legal issues involved, links to information about the individuals named, and a detailed analysis of its linguistic structure at the phonological, morphological, and syntactic levels. Archaic spellings could be flagged with their modern equivalents, and unusual words could be glossed, so the same text could be used either for advanced study by specialists or to produce a new-spelling handout with basic annotations for use in an undergraduate class. The specialist need not be distracted by the spelling modernizations and glosses intended for undergraduates, and the undergraduates need not be intimidated by the linguistic or historical apparatus: it is a simple matter for software to filter out and hide all the annotations intended for undergraduates, or to hide everything *but* the annotations for undergraduates.

Such analysis and markup is not the work of a day, of course, and need not be added in a day. For centuries, scholars have built up layer upon layer of commentary and analysis of important texts. SGML markup will not change that practice; it merely makes it possible for many such layers of analysis and interpretation to coexist in the same electronic form. As we work with our texts over the years, we will gradually enrich them with layer after layer of annotation. Eventually the electronic representation of the text will become a more adequate representation of the text and our understanding of it than even the most elaborately annotated printed page—because the electronic version can be directed to display or to conceal each layer in turn, so that the visual representation of the text can mirror our changing focus of interest as we study it.

Perhaps the most important implication of standardization of markup will be, however, that it will make it possible to integrate resources developed by separate projects into seamless electronic wholes. Currently, each electronic resource comes with its own software; to move from one to the other you must shut the first down and start the second up; if you are lucky you can simply close one window and open another, but even in the best of cases you must change context more or less completely. It is a bit as if the works of Ben Jonson and those of William Shakespeare not only did not circulate but were kept in different rooms of the library (or in different buildings entirely), so that to consult both you had to walk from one room to the other, or one building to another. One reason our libraries no longer chain books to the shelves is that scholarship is materially easier when we can have both books out on our desk at the same time for direct comparison.

Integration of editions into a virtual digital library is the electronic equivalent of getting both volumes onto our desk at the same time. And adoption of a common language for electronic text encoding is the way to make such integration feasible.

I said at the outset that the three general goals of any electronic edition must be accessibility, longevity, and intellectual integrity. In the light of the intervening discussion, it is now possible to enunciate some basic principles which can help electronic scholarly editions achieve those goals.

Strive for software and hardware independence. Tying an edition to one particular hardware or software platform erects an unnecessary technological barrier to users of other hardware and software and ensures that the edition will die when the platform on which it depends dies.

Distinguish firmly between the intellectual requirements of the edition and the requirements for convenient distribution and use of the edition. Our notions of what constitutes convenient use of an edition vary too much from individual to individual and will in any case change radically during the lifetime of any serious edition.

Create the edition in a software- and hardware-independent notation. Derive platform-specific versions of that archival form for distribution when and as necessary. Never confuse the edition itself with the temporary forms it takes for distribution and use. Otherwise, you fall into the same confusion as Benjamin, between the roles of the author and those of the printer and bookbinder.

Use documented, publicly defined, nonproprietary formats for the archival version of the edition. At this time, there is no serious alternative to SGML for this purpose. Use proprietary formats only for distribution versions.

Exploit the ability of the computer to provide multiple views of the same material. An electronic edition need not be limited to a single audience; much more readily than print editions, electronic editions can serve both general and specialized audiences. Where appropriate, provide the information needed to allow the user to read the text in new spelling or old, with or without the correction of obvious errors, with or without an apparatus of variants, including or excluding purely orthographic variants, with or without indications of text-critical, historical, literary, or linguistic commentary, with or without a literal or free translation into another language.

If as a community we ignore these principles, we will have electronic editions which do not capture the complexity and difficulty of textual transmission and textual variation, which run only on last year's (or the last decade's) machines, which impose on their readers a particular view of the material and brook no contradiction when they tell their readers what they ought to be interested in, which fall silent with every new revolution in computer hardware and software. If we attend to them, then we can hope to have editions which last longer than the machines on our desks, which can be used by a wide variety of users, from undergraduates to specialists, and which exploit the capacities of the electronic medium to render a full and useful accounting of the texts they represent, and the textual tradition to which we owe their preservation.

NOTES

1. "From a photographic plate it is possible to make a multitude of prints; there is no sense in seeking the authentic print." Walter Benjamin, *Das Kunstwerk im Zeitalter seiner technischen Reproduzierbarkeit* (Frankfurt am Main: Suhrkamp, 1963), par. 4, p. 21. All translations are my own.
2. "The enormous changes which printing, the technical reproducibility of writing, has called forth in literature, are well known." Benjamin, *Kunstwerk,* par. 1, p. 11. Not everyone distinguishes so carefully between literature and writing.
3. Florian Coulmas, *The Writing Systems of the World* (Oxford: Blackwell, 1991), 12.
4. "[T]he history to which it [the artwork] has been subject in the course of its existence." Benjamin, par. 2, pp. 13–14.
5. The discussions of Thomas Tanselle may be taken as emblematic of this point: in his essay on critical apparatus, he devotes much more space to considering how to make it easy to produce a student or lay reader's edition by photographically reproducing selected pages of the scholarly edition, than to considering how to ensure that the apparatus actually meets the needs of working scholars. See G. Thomas Tanselle, "Some Principles for Editorial Apparatus," *Studies in Bibliography* 25 (1972): 41–88; rpt. in his *Textual Criticism and Scholarly Editing* (Charlottesville: University Press of Virginia, 1990), 119–76. His purely typographic arguments need not apply to electronic editions, however, and computer-driven typesetting renders them irrelevant even to print publication. In a similar vein, cf. Peter L. Shillingsburg, *Scholarly Editing in the Computer Age: Theory and Practice,* rev. ed. (Athens: University of Georgia Press, 1986). Commenting on Tanselle's argument in favor of final authorial intention, which rests finally on the claim that "no critical text can reflect . . . multiple intentions simultaneously," Shillingsburg observes, "The practical difficulty of presenting multiple intentions in a book is seen as more important than the conceptual insight that multiple intentions are operative" (41).

The print-driven nature of much of Tanselle's editorial theory is also visible, though less egregiously, in the general statements on textual criticism his *A Rationale of Textual Criticism* (Philadelphia: University of Pennsylvania Press, 1989).

6. I say that Project Gutenberg objects in principle to the provision of apparatus, because it insists on distributing texts only in ASCII-only format, without any systematic explicit scheme of markup. Since the American Standard Code for Information Interchange (ASCII) makes no provision for textual apparatus, such apparatus can only be rendered in electronic form by means of some markup language such as the internal markup used by word processors like Word or WordPerfect, or the visible markup used by programs like LaTeX or Scribe, or the SGML markup defined by the TEI. By limiting itself to markup-free ASCII, Project Gutenberg systematically makes apparatus impossible to include in its texts.
7. "The basis of critical method is not an immediate judgment on the known readings; it is a historical reconstruction of the transmission of the text, using the oldest manuscripts." "As long as any error remains unexplained, the good reading remains tainted with a residue of uncertainty." Louis Havet, *Manuel de critique verbale appliquée aux textes latins* (Paris: Hachette, 1911), par. 17, p. 3; par. 67, p. 12.
8. "The editor of a text must account for the entire extant textual tradition, or more pointedly, for every single variant." Georg Steer, "Grundsätzliche Überlegungen und Vorschläge zur Rationalisierung des Lesartenapparats," in *Kolloquium über Probleme altgermanistischer Editionen, Marbach am Neckar, 26. u. 27. April 1966*, ed. Hugo Kuhn, Karl Stackmann, and Dieter Wuttke (Wiesbaden: Franz Steiner Verlag, 1968), 34.
9. The items given are gleaned from a variety of sources, including: Paul Maas, *Textkritik*, 3d ed. (Leipzig: B. G. Teubner, 1957); André Bataille, *Les Papyrus: Traité d'études byzantines II* (Paris: Presses Universitaires de France, 1955); [Louis Havet, rev. Jacques André], *Régles et recommandations pour les éditions critiques (Série latine)* (Paris: Société d'édition "Les belles lettres," 1972); [Louis Havet, rev. Jean Irigoin], *Régles et recommandations pour les éditions critiques (Série grecque)* (Paris: Société d'édition "Les belles lettres," 1972); and Georg Steer, "Grundsätzliche Überlegungen und Vorschläge zur Rationalisierung des Lesartenapparats," in Kuhn, Stackmann, and Wuttke, *Kolloquium*, 34–41, who describes a symbol system designed in Zurich and used in Erwin Nestlé's editions of the Greek New Testament.
10. On the Beowulf Workstation, see Patrick W. Conner, "The *Beowulf* Workstation: One Model of Computer-Assisted Literary Pedagogy," *Literary and Linguistic Computing* 6, no. 1 (1991): 50–58.
11. The case of Friedrich Hölderlin, whose works experienced two major editions within twenty years, is a slightly scandalous exception, the discussion of which lends a certain *frisson* of excitement to graduate seminars on German literature even now, thirty years later.
12. International Organization for Standardization, *ISO 8879-1986 (E): Informa-*

tion Processing—Text and Office Systems—Standard Generalized Markup Language (SGML) (Geneva: ISO, Oct. 15, 1986).

13. Association for Computers and the Humanities (ACH), Association for Computational Linguistics (ACL), and Association for Literary and Linguistic Computing (ALLC), *Guidelines for Electronic Text Encoding and Interchange*, ed. C. M. Sperberg-McQueen and Lou Burnard (Chicago, Oxford: Text Encoding Initiative, 1994). Available from the Text Encoding Initiative; further information may be obtained from the author.
14. The Thesaurus Linguae Graecae, at the University of California at Irvine, for example, makes no attempt to transcribe the apparatus of its source editions. I am told by Theodore Brunner that this is primarily because at the beginning of the project, the task of devising a usable encoding scheme for apparatus seemed insuperable. Two exceptions to the general neglect of textual variation in general-purpose systems should be mentioned. The general-purpose package TUSTEP, developed by Wilhelm Ott at Tübingen, does have built-in support for both collation and critical apparatus, but in this as in other ways it is unusually well designed. Manfred Thaller, of the Max-Planck-Institut für Geschichte in Göttingen, has developed notations for text-critical variation in connection with his general-purpose historical workstation software, κλειω. Together with various packages for version control in software development, these systems had direct influence on the TEI's recommendations for text-critical apparatus.
15. The claim that page layout and typographic features cannot be described at all in the TEI encoding scheme, as made by Jerome J. McGann elsewhere in this volume, is a misconception that cannot survive a serious examination of the text of the TEI guidelines.
16. The work of Jerome J. McGann on the Rossetti Archive, discussed elsewhere in this volume, may provide a useful starting point. The SGML document-type definitions developed for the Rossetti Archive, which are based on those of the first draft of the TEI guidelines, may be taken as demonstrating how the TEI's recommendations are compatible with extensions of widely varying types for different specialized interests.

Completeness and Adequacy in Text Encoding

John Lavagnino

People who edit texts for scholarly editions and people who create electronic texts do very similar things: they take existing texts and create new representations of them for scholarly use. But text encoders, in creating electronic texts, have not often drawn on the literature of textual editing, despite its relevance: perhaps because it's usually assumed that encoding is a technical process that doesn't require a scholarly examination of the text. Textual editing is seen as a producer of books to be encoded, or a consumer of encoded source texts, and not as an analogous pursuit. I will argue, however, that encoding is a form of editing, and that editorial theory suggests a change that's needed in our way of thinking about encoding: we should substitute a criterion of adequacy for the usual criterion of completeness, because completeness misleads us about the possible achievements of an encoding and is in the end unattainable.

Text encoders usually proceed without any theory, since encoding is most often thought of, by everyone involved, as a purely objective process. What most text encoders have instead is a criterion that they seek to have their texts meet: a criterion which I will call *completeness,* and which stipulates that an electronic text should reproduce exactly the written copytext. Completeness has similarities to the editorial criterion of *definitiveness,* as this was popularly understood for many years: the definitive edition of a work strives to be the last edition of that work, in the sense that it should establish the facts about the work once and for all. Here is a statement of this view from Fredson Bowers, with respect to his edition of Nathaniel Hawthorne's works, the Centenary Edition published by the Ohio State University Press:

> An important element in the definitive edition is the complete textual history that it records. A future editor may, for instance, disagree with a Centenary Hawthorne emendation (or refusal to emend) in *The Scarlet Letter,* but he will never need to collate the first, second, and third editions for variant substantive readings and a decision about their authority. That task has been fully and accurately performed in the definitive Ohio State edition down to the last plate changes made during Hawthorne's lifetime in the third edition text. In short, all the preparatory editorial work is over with and is properly listed in the edition. Nothing bearing on the authority of the Centenary text that any future editor could possibly wish to know about has been omitted.[1]

To rephrase this: it is possible that future editors will differ with Bowers's decisions on correcting suspected errors in the text of Hawthorne (as has indeed been the case). But there is a body of data from which any edition has to start, and that body of data has been collected definitively, once and for all. In the same way, it is commonly believed that an electronic text should simply capture the entire body of facts about the source text; and because most electronic texts are presented as unedited transcriptions rather than as critical editions, Bowers's strictures about the extent to which the term *definitive* applies don't come up. (The claim of scholarly editions by Bowers and others to be definitive was often criticized because many readers assumed that this extended to editorial decisions as well, despite Bowers's statements to the contrary; that question is not at issue with respect to electronic texts.) Completeness, like the aspects of scholarly editions to which definitiveness referred, is a criterion that is entirely objective and final: there is no possibility of disagreement if it's done right, and there is nothing about the text that is left unencoded.

Although most who believe in and use this criterion of completeness have not given any theoretical argument for it, it is nevertheless possible to consider what sort of theoretical basis can be found for it—especially because its application has proved to be a point of some contention among encoders, even though it looks like common sense at first to all involved. It is productive to look to current editorial theory for such a grounding, since editors are involved in a similar pursuit. From this point of view, completeness ceases to look like common sense, and instead looks rather odd, because it mixes together features of two very different ways of thinking about editing, which I will call *idealism* and *localism.*

I call by the name of idealism the view of texts that has long been dominant: this view is idealist in the sense of "not material," because on this view a text is an abstract thing. It is a theory most comprehensively elaborated by G. Thomas Tanselle in *A Rationale of Textual Criticism:* literary works are, in his term, "intangible" works, and may be physically realized in any number of ways.[2] On this view, a literary text can, as Gérard Genette puts it, "transcend in its essentials the particularities of its diverse materializations: phonic, graphic or other."[3] You can read it in a book, or you can hear someone else read it aloud, and it's reasonable to say that it's still the same text. Or, more significantly for the question of editing, you can take a printed text from a book and reprint it in another book, in a new typeface, with new pagination and a different binding, and still claim that you're presenting the same text—in the sense that, for example, a responsible scholar who wants to study that text can for a great many purposes look only at this new text. Genette acknowledges that texts often play with their sound or with their appearance on the page—but he doesn't think this undermines their ideal status. You don't have to hear a text spoken in order to appreciate its sound; a musical score means something to musicians even without a performance.

The example of the reprinted text illustrates the way this principle underlies the practice of scholarly editing; but the same principle is behind the commercial publishing industry as well, and indeed behind the systems on which many writers have depended for communicating their works to their audiences. In the European manuscript and print cultures alike, those systems have rarely delivered to the audience anything with a close physical resemblance to the author's manuscript or typescript; the author's text has always gotten translated into a different physical form. Indeed, those systems have typically been *more* idealist in their nature than scholarly editing: scholars tend to care a lot more about the preservation of nonideal features than the agencies of publication ever have. Today, it would often be more economical to reproduce an author's manuscript photographically rather than to set it in type, but this is almost never done *except* in publications intended for scholars: in microfilms and printed facsimiles of authors' manuscripts, all intended for study rather than reading. Some publishers ask their authors to submit camera-ready copy, but these are usually publishers of scholarly or specialized works, not publishers of general works, and in any case they specify formats for such submissions; they will not use manuscripts that haven't been tailored for such publication. But in any case scholarly editing does not pretend to avoid such transformations entirely. There is no scholarly edition—not even a facsimile—that does not ignore some features of previous editions. Many scholarly editions will list those things, though they will never list them all: such things as the type and size of paper used are rarely reproduced in a new edition, and it even more rarely seems necessary to state this. We all know without being told that, for example, the lineation of a prose work will be different.

We all know this without being told, and indeed we all tend to act on the claim of this theory—that there are aspects of the material manifestation of a text that may be ignored when that text is reproduced. It seems to be the natural state of things, so completely self-evident that it seems silly to set it out at such length. But there is a different tendency that is now embodied in a number of recent works on editorial theory. It has no accepted name; I choose to call it *localism,* a term used by Leah Marcus in her work that illustrates one form of this general approach.[4] Some people might say *materialism,* but this tendency isn't always tied to great knowledge of the material production of books or to Marxist thinking generally. Its distinctive feature is not attention to physical detail, since idealist textual scholars have that as well; it is instead the concern with incidentals, with details. It argues that idealist textual theory effaces those details in the name of theories about texts in general, or the meaning of the work in general, that don't do justice to these aspects. Its sensibility is similar to that of Clifford Geertz in favoring "local knowledge" over grand theoretical constructions.[5]

The argument of localists is that it's precisely the things which an idealist editor considers incidental to the ideal text that may be of the most interest. It is obligatory, in discussions of localism, to invoke William Blake—who illustrated and printed almost all of his own books, and whose practice implies very strongly that he considered this the one right way of issuing his work.[6] Nevertheless, comparatively few of his modern readers study Blake's works with their illustrations; idealist editors have considered it reasonable to issue versions of Blake's "complete poetry" that have few or no illustrations. David Erdman's edition, in its version of 1982, has four illustrations, and one more on the dust jacket.[7] It is hard to deny that this is, at the very least, not the only good way of representing Blake's writing.

But even when we consider texts without illustrations, we find great differences in the idealist and localist points of view. An important task in idealist editing, for example, is the correction of errors in transmission. Presumably nobody objects to the removal of simple mistakes—but in fact some localists do. Randall McLeod, in his work on English Renaissance texts, argues that some of the "errors" that editors have corrected in these texts were perfectly legitimate readings; that these editors have not corrected the texts, but garbled them. That much we could remedy, you'd think; but he goes farther than this. A facsimile of an early edition may have more "errors" in it than a modern reprint, but it also provides far more of the information we need to read as Renaissance readers did, with their understanding of what was right and what was wrong, and their awareness of the degree of uncertainty in the text; our corrected modern editions make it look as if we're quite certain about what the text is supposed to say, an error no contemporary reader would have made.[8]

In the view of localists, idealists go around saying, "This doesn't matter. You don't need to worry about that." And they smooth out the oddities and roughnesses of texts, when these features may be the most distinctive ones. The illustrations in Blake, or the errors in Renaissance texts, are two examples of this smoothing out or smoothing over at work. Idealists efface "difficult" features of these works and in so doing make them more like everything else; more ordinary. Another localist concern is with physical features of books that have (we tend to think) even less to do with the author's intentions and the text's meaning: such as a book's size, binding, and cost. Yet if you think about the books *you* buy, you know that in fact these things matter to readers.

McLeod and other localists think we should all read facsimiles, not new editions. And even facsimiles are not good enough for localists who particularly care about the physical features of books. Paul Mann points out that Blake, in publishing his own works, produced small and expensive editions for an audience that scarcely existed, and by a method that ensured that every copy was unique. And hence they are not the same works as modern machine-produced facsimiles, uniform in every copy and with a guaranteed audience. The modern facsimiles are *books* in a way that Blake's were not: Blake's editions are better thought of as we think of paintings, as unique art objects that cannot be reproduced. No Picasso scholar would consider a book of reproductions adequate for his or her work; Mann argues that a Blake scholar should feel the same way.[9]

I commented above that idealism was the "natural" view of things. But localism is natural too, at least for literary scholars today, because literary scholars are trained to pick up on tiny details and argue for their significance: so that once examples like that of Blake's works are forcefully presented, there will be people who've never thought much about editorial questions who will at once recognize their importance. Grace Ioppolo made the connection between criticism and localism:

> If we demand that our undergraduate students recognize the multiplicity of form and meaning and interpretation of a literary work, that they appreciate the multiple layers and structures, how can we demand that they use only fixed, limited, and copy-texted texts? Both textual and literary critics must now re-evaluate and re-define the idea of "the text"; it is no longer editorially or theoretically composite or finite, but multiple and ever-revising.[10]

It is true, however, that a fair number of people involved in literary studies still find this point of view almost incomprehensible—that is, not merely mistaken but totally unaccountable.[11] Such people tend to have the same reaction when they encounter the suggestion that collaboration and revision are widespread practices among writers.[12] Idealism, and a further belief in the determinate identity and single authorship of literary works, are for some very deeply held notions, fundamental to the way they think about literature.

If we turn back to the criterion of completeness in encoding, we can see elements of both idealism and localism in it. At first glance it appears to be very clearly a form of idealism, because it shares idealism's belief in the translatability of texts, in the possibility of reproducing them in a new medium technologically remote from that in which they were created; and indeed anyone who sets out to create electronic texts based on existing written texts must hold some such belief. But completeness also embraces the localist belief in the importance of every detail of original texts, and localism's reluctance to overlook any detail at all. Reports from the workshops conducted by the Text Encoding Initiative show that, once you direct the attention of scholars to a particular printed page that is to be encoded, they readily find many quite minute physical details that start to matter to them; if you kept such a group at it for a few weeks you would probably wind up with a few committed localists among them.[13] The problem, of course, is that this can easily lead to a position that is ultimately incommensurable with any attempt to create electronic texts. The encoder who follows this line of thinking is likely to create increasingly detailed transcriptions and, in the end, wind up forswearing encoding altogether in favor of an exclusive reliance on digital images, because it is always possible to imagine that you are missing something, even if you can't explain why it is important or even point to it.

Localist editorial theory does not actually lead in that direction, though; and the reason is that, unlike the usual idea of completeness, it is grounded in analytical bibliography. Both idealists and localists are well aware that photographs and digital images can never be perfect, and that in certain ways they are misleading; such reproductions convey information differently from the way a text encoding does it, but they aren't any more complete.[14] Localists who use reproductions in their articles and editions do so not because they imagine them to be perfect, but because they are better at displaying the features of the original artifacts that, in the light of their bibliographical and critical studies, appear most important; in the end, few scholars seem to have followed Paul Mann's rejection of all reproduction as corrupt, and localism is separated from idealism more by where it positions the balance of its concern than by an absolute theoretical difference. Completeness, however, substitutes for bibliographical knowledge the lingering fear of being wrong, which comes to dominate the entire project of encoding.

Localism, like any productive approach, implies a number of reasonable and interesting projects in the study of texts, even though editing is not one of them. And neither is encoding. But the fruits of localism can still be of value to encoders. If we disregard the claim that some localists will make, that texts should not be encoded at all, there remains a twofold message from localists to encoders: that they're ignoring features of great importance in their encodings, and that they're misinterpreting some of the evidence. The general truth behind these objections is that we don't know precisely what evidence from a particular physical instance of a text is going to matter, and we don't have a way of interpreting any evidence that is guaranteed to be free from error. As a general proposition this isn't news: the first half is recognized quite explicitly by astute encoders,[15] and the second half is a notion of considerable antiquity. For an idealist—and the text encoder must be an idealist—localist objections are therefore not fatal. But the localist dissatisfaction with what's left out of our encodings can be very helpful: just as localists like McLeod have helped textual editors, even while wishing they'd halt their activities, they can also help encoders by pointing out the things that they're missing.

For these reasons, the localist argument against idealism is not, I think, conclusive; but it does help to suggest the necessary limitations in any encoding. If we turn back to Bowers's statement on definitiveness, we recall his claim that the Hawthorne edition's establishment of the data about Hawthorne's texts would not be subject to modification. And yet one of the innovative features of this edition was that it collected data to which nobody else had ever paid any attention: this was the first edition of any work that included information on line-end hyphenation, and made clear its data and rationale for deciding whether the hyphen was to be retained or not when a word was no longer broken across lines.[16] A definitive edition prepared ten years before Bowers worked would *not* have collected all the necessary data for Bowers's work. Moreover, there are things about those early editions of *The Scarlet Letter* that some critics nowadays would consider quite important: to name only two, what was the physical appearance of those editions? What was their cost? None of this information appears in the Centenary Edition.

This suggests what is, I think, the important corrective made by localism to any idealist position. Yes, we are able to identify objective features of our texts: the problem is that there is no closed and determined set of such features. And that's true not only for texts in general, but even for any single text that you might choose. The contents of that set are in part determined by our critical interests: Bowers didn't think that the physical appearance of a book belonged in it, but a more localist editor might. The contents are also determined by the state of scholarly knowledge: there will always be further developments after we finish our work.

Anyone who has spent much time on reading or writing encoding standards should already have had something of the same perception: that any comprehensive set of textual features always winds up seeming incomplete. Nevertheless, we often hear statements from encoders similar to Bowers's: the insistence, for example, that our encoding should take care of the job for our chosen text once and for all. As in the case of the editions that Bowers prepared, this is often used as the justification for the great expense involved. But it is a justification we should reject. Bowers's editions, and our own text-encoding projects, are justified by the data that they make available and the scholarly work that they make possible. We should consider them successful if they generate enough work in the field to create a need and a desire for new editions or new encodings along new lines; and we should consider them failures if nobody cares enough to redo the work. Much of humanities scholarship involves endless reconsideration of the same works, further travels over the same ground; we should not expect editing and encoding to be different.

As a general guide for our work in encoding a text, a more useful criterion is ***adequacy:*** a consideration of just what features in the text to be encoded do and do not matter for the purposes of the encoding. Adequacy is a criterion of incompleteness; it recognizes that there is no limit to the amount of editorial and bibliographic labor that could be expended on a text, but stresses that, to achieve the practical end of completing an edition or an encoding that is useful for particular scholarly purposes, some restriction of scope is always necessary. If adequacy is our criterion, we accept that our encoding will not be final—that there will always be more details in our sources that we could have encoded, whether ones we saw but chose to ignore or ones that future scholars will identify. That should be regarded, however, not as an admission of failure but as a recognition of the true situation of all editions.

And, if completeness is not our justification, then we should also not see any particular merit in confining our encoding to objective features. The distinction between subjective and objective is often associated with completeness in encoding: what you'll often hear is that since we should be doing this encoding once and for all, and should provide for all possible uses of the text, we should therefore encode every objective feature and not mix in any subjective features. It is certainly foolish to ignore features of well-documented significance to large communities, if one can afford to encode them. And there is a difference between rejecting completeness and embracing relativism: to think our knowledge is incomplete doesn't mean that it's unfounded. But it is not necessarily foolish to ignore an "objective" feature in favor of a "subjective" feature in encoding. If the choice is between expending our resources on a clear-cut feature of no significance to us, but possible significance to someone, someday, or on an interpretive feature that we consider important but that isn't perceived by everyone in precisely the same way, we have good reasons to select the latter, particularly if it makes clearer what we believe is the text's meaning. And on the merely pragmatic level, we're bound to do a much better job at it; it's likely that the later students of that feature we thought was unimportant will decide we got it wrong—because we couldn't see what mattered about it—and will simply ignore our work. To do everything would require not only that we know what everything *is,* but that we also be able to adopt *all* critical positions ourselves.

The criterion of adequacy is already implicitly followed, in most cases, by those who seek to encode manuscripts. The *Canterbury Tales* Project has published the guidelines it is following in its effort to transcribe all the surviving manuscripts of Chaucer's masterpiece, and these guidelines provide an excellent example of the sort of scholarly work that is needed to establish a productive encoding approach, and of the kind of explanation of such an approach that all encoders should provide. The Chaucer editors explain why they chose to transcribe at this particular level of detail, and illustrate a large number of the sort of ambiguous or difficult cases that typically crop up. And they observe:

> In the course of our work we have come to realize that no transcription of these manuscripts into computer-readable form can ever be considered "final" or "definitive." Transcription for the computer is a fundamentally interpretive activity, composed of a series of acts of translation from one system of signs (that of the manuscript) to another (that of the computer). Accordingly, our transcripts are best judged on how useful they will be for others, rather than as an attempt to achieve a definitive transcription of these manuscripts. Will the distinctions we make in these transcripts and the information we record provide a base for work by other scholars? How might our transcripts be improved, to meet the needs of scholars now and to come? At the same time, we ask scholars to consider that decisions which may seem somewhat arbitrary might have a long history of argument and counter-argument behind them.[17]

Scholars who recognize that difficult choices are necessary in transcribing manuscripts are nevertheless inclined to be more reluctant to grant that this might be so for editions based on printed sources. I will conclude with an example of such a choice, based on the practice of the edition I am involved in creating: the edition of Thomas Middleton's collected works now in preparation for Oxford University Press, under the general editorship of Gary Taylor.

One form of our edition will be an electronic version; but it will not follow the usual approach of electronic editions today.[18] Most electronic editions are presented as archives of unedited documents, very often with digital images of those documents as well as transcriptions; but our electronic edition of Middleton will be an electronic version of a critically edited and modernized text, together with editorial and explanatory apparatus. It is our judgment that an edition that brings together all the works now acknowledged as Middleton's, and makes them accessible to the broadest possible audience, is more valuable today than an original-spelling edition or an archive of original materials would be. Our primary interest is to give a comprehensive account of Middleton's work as a writer, incorporating the developments of scholarship since the last collected edition of his work, in 1885; and unedited texts do that rather poorly in this case.

Leaving aside the problem of works that exist in multiple texts that need to be sorted out for readers in some way—such as *A Game at Chess,* which survives in eight independent versions (six manuscripts and two printed editions)—or that exist only in manuscripts that students and theatrical producers will find difficult to read, I turn instead to an example that helps to show what can be missed by an encoding that is too close to the sources, even when the source is a printed text. The play *Anything for a Quiet Life,* by Middleton and John Webster, was written in about 1621 but not published until 1662. The physical appearance of this edition systematically distorts the work. As Leslie Thomson, editor of this play for the Oxford edition, has shown, Thomas Johnson, the printer, made a practice of reworking the text of the plays he printed, simply to save paper. The text is extensively modernized to shorten the words—by omission of many final *e*s, for example—which also happens to bring them much closer to today's spellings; all unrhymed verse is printed as prose; and speeches do not always start on separate lines. Figure 1 illustrates the end of act 2, scene 1 and the beginning of act 2, scene 2, as it appeared in 1662; this passage mixes blank verse, rhymed verse, and prose in a way that is common enough in Middleton's work, but this texture is obscured by the presentation of the text. Here is Leslie Thomson's edited version for our edition of one exchange that looks like prose on the 1662 page:

CAMLET
Why Rachel, sweet Rachel, my bosom Rachel,
How didst thou get forth? Thou wert here, sweet Rac,
Within this hour, even in my very heart.
RACHEL CAMLET
Away—or stay still—I'll away from thee.
One bed shall never hold us both again,
Nor one roof cover us. Didst thou bring home—

The modernization in the 1662 edition renders the text's spelling particularly remote from that of manuscripts written by Middleton or by scribes of his time; the conversion of so much verse to prose means that the

Any thing for a quiet Life.

to ſteal ſome *Apricocks* my Husband kept for's own Tooth, and climb up upon his head and ſhoulders. Ile go to him, he will put me into brave Clothes, and rich Jewels; 'twere a very ill part in me not to go, his Mercer and his Goldſmith elſe might curſe me; and what Ile do there, a my troth yet I know not;

Women though puzzel'd with theſe ſubtile deeds,
May, as i'th Spring, pick Phyſick out of weeds. *Exit Lady.*

Enter (a Shop being diſcover'd) Walter Chamlet, *his Wife* Rachel, *two Prentices*, George *and* Ralph.

George. What iſt you lack, you lack, you lack?
Stuffs for the Belly, or the Back?
Silk-Grograns, Sattins, Velvet fine,
The Roſie-colour'd Carnadine;
Your Nutmeg hue, or Gingerline,
Cloth of Tiſſue, or Tobine,
That like beaten Gold will ſhine
In your Amarous Ladies eyne,
Whileſt you their ſofter Silks do twine: *Enter Rachel.*
What iſt you lack, you lack, you lack?

Rach. I do lack Content Sir, Content I lack: have you or your worſhipful Maſter here, any Content to ſell?

George. If Content be a Stuff to be ſold by the Yard, you may have content at home, and never go abroad for't.

Rach. Do, cut me three yards, Ile pay for 'em.

George. There's all we have i'th Shop; we muſt know what you'l give for 'em firſt.

Cham. Why *Rachel*, ſweet *Rachel*, my boſom *Rachel*, how didſt thou get forth? thou wert here ſweet *Rac.* within this hour, even in my very heart. *Rach.* Away, or ſtay ſtill, Ile away from thee, one Bed ſhall never hold us both agen, nor one roof cover us: didſt thou bring home

George. What iſt you lack, you lack, you lack?

Rach. Peace Bandog, Bandog, give me leave to ſpeak, or I'le

George. Shall I not follow my Trade? I'm bound to't, and my Maſter bound to bring me up in't.

Cham. Peace, good *George*, give her anger leave, thy Miſtriſs will be quiet preſently.

Rach.

Fig. 1

literary structure of the play is badly obscured. As a result, we can argue that our modernized edition is closer to the kind of text that a contemporary would have found meaningful than the original edition is; it is certainly more helpful to the modern reader. To transform the text in this manner is to unedit it, to remove the distorting changes made by its earliest editors. We are entirely aware that those whose primary interest is in the printing practices of 1662, rather than in authorial and performance practices of 1621, will not be happy with this decision; and those who wish to review the decisions in our edition about the verse lineation will also want to look at the 1662 edition. Yet the fact that my example above from our edition looks unremarkable—that it restores what we expect to see in a printed verse drama, and no more—suggests that this is the version of most general interest.

Another proposal might be that we could simply provide several versions: both a critical edition and a diplomatic transcript or digital image. We can certainly imagine that as a solution; and it is commonly believed that electronic editions free us from all the constraints imposed by paper publication. But they don't automatically bring us the money needed to do everything we can imagine; and in any case we may well choose as scholars to devote our own time to ends that seem more important. Once we recognize that, even in theory, we *cannot* encode every feature of our texts, we should see that the choice of *important* features becomes central to our work. In a limited world, we have to choose to do what matters most.

If all this makes encoding sound indistinguishable from editing, that is no more than my intent. Encoding is editing, in the sense that it involves informed thought about the meaning of texts and how it's embodied physically—not only in the documents that survive from our past, but also in the new representations of them that we seek to create. The encoder is not a person who has memorized a list of the important objective features of texts and can identify them in any book, but a person who is good at thinking critically about how a book fits into the spectrum of known practice, and about which things are significant in its typographical presentation—and which are not.

NOTES

1. Fredson Bowers, "Practical Texts and Definitive Editions," in Fredson Bowers and Charlton Hinman, *Two Lectures on Editing: Shakespeare and Hawthorne* (Columbus: Ohio State University Press, 1969), 21–70; reprinted in Fredson Bowers, *Essays on Bibliography, Text, and Editing* (Charlottesville: University Press of Virginia, 1975), 415.

2. G. Thomas Tanselle, *A Rationale of Textual Criticism* (Philadelphia: University of Pennsylvania Press, 1989).
3. Gérard Genette, *Fiction et diction* (Paris: Seuil, 1991), 13; my translation.
4. Leah S. Marcus, *Puzzling Shakespeare: Local Reading and Its Discontents* (Berkeley and Los Angeles: University of California Press, 1988).
5. Clifford Geertz, *Local Knowledge: Further Essays in Interpretive Anthropology* (New York: Basic, 1983).
6. See, for example, the discussion of Blake in Jerome J. McGann, "What Is Critical Editing?" *Text* 5 (1991): 15–29; reprinted in *The Textual Condition* (Princeton: Princeton University Press, 1991), 48–68.
7. David V. Erdman, ed., *The Complete Poetry and Prose of William Blake* (Berkeley and Los Angeles: University of California Press, 1982).
8. See "Unemending Shakespeare's Sonnet 111," *Studies in English Literature* 21 (1981): 75–96, and "Information on Information," *Text* 5 (1991): 241–81.
9. Paul Mann, "Apocalypse and Recuperation: Blake and the Maw of Commerce," *ELH* 52 (1985): 1–32.
10. Grace Ioppolo, "UnEditing Middleton." Paper delivered at the Society for Textual Scholarship conference, 1991, 15.
11. For an example, see Laurence Lerner, "Unwriting History," *New Literary History* 22 (1991): 795–815.
12. On revision and collaboration, see Grace Ioppolo, *Revising Shakespeare* (Cambridge, Mass.: Harvard University Press, 1991), and Jack Stillinger, *Multiple Authorship and the Myth of Solitary Genius* (New York: Oxford University Press, 1991).
13. See Donald Spaeth's account of the Oxford TEI workshop of July 1991: "'Living with the Guidelines': The First TEI European Workshop, Oxford University Computing Service, 1–2 July 1991," *ACH Newsletter* 13, no. 3 (1991): 1–3.
14. G. Thomas Tanselle, "Reproductions and Scholarship," *Studies in Bibliography* 42 (1989): 25–54.
15. See, for example, C. M. Sperberg-McQueen, "Text in the Electronic Age: Textual Study and Text Encoding, with Examples from Medieval Texts," *Literary and Linguistic Computing* 6 (1991): 36.
16. G. Thomas Tanselle, "Some Principles for Editorial Apparatus," *Studies in Bibliography* 25 (1972): 41–88; reprinted in G. Thomas Tanselle, *Textual Criticism and Scholarly Editing* (Charlottesville: University Press of Virginia, 1990), 153.
17. Peter Robinson and Elizabeth Solopova, "Guidelines for Transcription of the Manuscripts of the *Wife of Bath's Prologue*," *"The Canterbury Tales" Project,* Occasional Papers, vol. 1, ed. Norman Blake and Peter Robinson (Oxford: Office for Humanities Communication, 1993), 19.
18. On the assumptions behind, and typical design of, most electronic editions, see John Lavagnino, "Reading, Scholarship, and Hypertext Editions," *Text* 8 (1996), forthcoming.

Some Unrevolutionary Aspects of Computer Editing

Hoyt N. Duggan

My title makes sense, of course, only because we share a conviction that electronic technology *has* revolutionized our discipline. Many of us who work with computers in editing are convinced that we stand on the verge of a major reconceptualization of the nature of text, that like printers in the age of the incunabulum, we are initiators of a vast cultural project, the ultimate ends of which we cannot see. At the same time, any survey of electronic texts presently available will suggest that this has not yet become a golden age of textual editing. All too often in the preparation and publication of electronic texts, the chief criterion for choosing a text to be "input" for the electronic edition is expiration of copyright.[1] Computerized literary scholars have so far demonstrated a tendency to exploit the computers for quick-and-dirty textual solutions, to expend their efforts upon compiling massive amounts of textually uneven materials rather than upon producing reliable scholarly editions. Nevertheless, there is no intrinsic reason why the electronic archive should be the home of out-of-date and inferior texts.

Computer technology has enabled Thomas Cable and me to discover the underlying formal constraints governing composition of late Middle English alliterative, metrical constraints undiscovered and largely unsuspected in a century and a half of scholarship.[2] Larry Benson's sophisticated program for producing lemmatized concordances using the head words of the *Middle English Dictionary* offers extraordinary opportunities in stylistics and lexicography.[3] As the present volume alone makes abundantly clear, a number of important scholarly editorial projects are under way. Norman Blake and Peter Robinson's *Canterbury Tales Project,* already well begun, is being joined by other large projects, such as the Kevin

Kiernan, Andrew Prescott, and Paul Szarmach color digital facsimile edition of *Beowulf.*[4] Ralph Hanna, Thorlac Turville-Petre, and I are planning with members of the British Library staff a similar color digital facsimile edition of Cotton Nero A.x. Electronic editions of the Old English penitentials and psalter glosses are in progress or nearing completion. Yuki Matsumoto has recently completed an electronic text of *The Destruction of Troy;* Vincent McCarren is at work on the late Middle English/Latin *Medulla;* and a group of scholars headed by Greg Waite in New Zealand is producing a large computerized textbase of early Tudor verse, prose, and drama.

For the past several years I have worked with a team of scholars on an electronic archive designed to present in digital form the entire medieval and Renaissance textual tradition of the fourteenth-century dream vision *Piers Plowman.*[5] My interest in the text of the poem began in my attempts to determine whether Langland's metrical system and practice were consonant with those of other poets of the "Alliterative Revival." Though my comparisons of the Athlone A and B texts with the manuscripts increased my respect for the extraordinary care and intelligence of the editorial work in both editions, they also convinced me that George Kane and E. Talbot Donaldson—like pre-Tyrwhitt editors of Chaucer—had worked in essential ignorance of the poet's meter, mistaking both his alliterative practice and the rhythmic constraints that governed composition at half-line level.[6] In editing both the A and B texts, they occasionally rejected authorial manuscript readings and replaced them with unmetrical, and thus unauthentic, lections and conjectures. Moreover, in the B text, their very full list of variants did not always record metrically substantive variants. Other scholars at the same time pointed to yet other difficulties with the theory and execution of Kane and Donaldson's text.[7]

In 1987, Robert Adams and I began to consider collaborating to construct a new critical edition of the B text. Adams created a relational database of *Piers Plowman* manuscripts, designed to permit elaborate comparisons of the lections within the B tradition with those of the A, C, and Z versions.[8] Though his program at that time did not make machine collation feasible, Adams's preliminary efforts convinced us that the B archetype itself could be restored. Moreover, we found the reconstructed B archetype with notable frequency revealed a rationale for Langland's revision that had eluded Kane and Donaldson or had, perhaps, not been considered in their enthusiasm for using the agreement of the A and C versions to edit B. In focusing too narrowly on differences and agreements among the A, B, and C versions at the level of the half-line, Kane and Donaldson from time to time failed to account for possibly authorial changes at the level of the sentence or verse paragraph.[9]

In 1991 Adams and I were joined by Eric Eliason, Ralph Hanna, and Thorlac Turville-Petre, who also had an interest in the text of *Piers Plowman*. By then, we were coming to think that only an electronic edition could provide an adequate basis for a radically new approach to text editing, one that puts aside the traditional controversies on whether to create conservative "best text" editions of the poems or to exercise judgment to create more reliable critical editions. As we have continued to design and construct the *Archive*, we realized the degree to which the centuries-long dispute between conservative and interventionist editors has been technologically and economically constructed. Indeed, we now believe that the historical antagonism between textual conservatives and interventionists is inherent neither to editorial principle nor practice, but rather has been motivated by the limitations of print technology, limitations that need not constrain editors working with electronic media.

The economics of publishing printed codices have sustained the often acrid conflict between proponents of two partial editorial ideas, each in itself answering well to practical necessities, but neither in itself fully adequate. That is, the costs of setting, printing, storing, and merchandising books have tended to force editors and their publishers to decide among three practical alternatives: "best text" editions with full or selective variants recorded from other witnesses; parallel text editions (or entire series of "best" texts); or reconstructed critical texts. With any of these alternatives, the characteristically protean medieval text becomes fixed in print either as an editor's reconstruction of an author's putative "original" or as one or more of the "least bad" scribal copies. With each, the exigencies of print deprive the reader, who receives either a privileged editorial critical reconstruction or a privileged scribal version. The editor of the electronic edition need not privilege either kind of text.

The vast expanses of cyberspace permit editors to represent fully even very complicated textual traditions. Editors of works with complex textual histories, like that of *Piers Plowman,* can produce as many documentary or "best text" editions of individual manuscripts or early printed witnesses as their judgment (or patience) dictates. They can, moreover, produce digital facsimile editions of the original texts in 24-bit color with capacities for image manipulation that sometimes make electronic facsimiles superior to seeing the original in a good light. Moreover, each facsimile edition can be hypertextually linked to its documentary edition. In the case of the *Piers Plowman Electronic Archive,* we have decided to provide documentary texts of all fifty-four manuscripts and of the three authority-bearing sixteenth-century printed texts, each hypertextually linked with a color digital facsimile, each, moreover, accompanied by codicological, paleographical, and linguistic description as well as with textual notes. The scholar who wishes to do so may consult fifty-four "best" texts of the three versions of *Piers Plowman,* of the six A and C combinations, of the single A and B splice, and of the three combinations of AC with "a long B continuation."[10] Within a single large, hypertextually linked archive, scholars may interrogate the entire textual tradition of the poems.

Some scholars may conclude that the editorial project is completed with the production of accurate documentary and facsimile editions of all the witnesses. We take it only to have been well begun, for though the surviving manuscripts constitute the major evidential base from which an editor might attempt to reconstitute authorial texts, not one of the *Piers Plowman* manuscripts by itself reflects accurately what Langland wrote. Though some manuscripts are in general better witnesses to the authorial text than others, no one manuscript bears more a priori authority than any other. Therefore, if we are to read a text more nearly authorial than is represented in any one manuscript witness, it is incumbent upon editors to construct archetypal and critical editions of the authorial versions from this corpus of variants.

Scholars have reasonably complained of the losses and distortions of textual information in printed critical editions. The wealth of textual information conveyed in many *Piers Plowman* manuscripts by changes in hand, script, and color is ordinarily only hinted at in printed texts. That information will easily be represented in an electronic text both in relatively unmediated fashion in high-quality color facsimile editions and in machine-searchable form by sophisticated SGML (Standard Generalized Markup Language) markup in the documentary editions. Consider, for example, Corpus Christi College, Oxford, MS 201 (henceforth F), in which the scribe typically marked changes between the English alliterative text and the Latin quotations by changing the script from *anglicana bastarda* to a rubricated *textura fere,* marking the hierarchy both by color and by change of script. In some instances, the scribe further highlighted the Latin text by beginning a line of text with a Lombard capital. Larger structural divisions within the passus are set off with four-line ornamental capitals, and the smaller strophic divisions are indicated with alternating red and green or red and blue paraph signs. Important words and phrases within the English text are emphasized by red touches on initial letters or in some cases with red touches on every character and with red underlining. A color facsimile will put this textual information directly before those readers who cannot readily consult the manuscript itself. In addition, SGML markup within the transcribed text makes the distribution of such features machine searchable. In short, the customary loss of information from the hand-produced manuscript text by reduction to the printed text need not occur in the electronic text. Readers an ocean away from the originals may experience in a relatively unmediated form most of the physical qualities of the manuscript itself.[11]

Transcribing the manuscripts inevitably presents interpretive problems. Any transcription, no matter how literal an editor intends it to be, is an interpretive act, an abstraction from the brown and red and blue inks on vellum or paper, an attempt to represent the textual intentions of long-dead scribes. Every leaf presents many occasions for the exercise of editorial judgment. Late medieval *Piers Plowman* manuscripts differ in the number and density of suspensions and abbreviations the scribes utilized, the relative care with which corrections were noted and made, the care or lack of care with which letterforms were made. Most scribes use a variety of allographic forms. Should the editor distinguish sigma "s" from the long form? Should two-lobed "a" be distinguished from the single-lobed ɑ form? How should occasionally erratic word and morph divisions be represented? Should roman numerals be spelled out or left as is? Should abbreviations and suspensions be resolved or be represented graphically or by entity references?

Peter Robinson and Elizabeth Solopova are right to argue that editors should provide graphemic rather than graphetic transcriptions.[12] That is to say, editors will wish to use markup to represent just those graphic features that carry textual meaning and ignore other graphic features that do not convey such meaning. Distinguishing marks that carry meaning from meaningless flourishes is not always simple. In initial transcriptions editors must record all of the ambiguous graphic features so that they may be subjected to graphemic analysis. For instance, scribal flourishes, such as those frequently appearing on word-terminal <g> or <k>, must be recorded until it can be determined whether the scribe intended them to represent a final <e> or not.[13]

SGML markup permits editors of documentary texts to record discrepancies between scribal intention and performance. Lapses of the pen can be easily entered in dual form, one with the text as the scribe wrote it and another with his probable intention. For example, the F scribe refers to Christ as a "kaue child" in a context concerned with Christ's masculinity. This lection we have entered with a <*sic*> tag so that when the text is later collated with other manuscripts its true reading is reflected, but the same tag will include the intended reading "knaue child," so that a reader searching for *knaue* will be able to locate this occurrence. Neither version is privileged save by the interest of the user. Nor is either suppressed editorially. Both readings, what the scribe actually wrote and what the editor thinks he must have intended to write, are represented in the edited text.

Simple accuracy is perhaps the hardest thing to achieve in an edition, and electronic technology scarcely affects the labor of transcribing and proofreading. Transcription at a keyboard, like writing on animal skins with a quill, still takes place character by character. Optical character recognition software does not presently exist to shorten the task. Proofreading still requires serial rereadings to compensate for eye skip, arrhythmia, dittography, homoeoteleuton, or for the manifold other failures of concentration that have marred scribal efforts since literacy began. Our original plan provided for five separate readings of each transcription against the photocopies and a final proofreading against the original manuscript, but our practical experience with F suggests that in the case of a difficult or complex manuscript more readings will be necessary.[14]

The apparatus criticus of the electronic edition will differ inevitably from that of printed editions. For instance, traditional printed editions of Middle English texts include somewhere in the introduction a description of the paleographic features of the scribal hand, usually accompanied with a list, sometimes with illustrations, of the common abbreviations and suspensions used by the scribe. Frequently editors provide black-and-white photographic facsimile pages as part of the front matter of printed texts so that readers may see a representative page or two. In the electronic edition, the editor can supply, as I did in my Institute for Advanced Technology in the Humanities (IATH) research report on the World Wide Web, digital images of a full set of abbreviations and suspensions. The one in my research report is crude, even by the standards of present technology, taken as it is by cut-and-paste methods from xerox flow copy of the manuscript and then scanned on a flatbed scanner. In future, such paleographic descriptions can be constructed hypertextually with color facsimiles and with sufficient examples to produce for the user something approaching full analysis of the scribe's practice. Moreover, such descriptions, unlike their counterpart in printed texts, will in the completed *Archive* constitute fifty-four hypertextually linked databases of late medieval scribal practice.

When all fifty-four manuscripts have been transcribed with SGML markup, readers will have fifty-four "best text" documentary editions, each accompanied by and linked to a color facsimile edition. How many scholars, including those most insistent upon privileging scribal versions of the poem, will read fifty-four editions of very similar poems? Even in the case of a culturally important work such as *Piers Plowman,* it is not at all clear that so many marginally different "poems" will find readers. As it stands, few have read all three published versions with the same attention they have given B. How many scholars will wish to read several dozen manuscript witnesses differing in quite minor ways one from another? This profusion of textual material, even with meticulous hypertextual linking, is at once too much and too little.

Too much, certainly, if one thinks of the text only as an aesthetic object. Such a view of text is, of course, more than a little parochial, since literary texts serve a variety of other functions in modern attempts to re-create and understand our past. Less parochially, fifty-four electronic transcriptions and facsimiles—perhaps none of them ever serving as a traditional reading text—will offer scholars not only new ways to study the text and the textual tradition of the poem but also possibilities for gaining fresh insights into other aspects of late medieval literary culture. Students of text reception may readily access formerly inaccessible marginal and interlinear annotations or significant scribal changes to the text itself. The *Archive* will enable study of the changes both in language and literary focus wrought by the revising sixteenth-century scribe who created Toshiyuki Takamiya, MS 23, or by Robert Crowley's Protestant rebaptism of the poem in his three 1550 printed editions of the B text, each converting Langland's Middle English into something more appropriate for its Tudor audience. Since *Piers Plowman* was copied in virtually every late Middle English dialect, historical linguists will be able to study patterns of regional variation in lexicon, phonology, and orthography. The facsimiles will be useful to students who once lacked access to large collections of primary manuscript materials. Moreover, students of form and style and meter can add their own markup for other, as yet unimagined, kinds of study. It matters little that no one is ever likely to want to *read* all fifty-four documents. Many will want to *use* them.

Even so, despite the proclaimed "death of the author," many readers still want to read the poems that Langland wrote, as he wrote them and without scribal lapses or accretions. Medievalists, of course, have never had occasion to celebrate the kind of author whose demise has been announced.[15] We know, for example, virtually nothing about the historical poet who composed the three versions of *Piers Plowman*. The autobiography of Long Will, the dreamer-protagonist, is constructed as much by thematic considerations as by knowable events in the poet's life and may well be completely fictional. Whether *Langland* means anything to us other than a name to attach to the three poems, we recognize in those poems the work of a poet of extraordinary power. We want to read his words. Without wishing for one moment to deny the intrinsic interest of scribal practice to bibliographers, students of reception, linguists, metrists, or cultural historians, we recognize that scribal accretions are of secondary interest to most readers. In any case, the import and direction of scribal changes are recognizable only in relation to a concept of the authorial text. That is, we cannot study the reception history of texts like *Piers Plowman* as it is reflected in the manuscript witnesses until editorial work distinguishes what each scribe or editor did from what was inherited from an exemplar. Without doing collations, without establishing archetypal or critical texts, without an attempt to construct a stemma, textual variation is difference without significance. Though the fifty-four documentary editions constitute necessary groundwork for critical editing, each witness with its own set of differences will not be fully meaningful until its relationship to the other texts in the tradition can be established.[16] That requires critical editing.

This reference to constructing archetypal and critical texts moves us into the "unrevolutionary aspects of textual editing," even into what some will consider hopelessly outdated notions of editing. It is currently fashionable to think claims to literary knowledge vestigial remains of an earlier, more naive and optimistic age.[17] A fashionably automatic rejection of archetypes and critical texts prevails among postmodernists and some romantically inclined traditional scholars. One traditional scholar has complained of "the sterile operating room (or terminal intensive care unit) of the modern critical edition" of medieval poems, complaining that they have functioned to suppress and distort "the realities of medieval texts and manuscript production."[18] Scholars influenced by Jerome McGann's work with nineteenth-century authors and his sociological critique of the Greg-Bowers school of critical editing also reject the possibility of rescuing medieval texts from the depredations of scribes. Still others, inspired by poststructuralist "theory," proclaim their indifference to authorial texts and reject critical editing as a viable scholarly project.[19]

Though readers understandably want to read authorial texts, editors of *Piers Plowman* have always known that the authorial text has disappeared, lost to the accidents of time and of hand copying. Even if, miraculously, we were to reconstitute from the maze of scribal witnesses Langland's final texts precisely as he intended to leave them, we would never be confident that we had done so. This situation, of course, does not distinguish the texts of *Piers Plowman* from those of Chaucer or of most other medieval authors. Lacking autograph manuscripts, editors of medieval texts inevitably engage in an attempt to understand the relationship of the extant witnesses to a lost text. Inevitably they will create a new text, something of their moment in history, using all of the available documentary evidence or some portion of it to attempt to re-create what we have lost to time. In this important respect, editors of medieval texts differ from editors of more recent texts such as my colleague Jerome McGann deals with in the Rossetti Archive.[20] Unlike the editor of a medieval work, he enjoys a surfeit of authority. McGann works with texts either handwritten by the author or printed under his supervision, where differences between and among versions are, for the most part, differences between authorial texts. In the case of *Piers Plowman,* we have not separate versions of the poet's work but flawed documentary witnesses to the work.

The attempt to re-create a perfect authorial text is, under the circumstances, quixotic. Textual scholars—both conservative traditional scholars and progressive poststructuralist theorists—agree at least on that. Typically, the conservative critique consists of the following points: the empirical observation that modern critical editors not infrequently reach diametrically opposed conclusions from the same set of basic data, a reminder that medieval scribes, whatever their deficiencies of intellect or attention, nevertheless knew the language in ways that modern scholars can never know it, and the claim that a conservatively edited, well chosen "best text" at the very least provides a genuinely medieval document that some medieval readers could have read, whereas the critical edition is a hybrid modern monster, one that never existed before the cultural project of modern scholarship.[21] Postmodern theorists have added the further objection that the critical edition fetishizes the author. Tim Machan, for instance, though he does not deny that someone called William Langland "may have been the efficient cause of the text, or that it is possible to recover the text he was responsible for, or that his own efforts may be superior to others' according to certain aesthetic standards," argues that "the valorization of *his* text is necessarily an interpretive imposition on the manuscript evidence."[22] Machan characterizes the goal of traditional textual criticism, the establishment of an authorial text, as "only one of the things, and perhaps the most historically problematic, which one can do with a medieval work" (13). The traditional privileging of the authorial is vicious, from Machan's point of view, largely because it "precludes—pronounces 'wrong' or 'other'—other kinds of evidence and analysis which may in fact be less historically problematic and are, in any case, equally valid as aesthetic activities" (14). Machan's objections, occasioned by printed critical editions are, of course, made irrelevant by the electronic archive. I think they are irrelevant to good critical editing in printed texts to the degree that they rely upon Machan's creation of an unnecessary and false disjunction between an editor's respect for the material objects in which texts survive and his or her desire to reconstitute the authorial text. Good critical editing requires that a competent editor pay minute attention to the manuscript as a physical object, recording and analyzing its physical features, its *ordinatio,* its provenance, its original audience, its punctuation—in brief, its *thingness.* An editor's preliminary attention to codicology and paleography is not exclusively preliminary. Ralph Hanna wrote a description of the casting-off procedures of the scribe who copied MS Lambeth Palace 491, but it was only after he and David Lawton had completed their critical edition of the poem that they were able to explain Hanna's observations of the physical text.[23]

In the electronic archive, the reconstituted authorial text is privileged only at the level where such privileging is appropriate. At such a level, the *Piers Plowman* team will attempt to recuperate the authorial texts of the three versions. At a different level of the archive, we will attempt to represent the scribal versions of the text—their *ordinatio* of the page, their passus divisions and rubrications, their verse paragraph markers, their hierarchy of scripts, their use of color and line in emphasizing and presenting text, their choice of dialect terms, spellings, and so forth. An electronic archive can and should be as faithful at this level to scribal intentions as—on a different level of abstraction—it is to the author's text. In the electronic archive, the user/reader will be able to move easily between levels, but the editors must first do the traditional editorial work and supply the linkages.[24]

In the case of many medieval texts, attempts to publish a reconstructed authorial text are misguided. When, for example, the evidence shows that the extant copies are not derived from a common written original—as is frequently the case with lyric poems, some popular romances, tropes, learned commentaries, saints' lives, to name only a few genres in which textual *mouvance* represents the ordinary state of affairs—there is no original to be derived from the mass of variants.[25] However, until the editor has analyzed the evidence, until she has undertaken the fundamental activities of critical editing, she cannot know whether—or to what extent—the textual tradition is monogenous or not. Critical editing does not always mean that a single authorial text will be reconstituted, only that the editor has thought in a systematic and disciplined way about the documents and other textual evidence.

Under some circumstances, reliable authorial texts cannot be reconstructed by critical methods from scribal copies, but in many cases something approaching the authorial text can be restored. Thorlac Turville-Petre and I edited one such text, *The Wars of Alexander,* in which the accidental survival of two good manuscripts, the relative fidelity of the poet's translation to a known source that itself survives in many witnesses, and our knowledge of the metrical constraints under which the poet wrote all conspired together to make a critical edition possible.[26] We know, of course, that we did not reconstruct the original poem, only a modern version of it, but that modern version is closer to that original poem than either of the extant witnesses. Ralph Hanna and David Lawton have similarly just completed a critical edition of *The Siege of Jerusalem,* a poem with known sources and nine surviving witnesses.[27] Their text, like the text of *The Wars of Alexander* that Turville-Petre and I edited, which is not the original, has exactly as much authority as its editors can persuade readers that it carries. That is, the reconstructed text, like interpretive scholarship in literature—or for that matter in physics or history—is a rhetorical construct within the framework of an intellectual discipline.

Our preliminary work with *Piers Plowman* supports Skeat's theory that the poem survives in three different versions, but we are willing to forsake that theory if the evidence should require that we do so. Our work so far with the B text supports the Kane-Donaldson view that the extant witnesses are all descended from a single archetype, an early document already textually at some remove from Langland's poem. We are skeptical of various claims that any large number of textual variants represent authorial revisions, though again that is a position that can be reversed when all the evidence is available and subjected to analysis.[28] We are inclined to think that the Athlone editors and A. V. C. Schmidt were correct in finding two major families of manuscripts in the textual tradition of the B version, though again we will cheerfully change our minds if the evidence should require it.[29] Once all the manuscripts have been transcribed with SGML markup, we will have immediate access to all the relevant textual evidence, more accessible and usable than it ever has been before because the computer puts at the editor's immediate disposal a vast array of materials minutely searchable.

I will use a single example to indicate the range of evidence electronic editors will be able to bring to bear upon textual problems. It should be remembered that the archival base for our editorial decisions is still in preparation. We have, so far, only a tiny fraction of the textual information we plan to accumulate, especially from the textual tradition of C. The following example, therefore, is a provisional hypothesis, and can only suggest how we will distinguish authorial from scribal lections.[30]

In passus 13.140, the B witnesses are about evenly divided on the reading of the a-verse:

> With wordes and with werkes, quod she . . .
> and with] WHmCrLMRF; and YGOC^{2}CB

Kane and Donaldson, probably on aesthetic grounds (they almost invariably select the more laconic or syllabically shorter variant), select the reading of YGOC^{2}CB.[31] A similar set of variants occurs at B 3.2:

> Wiþ Bedeles and with baillies . . . WHmYCLR
> With bedellus and baillifs . . . MHm^{2}CrGOC^{2}BH

In this instance, both A and C versions agree with the more laconic reading, and Kane-Donaldson again select the shorter lection. If our final analysis—including use of cladistic analysis—continues to show but two main textual families, the archetypal reading here cannot be determined by recension.[32] The logic of attestation, however, tends to support the first reading, with its agreement of four of the best beta manuscripts (CHmLW) with the better alpha witness R. F's characteristic eccentricity complicates the situation with its reversed a- and b-verses. F's b-verse "with bedel and bayly" offers weak support to the group without the second "with."

The poets of the Alliterative Revival composed in phrasal units of metrically regular half-lines.[33] Their wonderfully flexible grammar of composition represents a metrically defined subset of the syntactic possibilities of Middle English. These poets, Langland included, tended not only to say the same things in the same way in lexical formulas but also used the same syntactic-rhythmic frames over and over in the course of a long poem. The poems manifest multiple rhythmic realizations of the same grammatical collocations. The relevant grammetrical pattern for the preceding example can be described as follows:[34]

$$\text{prep} + \text{NP}^{\text{obj}} + \left\{ \begin{array}{c} \text{prep} \\ \text{cj} + \text{prep} \\ \text{cj} \end{array} \right\} + (\text{art})\ \text{NP}^{\text{obj}}$$

With presently available software, it is a tedious but relatively simple matter to assemble all instances of this pattern in all three versions of *Piers Plowman*.[35] Both Langland's *usus scribendi* and the rhythmical rationale for the usage become instantly clear. Though he composed a number of a-verses in which only one strong dip appears, he generally preferred to provide three or four syllables in the one strong dip.[36] The preposition is repeated where it is needed to provide a second or third unstressed syllable in a single strong medial dip:

A 5.68 B 5.86   With werkes or with wordes . . .
A 10.4 B 9.4   With wynde and with water . . .
C.8.321   With craym and with croddes . . .
B 13.289   With inwit and with outwitt . . . /V/
B 17.69   Wyth wyn and with oyle . . .

It is also repeated when it provides a syllable to make a strong medial dip:

B 5.600   With no lede but with Loue . . .

The second *with* tends to be omitted when the noun head of the prepositional phrase is trisyllabic or when other unstressed syllables intervene, for example:

B 5.89   With bakbitynge and bismer . . .
B 7.12   With patriarkes and prophetes . . .
C.2.91   With vsurye and auaryce . . .

The second preposition is also omitted generally when the first noun phrase contains both a stressed adjective and a noun:

AB P.16	Wiþ depe dikes & derke . . .
A 7.285	Wiþ good ale & glotonye . . .
B 6.300	With grene poret and pesen . . .
B 13.359	With false mesures and mette . . .
C.18.154	With fyue fisches and loues . . .

However, it appears to be required when the second noun phrase has two stresses:

A 7.205	Wiþ fuyr or wiþ false men . . .
B 18.30	With glorie and with grete liȝte . . .
C 19.243	With wyles and with luyther wittes . . .

Since the language permits that the conjunction or the preposition may be present or omitted, depending upon the rhythm of the verse, it should not surprise us that scribal variation is common. The set of variants that began this investigation appear again in the poem:

1.	A 5.68	Wiþ werkis [or wiþ] wordis . . . or wiþ] UVHEKWM; or DLN; and with R	
	B. 5.86	With werkes or with wordes . . . with (2)] om. GH	
2.	A 7.210	Wiþ mete or [wiþ] mone . . . wiþ (2)] RUDChVHJLKNMH³; in E; om. TW	
3.	A 10.4	Wiþ wynd & wiþ watir . . . wiþ (2)] om. DJW	
	B 9.4	With wynde and with water . . . No variants.	
	C 10.130	With wynd and with water . . .	(Pearsall)
	C.11.130	With wynd & water . . .	(Skeat)[37]

In the case of B 13.140, the agreement of both alpha and beta families shows the lection rejected in the Athlone text to have been archetypal, and the grammetrical evidence suggests Langland himself is responsible for the repetition of the preposition.[38] In the case of B 3.2, agreement of versions A and C, added to the grammetrical evidence, indicates that the archetypal reading is in error and that the repeated *with* is scribal.

The arguments advanced here are, I repeat, provisional. Only a portion of the evidence is now available in machine-searchable form, and a search of other monosyllabic prepositions, for instance, may complicate or controvert this hypothesis. Consideration of *with* alone reveals a few anomalies. An apparent exception appears in Skeat's text at B 20.124:

> With glosynges and with gabbynges . . .

In that verse, about half the witnesses also omit the metrically and syntactically otiose second *with:* C²GYOCBR lack it; WHmCrLMF have it. It is worth remarking that the variation occurs in both alpha and beta families, as it did at B 3.2. In this verse, Kane's and Donaldson's preference for the more laconic reading led them to the correct reading, rejecting the second *with*. More problematic verses appear in which all of the witnesses agree in a reading inconsistent with the patterns observed above:

B 15.520	With londes and ledes . . .
B 19.230	With sellyng and buggynge . . . (also C.21.235)

Whether such verses reflect corruption of the archetype or constitute important evidence against the hypothesis advanced here must await analysis of the larger corpus we are assembling.

I chose this particular a-verse pattern, partly to demonstrate how swiftly and reliably the computer permits us to order a substantial base of evidence, and partly because it raises the critical issue of the recovery of authorial intention. Did Langland intend to write "*With* x and *with* y" or "*With* x and y"? Indeed, can he be said to have had any particular intention at all in regard to these syntactically and semantically redundant monosyllables? How would Langland have explained his choice? Would he have known consciously what he intended? Or would he have had to speak the verse to hear what "sounded" right? I suspect it would have been the latter, that he and other fourteenth-century alliterative poets would not have made conscious decisions to include or elide prepositions in such half-lines any more than we do in ordinary speech. Nevertheless, one may argue that Langland intended to compose alliterative verse and that his conscious intention to do so immediately involved him in thousands of unconscious intentions entailed by the metrical grammar of composition.

Generative metrists in recent years have shown that very powerful unconscious linguistic rules underlie and govern poetic composition, just as similar rules determine the shape of our every utterance, rules inaccessible to most of us, though no less powerful for being so.[39] Such rules are rarely broken because they do not rise to a level of conscious control. The full set of such rules for alliterative poetry has not been discovered, though we have recently made some steps in the direction of understanding them. The hypothesis proposed here is not such a rule, though it may be preliminary to discovery of such a rule. Within the limitations imposed by the surviving evidence, we can recover and describe some of the linguistic and metrical rules governing composition. In the instances we have just examined, if the tentative hypothesis proposed to account for Langland's practice with respect to this grammetrical frame should hold up when all the evidence has been collected and considered, we will have another basis for determining what Langland "intended" to write.

Electronic technology offers powerful new tools to scholars who want to distinguish what Langland and other poets wrote from scribal changes. Degrees of accuracy and consistency formerly unattainable by even the most scrupulous editors are enabled by the computer. Machine collations, unmarred by the inevitable human failures of eye, attention, and memory, will replace hand-produced collations. Deliberations on archetypal and critical texts will be speeded by virtually instantaneous access to all the other manuscript versions, to concordances of each manuscript version as well as to machine-readable texts of other modern editions of all three versions. In addition, we and other scholars will have access to electronic texts of every other major Middle English alliterative poem and to electronic concordances to each of those texts. Presented with a set of variant readings, we can in a matter of moments examine all of the contexts in which the alternative lections appear, either elsewhere in *Piers Plowman* or even within the whole tradition of alliterative verse. It would be a pity if the postmodern distrust of empirical evidence and distaste for the methods of the harder sciences should cause us to turn our backs on critical editing just as the tools become available that will help us do it better than ever before.[40]

NOTES

1. The editor of the *European English Messenger* 3 (1994): 86–87, describes his experience with an inaccurate electronic edition of Virginia Woolf's *The Waves* and the absence of any response to a "set of letters to literary critics and media experts at other universities, asking what on earth one is to do with all this electronically stored textery." He concludes with an appeal to readers "who have discovered what to do with or to a text on the computer [to] advise us as to what pleasures those of us miss who are puzzled by all these oysters that refuse to yield the pearls they had promised. Surely the emperor of CD does have some clothes on?"
2. Thomas Cable, *The English Alliterative Tradition* (Philadelphia: University of Pennsylvania Press, 1991); Hoyt N. Duggan, "The Shape of the B-Verse in Middle English Alliterative Poetry," *Speculum* 61 (1986): 565–67, "Alliterative Patterning as a Basis for Emendation in Middle English Alliterative Poetry," *Studies in the Age of Chaucer* 8 (1986): 73–105, and "Final -*e* and the Rhythmic Structure of the B-Verse in Middle English Alliterative Poetry," *Modern Philology* 86 (1988): 119–45. "Notes toward a Theory of Langland's Meter," *Yearbook of Langland Studies* 1 (1987): 41–70; "Langland's Dialect and Final -*e*," *Studies in the Age of Chaucer* 12 (1990): 157–91; "Stress Assignment in Middle English Alliterative Poetry," *Journal of English and Germanic Philology* 89 (1990): 309–29.
3. For a description of the program, see Larry Benson, "A Lemmatized Concordance of Chaucer," in *Computer-Based Chaucer Studies,* ed. Ian Lancashire, CCH Working Papers 3 (Toronto: University of Toronto Centre for Computing in the Humanities, 1993), 141–60.
4. For the *Beowulf* facsimile project, see Kevin Kiernan's research report "Digital Preservation, Restoration, and Dissemination of Medieval Manuscripts," published on the World Wide Web at the following URL: http://www.uky.edu/~dhart/.html. For the *Canterbury Tales* Project, see Norman Blake and Peter Robinson, eds., "*The Canterbury Tales*" *Project,* Occasional Papers, vol. 1 (Oxford: Office for Humanities Communication, 1993).
5. For a description of the project, see my "The Electronic *Piers Plowman:* A New Diplomatic-Critical Edition," *Æstel* 1 (1993): 1–21, and my hypertextual research report "Creating an Electronic Archive of *Piers Plowman,*" *Publications of the Institute for Advanced Technology in the Humanities,* Research Reports, 2d series (1994) on the World Wide Web at the following URL: http://jefferson.village.virginia.edu/home.html.
6. George Kane, ed., *Piers Plowman: The A Version* (London: Athlone Press, 1960); George Kane and E. Talbot Donaldson, eds., *Piers Plowman: The B Version* (London: Athlone Press, 1975).
7. David C. Fowler, "A New Edition of the B Text of *Piers Plowman,*" *Yearbook of English Studies* 7 (1977): 23–42; Charlotte Brewer, "The Textual Principles of Kane's A-Text," *Yearbook of Langland Studies* 3 (1989): 67–90; "Authorial vs.

Scribal Writing in *Piers Plowman*," in *Medieval Literature: Texts and Interpretation,* ed. Tim William Machan, Medieval and Renaissance Texts Society Texts and Studies 79 (Binghamton, N.Y.: Medieval and Renaissance Texts Society, 1991), 59–89; and "George Kane's Processes of Revision," in *Crux and Controversy in Middle English Textual Criticism,* ed. A. J. Minnis and Charlotte Brewer (Woodbridge, England: D. S. Brewer, 1992), 71–96; Robert Adams, "Editing *Piers Plowman* B: The Imperative of an Intermittently Critical Edition," *Studies in Bibliography* 45 (1992): 31–68; Thorlac Turville-Petre, "Review of Kane-Donaldson, *Piers Plowman: The B Version,*" *Studia Neophilologica* 49 (1977): 153–55.

8. For the controversy on the so-called Z version, see William Langland, *Piers Plowman: The Z Version,* ed. A. G. Rigg and Charlotte Brewer (Toronto: Pontifical Institute of Mediaeval Studies, 1983), and George Kane, "The 'Z Version' of *Piers Plowman,*" *Speculum* 60 (1985): 910–30. Kane makes the more compelling case.
9. "Editing *Piers Plowman* B: The Imperative of an Intermittently Critical Edition," *Studies in Bibliography* 45 (1992): 31–68.
10. George Kane, "The Text," in *A Companion to Piers Plowman,* ed. John A. Alford (Berkeley and Los Angeles: University of California Press, 1988), 178.
11. Murray McGillivray, "Electronic Representation of Chaucer Manuscripts: Possibilities and Limitations," in Lancashire, *Computer-Based Chaucer Studies,* 1–15, predicts that electronic technology will bring virtual reality to manuscript studies so that readers can be given the smell and feel of turning the pages of the virtual manuscript. At the rate of technological change, that prediction cannot be dismissed as hopelessly utopian.

    We considered for a time producing our digital facsimiles from black-and-white microfilm. There are some obvious reasons for doing that: in many cases, microfilm copies already exist and thus do not require further handling of the originals. They are, furthermore, relatively inexpensive to purchase initially and to reproduce in quantity. For many documents, the images produced are clear and entirely readable. Readers of microfilm lose, of course, all of the textual information encoded in color. However, editors have used microfilm copies of manuscripts for editorial work for decades, and digitized microfilm is likely to continue to provide a basis for many editions. For instance, the editors of the *Canterbury Tales* Project are preparing some of their digital facsimiles from black-and-white microfilm. However, we have come to believe that digitizing black-and-white microfilm is a second-best, make-do solution and that editors will wish, where it is at all possible, to produce 24-bit color facsimiles.
12. "Guidelines for Transcription of the Manuscripts of the Wife of Bath's Prologue," in Blake and Robinson, *"The Canterbury Tales" Project,* 19–52.
13. Scribal behavior is frequently inconsistent. The scribe who copied F from time to time adds a flourish to words ending in <g, k, t>. When the end of the word coincides with a phrasal boundary or the caesura, the scribe not infrequently uses that flourish to serve in place of his usual virgule, but in other instances, as at the top of fol. 24^{v}, the flourish appears to be utterly meaning-

less, and in some other instances, he writes both the flourish and a virgule at a phrasal boundary.

14. Since graduate student members of my team of assistants were learning both how to read medieval handwriting and to insert SGML markup while they were transcribing and proofreading, it appears likely that with more experience fewer passes will be necessary.
15. For thoughtful comment on this formalist gambit, see Seán Burke, *The Death and Return of the Author: Criticism and Subjectivity in Barthes, Foucault, and Derrida* (Edinburgh: Edinburgh University Press, 1992).
16. Robert Adams decries "the recent penchant for . . . treating scribal errors as instances of medieval literary criticism" ("Editing *Piers Plowman* B," 33). Cf. Barry Windeatt, "The Scribes as Chaucer's Early Critics," *Studies in the Age of Chaucer* 1 (1979): 119–41, and Derek Pearsall, "Editing Medieval Texts: Some Developments and Some Problems," in *Textual Criticism and Literary Interpretation,* ed. Jerome J. McGann (Chicago: University of Chicago Press, 1985), 103, with Kane, "The Text," 194.
17. For critiques of the hermeneutic suspicion characteristic of the postmodern establishment, see Paisley Livingston, *Literary Knowledge: Humanistic Inquiry and the Philosophy of Science* (Ithaca, N.Y.: Cornell University Press, 1988); Umberto Eco, *The Limits of Interpretation* (Chicago: University of Chicago Press, 1990); *Interpretation and Overinterpretation,* with Richard Rorty, Jonathan Culler, and Christine Brooke-Rose (Cambridge: Cambridge University Press, 1992); and Paul R. Gross and Norman Levitt, *Higher Superstition: The Academic Left and Its Quarrels with Science* (Baltimore: Johns Hopkins University Press, 1994).
18. Pearsall, "Editing Middle English Texts," 104, 102.
19. Some students of medieval texts have misread McGann, who distinguishes between the textual situation in preprint societies and that after printing houses had been established. McGann is aware that, whereas the editor of a nineteenth-century poet must select his or her text from a variety of authorial texts, the editor of the classical or medieval text may lack any authorial document. Though medieval poets may have expected scribes to make mistakes and change their texts—and we know what Petrarch and Chaucer thought of meddling or careless scribes—such an expectation hardly constitutes an analogy with a publishing house's style sheet. As John Bowers has recently shown in "Hoccleve's Two Copies of *Lerne to Dye:* Implications for Textual Critics," *Papers of the Bibliographical Society of America* 83 (1989): 437–72, even authorially produced texts can often lack textual authority. I believe that Bowers has drawn the wrong implications from Hoccleve's scribal practice and that the poet, acting as his own scribe, worked from a scribal rather than authorial mind-set. Others who have less difficulty than I do in proofreading my own work may be more receptive to Bowers's take on the evidence.
20. An elegant hypertextual demonstration of the textual principles at issue in constructing the *Rossetti Archive* is available on the World Wide Web at the following URL: http://jefferson.village.virginia.edu/home.html. Click on "Publications of the Institute."

21. For a cogent critique of critical editing from a conservative position, see E. G. Stanley, "Unideal Principles of Editing Old English Verse," *Publications of the British Academy* 70 (1987): 231–73.
22. Tim William Machan, "Late Middle English Texts and the Higher and Lower Criticism," in Machan, *Medieval Literature,* 11. Machan's fuller development of his theoretical stance, *Textual Criticism and Middle English Texts* (Charlottesville: University of Virginia Press, 1994), arrived too late to be considered here. Similar textual positions, informed by recent critical theory, have been staked by Robert S. Sturges, "Textual Scholarship: Ideologies of Literary Production," *Exemplaria* 3 (1991): 109–31, and Bowers, "Hoccleve's Two Copies."
23. Ralph Hanna III, "Booklets in Medieval Manuscript: Further Considerations," *Studies in Bibliography* 39 (1986): 100–111. The Hanna-Lawton edition of *The Siege of Jerusalem* is forthcoming (Colleagues Press, 1995).
24. Bernard Cerquiglini, *Eloge de la variante; Histoire critique de la philologie* (Paris: Seuil, 1989), imagines a new kind of electronic text not unlike that proposed here, though he appears to be content with the archival element of compiling vast collections of linked data but without considering it necessary to move beyond accumulation of data. As Mary B. Speer trenchantly remarks, "What Cerquiglini envisions is a decentered, pluralistic collection of transcriptions, accompanied by the mechanisms for comparative searches: medieval texts defined, in effect, as the raw material for linguistic enquiry. Criteria of authorial or redactional authenticity, philological truth, and scribal error or idiosyncrasy would be replaced by mere usefulness" ["Editing Old French Texts in the Eighties: Theory and Practice," *Romance Philology* 45 (1991): 22].
25. Rupert Pickens, "Jaufré Rudel et la poétique de la mouvance," *Cahiers de civilisation médiévale* 20 (1977): 323–37; Rupert Pickens, ed., *The Songs of Jaufré Rudel,* Studies and Texts 41 (Toronto: Pontifical Institute of Mediaeval Studies, 1978); A. C. Baugh, "Improvisation in the Middle English Romance," *Proceedings of the American Philosophical Society* 103 (1959): 418–54, "The Middle English Romance: Some Questions of Creation, Presentation, and Preservation," *Speculum* 42 (1967): 1–31; Murray McGillivray, *Memorization in the Transmission of the Middle English Romances,* Albert Bates Lord Studies in Oral Tradition, 5 (New York: Garland, 1990); Sherry L. Reames, "*Mouvance* and Interpretation in Late-Medieval Latin: The Legend of Saint Cecilia in British Breviaries," in Machan, *Medieval Literature,* 159–89; Julia Boffey, "Middle English Lyrics: Texts and Interpretation," in Machan, *Medieval Literature,* 121—38; Gunilla Iversen, "Problems in the Editing of Tropes," *Text* 1 (1981): 95–132; Marjorie Curry Woods, "Editing Medieval Commentaries: Problems and a Proposed Solution," *Text* 1 (1981): 133–45.
26. *The Wars of Alexander,* Early English Text Society Special Series 10 (Oxford: Oxford University Press, 1989).
27. See David Lawton's discussion of their editorial use of metrical theory in "The Idea of Alliterative Poetry: Alliterative Meter and *Piers Plowman,*" in *Suche Werkis to Werche: Essays on Piers Plowman in Honor of David C. Fowler,* ed. Míċeál F. Vaughan (East Lansing, Mich.: Colleagues Press, 1993), 147–68.

28. Charlotte Brewer has argued for extensive authorial revisions in the texts of *Piers Plowman* in "The Textual Principles of Kane's A-Text," *Yearbook of Langland Studies* 3 (1989): 67–90, and in "Authorial vs. Scribal Writing." For a critique of Brewer's argument, see Adams, "Editing *Piers Plowman* B," 64–65; Ralph Hanna, "Producing Manuscripts and Editions" in *Crux and Controversy in Middle English Textual Criticism,* ed. A. J. Minnis and Charlotte Brewer (Woodbridge, Suffolk: D. S. Brewer, 1992), 109–30; and my review of Machan's *Medieval Literature* in *Studies in the Age of Chaucer* 15 (1993): 234–35.
29. A. V. C. Schmidt, ed. *William Langland: The Vision of Piers Plowman* (London: Dent, 1984), xxxv–xxxviii; Kane and Donaldson, *Piers Plowman: The B Version,* 16–69.
30. Citations from A are taken from Kane's edition. Those from B are from my computerized copy of W. W. Skeat's edition, *The Vision of William Concerning Piers the Plowman in Three Parallel Texts,* 2 vols. (Oxford: Oxford University Press, 1886), while quotations from the C version are from Derek Pearsall's edition, *Piers Plowman by William Langland: An Edition of the C-Text* (London: Edward Arnold, 1978). The variant lections are supplied from Kane's A text and the Kane-Donaldson text of B.
31. Both Schmidt and Kane and Donaldson tend to prefer the syllabically shorter reading when other evidence cannot be adduced. In general, that preference is shaped by both classical poetry and by post-Renaissance verse traditions, traditions perhaps not fully relevant to Middle English alliterative poetry.
32. Cladistic analysis is a methodology developed over the past three decades by evolutionary biologists to reconstruct the descent of related species. Both evolutionary biologists and textual critics seek to explain the existence of a varied population as the product of branching descents over time from a common ancestor. For cladistic theory, see Elliot Sober, *Reconstructing the Past* (Cambridge, Mass.: MIT Press, 1988), and N. I. Platnick and H. D. Cameron, "Cladistic Methods in Textual Linguistic and Phylogenetic Analysis," *Systematic Zoology* 26 (1977): 380–85. For successful attempts to use cladistic analysis to determine lines of manuscript descent, see Peter M. W. Robinson and R. J. O'Hara, "Cladistic Analysis of an Old Norse Manuscript Tradition," *Research in Humanities Computing* 4, ed. Nancy Ide and Susan Hockey (forthcoming), and the same authors' "Computer-Assisted Methods of Stemmatic Analysis," in Blake and Robinson, *"The Canterbury Tales" Project,* 53–74.
33. For the notion of grammetrical frames, see R. F. Lawrence, "The Formulaic Theory and Its Application to English Alliterative Poetry," in *Essays on Style and Language,* ed. Roger Fowler (London: Routledge and Kegan Paul, 1966), 166–83; R. F. Lawrence, "Formula and Rhythm in *The Wars of Alexander,*" *English Studies* 51 (1970): 97–112; and my "The Rôle of Formulae in the Dissemination of a Middle English Alliterative Romance," *Studies in Bibliography* 19 (1976): 265–88.
34. Optional elements are in parentheses. The central stacked elements indicate that the conjunction or preposition may be omitted, but not both. In this frame, both the conjunction and second preposition are elidable because they are strongly implied. NP = noun phrase; art = article; cj = conjunction; prep

= preposition; unstressed elements are indicated in lowercase. One syllable in the noun head of NP carries both stress and alliteration.

35. Over three dozen a-verses of this form with the preposition *with* occur in the three versions of *Piers Plowman,* counting verses repeated in two or three versions only once. Shortly after I had laboriously assembled the data presented here using a word processing program and a set of macros, Thornton Staples and Susan Gants at the Institute for Advanced Technology in the Humanities began to plan with present and former Fellows to develop a search-and-display program to facilitate precisely this kind of textual search.
36. A weak dip consists of a single unstressed syllable. A strong dip in the a-verse consists of two to six or (rarely) seven metrically unstressed syllables. The preponderance of a-verses display two strong dips in Langland's verse as well as in the a-verses of other Middle English alliterative poets, but some verses of the form x/xx/x appear in all three versions of *Piers Plowman*.
37. Similar variants appear in A 3.2, B 3.2; A 6.78, B 5.600, C 7.238; B 5.89; B 13.140; B 13.289; B 20.124; C 6.116.
38. Langland uses "quod he/she/I" in this position in ways uncharacteristic of other alliterative poets. My sense, based on uncompleted research, is that such fillers are extrametrical and do not affect the argument here.
39. The literature on generative metrics is extensive. A good place to begin is Gilbert Youman's essay "Introduction: Rhythm and Meter," in *Phonetics and Phonology,* vol. 1., *Rhythm and Meter,* ed. Paul Kiparsky and Gilbert Youmans (San Diego: Harcourt Brace Jovanovich, 1989), 1–14.
40. For the ongoing debate between the proponents of the "new" and "old" philologies, see Siegfried Wenzel, "Reflections on (New) Philology," *Speculum* 65 (1990): 11–18. The entire issue, entitled *The New Philology,* was edited by Stephen G. Nichols. See also Kevin Brownlee, Marina Brownlee, and Stephen G. Nichols, eds. *The New Medievalism* (Baltimore: Johns Hopkins University Press, 1991), and Keith Busby, ed., *Towards a Synthesis? Essays on the New Philology* (Amsterdam: Rodopi, 1993).

Is There a Text in These Variants?

Peter M. W. Robinson

In his essay "The Philistinism of 'Research'" F. W. Bateson asks a tantalizing question: "if the *Mona Lisa* is in the Louvre in Paris, where is *Hamlet*?"[1] Bateson himself answers this question by suggesting that the original *Hamlet* existed "physically in a substratum of articulated sound," and that all the printed versions of *Hamlet* are imperfect translations of this original. Other critics are not satisfied with that answer: McLaverty suggests that Pope's *Dunciad* is not just a translation of a substratum of articulated sound but is to be found in all the editions and printings: in all the various forms the text, any text, may make.[2] In this essay I take up McLaverty's suggestion and consider how the new possibilities opened up by computer representation offer new ways of seeing all the various forms of any text—and, with these, the text beneath, within, or above, all these various forms. The text itself alters as we look at it from different points, just as the mass and dimensions of subatomic particles vary as they are examined from different points. The holding of multiple texts in the computer, in multiple forms, may dramatize this variance and better permit us to search for a one among the many; or not, as we prefer.

Jerome McGann has declared that the one constant fact about texts is their inconstancy: "The textual condition's only immutable law is the law of change."[3] His own writings have tended to focus on the different physical and social expressions of texts: on their printing, the "bibliographic codes" of layout, paper, and binding; the differing meanings created by different social contexts.[4] D. F. McKenzie, through a series of influential articles and lectures, has developed similar arguments: the history of the book is a history of its various actual printings and of its various readings and misreadings.[5] These scholars, and others, have tended to focus on the physical expression of the book, rather than on its textual variation: McGann, discussing Byron's "Fare Thee Well!" remarks on the "misleadingly calm appearance" of the poem's "linguistic text" and contrasts this apparent stability with the radically different meanings he extracts from the "bibliographic codings" implicit in its various publications.[6] In cases like this, where the linguistic text does not change although its physical expression does, there is no problem (on this one "linguistic" level, at least) in answering the question of the title of this essay. There is a single text, a linguistic text at least, among these variants: one can point at a sequence of words and lines in the different printings of Byron's poem and say: here is a text, the same text. But what of texts where the linguistic text is not so stable at all, but varies so greatly that one cannot even point to a single word the various texts might have in common? If all the texts differ, where is the text?

Let us take a rather extreme example of this problem: the medieval vision work, the *Visio Pauli.* Scholars believe this was composed in Greek around the second or third century, and it is now extant in some two hundred manuscripts, written all over Europe throughout the medieval period.[7] There are at least three different Latin versions of *Visio Pauli,* and Theodore Silverstein and Mary Dwyer have identified twelve different redactions of just one of these three versions. In addition to all these Latin versions and redactions, there are versions in Greek, Irish, English, French, Slavonic, Provençal, Coptic, Armenian, Arabic, Syriac, and various other languages: it is a polyglot's delight. The matter does not end here: within redaction IV, just one of the twelve redactions identified by Silverstein and Dwyer of just one of the Latin versions, there is such extreme variation as to make one wonder just how many redactions there really are. Sentences and blocks of sentences are shuffled about, omitted, or added, in bewildering fashion; scribes enthusiastically improved the text in all directions; they imported materials from other manuscripts, even interpolating whole passages from sources quite outside the *Visio Pauli* tradition. Here is the textual condition in extremis. What is an editor to do with all this?

Presumably, there was once just one version, one authorial original perhaps, of the *Visio Pauli.* But what is most interesting about *Visio Pauli* actually is the variation: all the different versions, in all these different languages, and what this tells us about medieval notions of the other world. For example, at one point it appears that the original of redaction

IV described breakers of the fast as suspended "super canalia," over watercourses, with fruit dangling just out of reach. Thus, the fast-breakers suffer torment by thirst and hunger: this is the version preserved in many manuscripts. But some manuscripts write for "canalia" the word "canulas" or "canelas." By minim error we then get "camelos": the breakers of the fast are no longer suspended over water, they are now riding through hell on camels. Do not forget the fruit: this now has a new function, as it dangles forever just in front of the camels as they pursue it perpetually.[8]

What, if anything, is the *Visio Pauli*? It is the text of two hundred manuscripts, of the three Latin versions, of the twelve redactions of one of them, of the various translations, and of the now lost original from which all this grew: it is also the text of all the editors who have attempted to make sense of it all. Because it is all these, it is no one thing at all. Yet we persist in using the title as I have, to denote some entity that is determinate and definable. We can distinguish *Visio Pauli* from other vision works: it is not the book of the Revelation of St. John, or *Visio Tnugdali,* or Coleridge's "Kubla Khan." We have the odd situation that we can identify a sequence of words as being those of *Visio Pauli,* even though not all these words or even any of these words actually occur in any one other manuscript or source labeled *Visio Pauli.* On what basis do we identify any one text, in any one manuscript, as *Visio Pauli*?

Let us take a more modern example and return to Bateson's question: if the *Mona Lisa* is in the Louvre, where is *Hamlet*? Tom Stoppard has produced a one-minute *Hamlet,* originally devised to be performed from a bus as it traveled about London.[9] But it is recognizably *Hamlet:* the play about a prince who has to avenge his father's death upon his uncle. Some may find even the one-minute *Hamlet* too long. Here is a ten-second *Hamlet,* ideally suited to the world of video sound-bytes:

> *Ghost.* The serpent that did sting thy father's life
> Now wears his crown.
> *Hamlet.* To be or not to be! This is I, Hamlet the Dane.
> Then, venom, to thy work! Thou incestuous, murderous, damned Dane!
> Horatio, I am dead. [Exeunt]

We can all recognize this as a text of *Hamlet* and not *Macbeth* or *Bewitched.* One could stitch together many other phrases from *Hamlet* without people realizing that it is *Hamlet*. This is the deconstructed ten-second *Hamlet,* of phrases taken at random from the play:

> *Marcellus*. Good now, sit down.
> *Hamlet*. But your news is not true.
> *Horatio*. Twere to consider too curiously, to consider so.
> *King*. Here's to thy health! Give him the cup.

This deconstructed ten-second *Hamlet* actually has more claim to be the "real" *Hamlet* than the first ten-second *Hamlet*. The first version contains one word, "murderous," that is not found in both the folio and quarto versions. Yet, despite its relative textual inauthenticity, I think most people would agree that the first version, containing "To be or not to be" and various other well-known phrases from the play, is more *Hamlet* than the second.

This opens the interesting possibility that a variant text may have a reality even though it has no authority. The most famous line in *Casablanca* is Humphrey Bogart's saying, "Play it again, Sam," even though he never did say this in the film. Similarly, through all the many series and films of *Star Trek,* no one ever did say, "Beam me up, Scotty."[10] These lines have no authority as part of the literal text of these works; yet they are completely associated in the minds of millions with the works. One may argue that some future scholarly editor of these works would have to include, somehow, these variant readings in the text: in a real sense, these are the text.

In just this way, a biographer of T. H. Huxley or a historian of the controversies surrounding evolutionary theory must take account of what Huxley is supposed to have said to Bishop Samuel Wilberforce in the debate about Darwin's theories at the University Museum in Oxford on 30 June 1860. The legend is that Wilberforce asked Huxley rhetorically whether he (Huxley) was descended from an ape on his mother's or his father's side; Huxley is supposed to have replied that he would "rather be descended from an ape than a Bishop who so misused his intelligence," a reply felt to be so crushing that a woman fainted and the whole audience felt at that moment the victory of Science over Ignorant Superstition.[11] In fact, Huxley himself disclaimed these words in an erratum note he sent to Wilberforce's biographer, and contemporary accounts give a very different version of Huxley's speech and its reception. Hooker, writing to Darwin in the next days, remarks that Huxley "could not throw his voice over so large an assembly, nor command the audience . . . nor put the matter in a way that carried the audience," and newspaper accounts confirm this.[12] As for the words themselves: while all agree on Huxley's meaning, the exact wording seems lost. Huxley himself declared in a letter written a few months later that he actually said, "if . . . the question is put to me I would rather have an ape for a grandfather or a man highly endowed by nature and possessed of great means & influence & yet who employs these faculties & that influence for the mere purpose of introducing ridicule into a grave scientific discussion I unhesitatingly affirm my preference for the ape": a rather more diffuse phrasing.[13] The significance of the incident is not in the exact words Huxley said, or even what actually happened that day in Oxford, but in the need for later writers to find a turning point, a watershed in history. As Darwinism triumphed, there needed to be a decisive instant when the forces of scientific right faced down and crushed the forces of dogmatic wrong: Huxley's retort to Wilberforce, regardless of what actually was said and how it was actually received, became that instant. So Wilberforce becomes "Soapy Sam," the pattern of a complacent and clubbable Victorian vicar and not the open-minded, intelligent, and well-informed critic of Darwinism he actually was.[14] Here, it is the aftertext, the misreadings of its historic reception, that are all-important: the text is nothing if it is not this aftertext.

In these cases, there is at least some semantic connection between the variant texts, between what was actually said and what everyone thinks was said. But there may not even be that connection between variants of the one text. Tom Stoppard, not satisfied with his various Hamlets, also presents a version of *Macbeth* written in Dogg language. Here is part of Dogg's *Macbeth:*

> dominoes et dominoes et dominoes

Once more, we have no trouble recognizing this, through all the distortions and noise, as Macbeth's "tomorrow and tomorrow and tomorrow." By repetition and rhythm alone, this variant text achieves a kind of authenticity.

In these examples, we meet text that seems the thing itself even though it is savagely abbreviated, as in our *Hamlet* examples, or even though it never was part of the text or of any source for the text. The reverse is true: all the sources could agree, but the text have no weight. Consider the first three lines of Chaucer's *Wife of Bath's Prologue.* In the *textus receptus,* Benson's Riverside edition,[15] the *Wife of Bath's Prologue* begins thus:

> Experience, though no authority
> Were in this world, is right enough for me
> To speke of wo that is in marriage.

In obedience to the strictest concept of textual authority, that only those words found in all significant witnesses may be regarded as authentic, I give here only those words that occur in every manuscript.[16] All other words I will replace by *beep.* Thus:

> beep beep beep authority
> beep beep beep world is beep beep beep
> beep beep of beep beep beep beep beep

I have cheated here by disregarding fragmentary manuscripts. If I decide to include only text that is present in every extant manuscript, this authoritative text of the *Wife of Bath's Prologue* dwindles to nothing. There are fifty-eight manuscripts and early printed editions of the *Wife of Bath's Prologue;* there is not one line that is actually present, in some form or other, in every one of these fifty-eight early witnesses. The text of *Wife of Bath's Prologue* found in every manuscript is a long beep.

The one true fact of editing is, then, variation. It is unavoidable within the texts we edit, and even as we edit we make more variation. Indeed, one of the lessons of the concentration of McGann and others on what are called "bibliographic codes," loosely the different physical manifestations of the text, is that there is far more variation within texts than can be conveyed by a standard critical apparatus, with its concentration on the words of the text, its "linguistic code." In medieval vernacular texts such as those of Chaucer, there is actually far more variation even within the words of the text than is commonly reflected in critical apparatus. Here is the text of part of line 11 of the *Wife of Bath's Prologue* from the Ellesmere (El) and Corpus (Cp) manuscripts, as it might appear in a regularized edition of these manuscripts:[17]

> To weddyng in the Cane of Galilee (El)
> To weddyng in the Cane of Galilee (Cp)

El:

Cp:

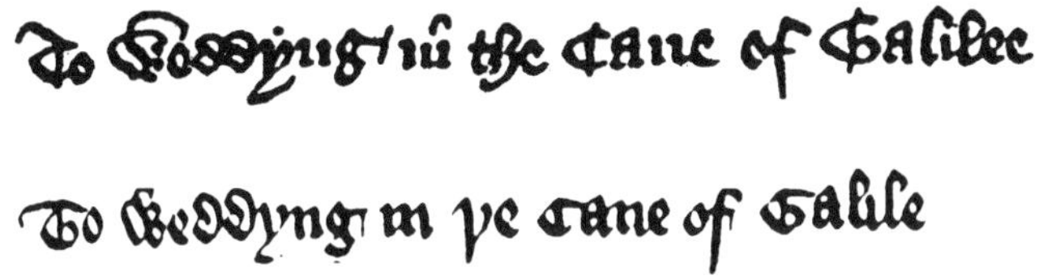

Fig. 1. Line 11 of the *Wife of Bath's Prologue* in the Ellesmere and Corpus manuscripts

There is no variation to be seen here, and so far as I know, no editor has ever reported these lines in these manuscripts as variants of one another. Figure 1 shows what is actually in the manuscripts.

Clearly, these two lines are not identical in the two manuscripts. We can identify at least three levels of variation. Firstly, there is graphemic variation. If we transcribe the text not in regularized form, as above, but in a form that preserves the spelling information, we have a graphemic transcription of the two manuscripts (fig. 2).

Observe the different spellings of *the, of,* and *Galilee* in the transcription. We might record all these different spellings in an apparatus; suddenly our apparatus has grown rather big. Below this first level of graphemic variation is a second level, that of graphetic variation. In the graphemic transcription above, we ignore the fact that the letter *y* actually occurs in two different forms in these lines, with a dot over it in El and without a dot in Cp. If we carried out a graphetic transcription, we would have to identify every different form of every letter and record all these in our transcription. Again, we might have to record all these different letterforms in an apparatus; the apparatus has now grown from rather big to rather huge.[18]

Now below this second level, of graphetic variation, one may identify yet a third level, which we can call graphic variation. Look closely at the *G*

El: To weddyng⁊ in the Cane of Galilee

Cp: To weddyng⁊ in þe Cane of⁊ Galile

Fig. 2. Graphemic transcription of line 11 of the ***Wife of Bath's Prologue***

in the two manuscripts. There is, I think, no graphetic distinction: both are the same form of *G,* the form made up of a loop open to the right, with the top right opening of the loop slightly flattened and the bottom right curved back, with a single vertical stroke through the middle of the letter. But graphically, the marks on vellum that make up the two forms of *G* are not identical. There is a greater variation of thickness in the loop in the Corpus manuscript, and the vertical stroke is slightly longer in this manuscript. Again, if we were to try and record all these graphic variants in an apparatus, the apparatus would grow from rather huge to rather enormous.

In fact, the closer we look at a text, the more variation we see. It is not only that there is more variation: the text itself changes depending on how closely we are looking at it. This is the answer, in part, to the question posed by the title of this essay, "Is There a Text in These Variants?" The answer is: yes, depending on what you are looking at. If we see *Hamlet* just as a play about a prince who avenges his father's death, then there is only one text and no variants. The folio, the quarto, all the printed and staged versions, Tom Stoppard's fifteen-minute and one-minute versions, and my ten-second version: all these are *Hamlet.* Seen from a great distance, as through the wrong end of a telescope, all the variations in these texts disappear: they all tell the story of the avenging Prince Hamlet. For many people, the wrong end of a telescope is as near as they want to get to Shakespeare and *Hamlet;* hence the lack of popular interest in textual variation. Come closer to *Hamlet,* and variation begins to appear between quartos and folios: different orders of scenes, different words, different stage directions; text missing or added. Come closer yet, and enter the shadowy world of foul papers, memorial reconstruction, and compositor identification: the text explodes into fragments, this speech as remembered by this actor, that scene as set by that compositor, this speech as reconstructed by this editor. You can come closer yet, and measure the degrees of type better, or trace the use of a single printer's character through the different formes. Still you can come closer even, and place the pages in a cyclotron to determine the atomic composition of the paper and inks, and then compare different printings, or different parts of the one printing, atom by atom.[19]

The text, then, changes depending on how we look at it. There is an interesting analogy to this in the exotic worlds of subatomic physics and fractal geometry. When scientists first began to measure the mass or charge of quantum particles, they found something very strange.[20] If you looked at the quantum particle from a long distance, it had a definite mass. But if you looked at the particle from a microscopic distance, as in a high-energy accelerator, the effective mass of the particle changed: it might be either greater or smaller than its mass as seen from a long distance. How can something as apparently fixed as mass change, depending on whether we look at it from close-up or from a distance? Physicists explain this by reference to fractal geometry. Look at the line in figure 3. Viewed at a great distance, its length is one inch, as shown on the scale. In figure 4, we see that the line is not perfectly straight: it has bends within it; it has variants. To get the length of the line, we have to measure along the bends: the line grows to over an inch in length. One could come closer yet, and we see yet more bends, more variants, and the line grows still longer.

The texts we edit are just like this line, or like quantum particles: they change as we look at them, depending on where we are looking from and what we are looking at. This suggests how we might cope with the problems of massive textual variation, in traditions like *Visio Pauli* or the *Wife of Bath's Prologue*. Many of the problems editors have had with textual variation are to do with the limitations of printed editions. Essentially, a printed edition allows one to look at the text from one distance, and one distance alone. Usually, this is at the level of the regularized text: we see only the linguistic codes, the words as they are distributed across the various witnesses. We see little or nothing of the bibliographic code, the text's physical presentation; for medieval texts, we see little or nothing at the levels of graphemic, graphetic, or graphic variation.

The potential of electronic editions is that they free us, as editors, from the necessity of showing the texts we edit from one distance and from one distance alone. In an electronic edition of Chaucer's *Canterbury Tales,* in which I am now involved, we plan to show at least seven different views of the text.

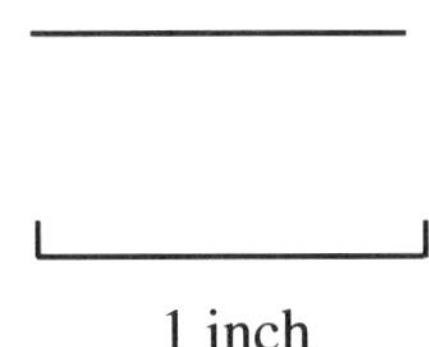

Fig. 3. An apparently straight line, one inch long

Fig. 4. The same line, but with magnification showing it is actually slightly bent, and therefore longer

First, we will have something like a standard printed edition: a single text, with completely regularized spelling, modern punctuation, and so forth. It will be this that users of our edition will normally first encounter. Behind that text there will be the second view: a critical apparatus recording the level of support for each reading in this single text. Behind that there will be the third view: regularized transcriptions of each manuscript. Behind this will be the fourth view: a graphemic, unregularized transcription of each manuscript, preserving all the information about the manuscript spellings. Behind the third and fourth views will be the fifth view, a spelling database. This will collect together all the various spellings in the graphemic transcriptions of each word in the regularized text, so that the history of the spelling of each word can be traced through the manuscripts. Behind these first five views there will be a sixth view: a collection of analyses describing the manuscripts and surveying their relationships. This view will also provide analytic tools to permit scholars to make their own analyses. Finally, at the base of all this is the seventh view, computer images of the manuscript pages themselves.

These seven views will be linked together by a hypertext interface, so that one can move easily between text, collation, transcriptions, manuscript images and databases, and so on. For example, see figure 5.

At the top of this window, we see a line of the base text. You can discover the support in the manuscripts for any one word in the base text just by clicking on that word: here "telle." This brings up a window showing that the manuscripts Hg El Dd Gg Cp have that word, and the manuscript Ha4 has the variant spelling "tel." Clicking on the sigil Cp brings up a window with the transcript of just the line in the transcript for that manuscript which contains that word. Then, to see the image of that page in the manuscript that has this word, click on the photo icon immediately preceding, and an image of the manuscript page appears.

Through all this, we will make available to scholars the evidence of variation within the manuscripts of *The Canterbury Tales*. We will also eventually make available some tools to explore this variation: for example, to collate the transcriptions, and then to discern the flow of readings through the tradition by analysis of the manuscript agreements and disagreements. The provision of all this material for any one text raises some

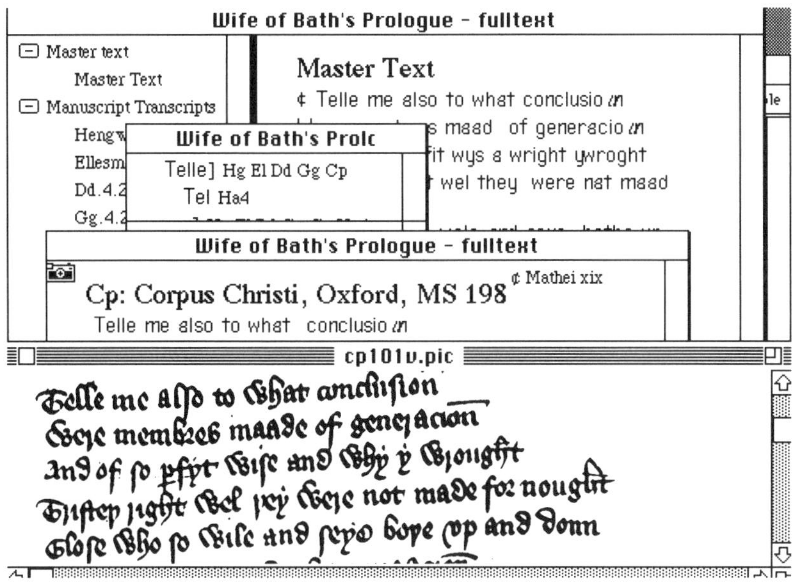

Fig. 5. Different views of the one text in an electronic edition

interesting questions. Historically, textual editors have been most concerned with the text as a literary object. The presentation of the text of editions and the selection of variants within the apparatus have reflected that bias. Yet the great bulk of the variants within the many texts of *The Canterbury Tales* are not "literary." The different ways scribes spell any one word, the different letterforms they use in these spellings, the different ways they inscribe these letterforms, the different inks they use: except in quite rare cases, none of this has any bearing on the text most people will read. Why then, for a literary text like *The Canterbury Tales,* do we open the door on all this variation?

There are many answers to this. One answer is to do with the narrowness of the idea of a purely conceived "literary text." As well as a literary text, *The Canterbury Tales* is a cultural entity: the history of its reception through the hundred years of the manuscripts is in miniature a history of England. You can see this even in the one page of the Corpus Christi Oxford MS we reproduce as the frontispiece to the first volume of the project's Occasional Papers Series. In the decorations, the formal presentation of the text upon the page, you can see the honor accorded to Chaucer's text by this early contemporary scribe. With that, you can see the confidence of this English scribe in this new English vernacular literature: Chaucer's work deserves all the care he can give it. To read Chaucer in manuscript, like this, is a very different experience from reading Chaucer in any printed edition. Very few people have the opportunity to read Chaucer either in manuscript or in high-quality facsimiles of them. We want to give more people this experience.[21]

Another reason for providing all this variation is that some of it may indeed give crucial information about the early history of Chaucer's text. We think we can see already, from the patterns of variation at both graphemic and regularized levels, evidence of an intense cooperative scribal effort to polish Chaucer's unfinished text. Resolution of just what happened in and before the earliest manuscripts of *The Canterbury Tales* may rest on just a few spellings in a few manuscripts. We do not yet know just which spellings in which MSS; therefore we have to trawl in vast quantities of plankton to catch a few fish.

Further, we can justify the provision of the graphemic transcriptions and the spelling databases by the types of research these will enable. The spelling database of the fifty-eight manuscripts and early printed editions of the *Wife of Bath's Prologue,* which will be the first part of our edition of *The Canterbury Tales* to be issued, will contain tables linking around two hundred thousand words in the manuscripts to their appropriate regularized form. It will be possible to trace the different spellings of each word through place and time. It will be possible to examine the distribution and use of marks of abbreviation within and across the manuscripts. Especially, scholars will be able to gather information relating to the presence or absence of final *e* in the manuscripts.

All this material leaves unanswered one simple question: what is the best way to read *The Canterbury Tales*? In one sense, the electronic edition of *The Canterbury Tales* will be an evasion of the question. A traditional, single-text printed edition says: read me; I am the best text. By giving at least seven different views onto the fifty-eight manuscripts and early printed editions of *The Canterbury Tales,* we may seem to be leaving the reader drowning in a sea of variation: as if we were saying, there is no one text; there are just all these variants. The challenge for our edition is to find a way to help readers into this textual labyrinth. Of course, we might refuse to help the reader at all, but simply present, much as does Michael J. Warren for *King Lear.*[22] There are many (including perhaps some others writing in this volume) who believe, following this model, that an electronic edition might not be an edition at all, but might be an electronic "archive," a "resource," an accumulation of materials without any editorial "interpretation" at all, without the privileging of any one text at all.

We—Norman Blake and I; the whole *Canterbury Tales* endeavor—are not of this party. Concerning the first point, the accumulation of materials without any editorial interpretation: our transcriptions of the manuscripts are profoundly interpretative. The casual reader may not think them interpretative, in that we do not introduce gross emendation; but they are interpretative in that we have decided a level of transcription (graphemic, rather than graphic or graphetic) and we are aware of many arbitrary choices in our implementation of this transcription. Elizabeth Solopova and I put it thus in our account of the project's transcription system:

> Transcription of a primary textual source cannot be regarded as an act of substitution, but as a series of acts of translation from one semiotic system (that of the primary source) to another semiotic system (that of the computer). Like all acts of translation, it must be seen as fundamentally incomplete and fundamentally interpretative.[23]

We are used to thinking that because we all agree that a short vertical stroke with a dot over it is an *i*, then this is not a matter of interpretation. But it is: an interpretation does not cease to be an interpretation just because we all agree on it. Interpretation is present even in the making of manuscript facsimiles: we have to choose how much color, how much resolution, and our choices are guided by what we see as important in the manuscripts.

Concerning the second point, that one might present the many texts without privileging any one text: it is possible that long exposure to the text in its earliest forms might lead the editor to strong opinions about what is the best way to read and present the text, and what is the result of mistake enshrined by long tradition. This was certainly the case of the Oxford Shakespeare, where Stanley Wells and Gary Taylor found themselves induced to radical opinion from study of the earliest states of the text, and I think this might well be the case for Norman Blake and myself.[24] We have already decided that all previous systems of division and lineation of the *Canterbury Tales* are invalid and devised our own system that we think far better represents what actually happens in the manuscripts. This does not mean that we will eventually impose our own text on the tales and call it definitive. But we certainly do not think our duty as editors ends with the gathering of manuscripts. There are many other ways that one can be an active editor, indeed an opinionated editor, beside the making of a single text. Already, even from the fragment of the tales contained in the *Wife of Bath's Prologue*, we have some sense of what we think is happening in the manuscripts, and we will take the opportunity to say this. It is quite likely that some scholars will not like what we say. The presentation of original materials alongside our opinion will make it easy for these scholars to ignore what we say but still make use of our edition, and that is how it should be.

For these reasons, we believe we are not making an archive, or a resource bank (though our work has something in common with these): we are making an edition. As editors, we transcribe, mediate, interpret: we too are present in the text; the text is Chaucer; the text is the scribes; the text is the Wife of Bath; the text is us. It is a continual delight to make an edition such as this: there is the beauty of the manuscripts, the serendipity of recovering what the scribes did from the variants, and of seeing unseen patterns of manuscript relations emerge; and then there is through all this the Wife of Bath herself speaking. If our edition brings others a fraction of this delight, then it will have done well. In Bateson's terms: we are not providing a single answer to the question "where is the Wife of Bath?" but we are providing a collection of places where you might look for her. There will be many texts among these variants; within these, each reader is free to find the one text they seek.

NOTES

1. In *Essays in Critical Dissent* (1972): 7–10; reprinted from "Modern Bibliography and the Literary Artifact," *English Studies Today,* 2d ser. (1961): 66–77. A version of this paper was delivered at the Liverpool, U.K., conference on textual editing in July 1993.
2. John McLaverty, "The Mode of Existence of Literary Works of Art: The Case of the *Dunciad* Variorum," *Studies in Bibliography* 37 (1984): 82–105. For a dissenting approach, see Peter L. Shillingsburg, "Text as Matter, Concept, and Action," *Studies in Bibliography* 44 (1991): 31–82.
3. Jerome McGann, *The Textual Condition* (Princeton: Princeton University Press, 1991).
4. For example, in his *Black Riders: The Visible Language of Modernism* (Princeton: Princeton University Press, 1993); in *Social Values and Poetic Acts: The Historical Judgment of Literary Work* (Cambridge: Harvard University Press, 1988). The subtitles well show the focus of each book. See also his article "What Is Critical Editing?" *Text* 5 (1991): 15–30.
5. Especially, his *Bibliography and the Sociology of Texts* (London: British Library, 1986); cf. the review by T. H. Howard-Hill in *Library,* 6th ser., 10 (1988): 151–58.

6. McGann, "What Is Critical Editing?" 22.
7. The fullest modern edition is T. Silverstein, *Visio Sancti Pauli: The History of the Apocalypse in Latin together with Nine Texts,* Studies and Documents 4 (London, 1935). Other editions and studies include H. Brandes, ed., *Visio S. Pauli* (Halle: M. Niemeyer, 1885); T. Silverstein, "The Graz and Zürich Apocalypse of Saint Paul," in *Medieval Learning and Literature: Essays Presented to R. W. Hunt,* ed. J. J. G. Alexander and M. T. Gibson (Oxford: Clarendon Press, 1976), 160–80; M. E. Dwyer, "An Unstudied Redaction of the *Visio Pauli,*" *Manuscripta* 32, no. 2 (1988): 121–38; C. D. Wright, "Some Evidence for an Irish Origin of Redaction XI of the *Visio Pauli,*" *Manuscripta* 34, no. 1 (1990): 34–44. I thank Mary Dwyer of the University of New England, Armidale, Australia, who has commenced the textual battle of editing redaction IV of the *Visio,* and who has cheered me greatly over the last few years with her tales of the horrors of the *Visio Pauli.*
8. These variants, reported by Silverstein, *Visio Sancti Pauli,* 114, were pointed out to me by Mary Dwyer.
9. The one-minute *Hamlet* is an encore for the fifteen-minute *Hamlet,* "written (or rather edited) for performance on a double-decker bus" (Tom Stoppard, *Dogg's Hamlet, Cahoot's Macbeth* [London: Faber and Faber, 1980], 7).
10. A. J. Augarde, *Oxford Dictionary of Modern Quotations* (Oxford: Oxford University Press, 1991), 77, 182. The Press went to considerable lengths to trace "Beam me up, Scotty," having every episode of *Star Trek* scrutinized and writing to its producers, but were unable to find even a single occurrence of this phrase in the series. The nearest they found was "Beam us up, Mr. Scott."
11. J. R. Lucas, "Wilberforce and Huxley: A Legendary Encounter," *Historical Journal* 22, no. 2 (1979): 313–30.
12. On Huxley's erratum note in Wilberforce's biography see Lucas, "Wilberforce and Huxley," 324; the note is in volume 3 of P. G. Wilberforce, *Life of Bishop Wilberforce* (London, 1881). Hooker's letter to Darwin is dated 2 July 1860 and is quoted in A. Desmond and J. Moore, *Darwin* (London: Michael Joseph, 1991), 494–96; for contemporary newspaper accounts see 721 n. 27.
13. Letter to F. Dyster, 8 September 1860, cited by Lucas, "Wilberforce and Huxley," 326, and by Desmond and Moore, *Darwin,* 497 (they give the date of letter as 9 September).
14. Lucas, "Wilberforce and Huxley," 318–21.
15. L. D. Benson, ed., *The Riverside Chaucer,* 3d ed. (Boston: Houghton Mifflin, 1987).
16. The examples from the *Wife of Bath's Prologue* draw upon the transcriptions and collations done for the *Canterbury Tales* Project. This project is based at the Universities of Sheffield and Oxford; Norman Blake (Sheffield) is its director and I am the executive officer. Our aim is to publish transcriptions, analyses, and images of the full text of every one of the eighty-eight fifteenth-century witnesses to the text of the *Canterbury Tales.* These are to be published in CD-ROM form by Cambridge University Press, commencing with the *Wife of Bath's Prologue* in March 1996. The project's aims, methods, and findings are

also described in our Occasional Papers Series, edited by Norman Blake and myself and published by the Office for Humanities Communication, Oxford. The first Occasional Papers volume was published in November 1993.

17. Ellesmere: Huntington Library, San Marino, Calif., MS 26.C.9; Corpus: Corpus Christ College, Oxford, MS 198. Dan Mosser of Virginia Polytechnic and State University is working on a new electronic catalog of the early witnesses to the *Canterbury Tales,* to be published in CD-ROM form by the *Canterbury Tales* Project.
18. A graphetic transcription of Chaucer manuscripts is currently being performed for the manuscripts of the *Book of the Duchess* by Murray McGillivray of the University of Calgary. See his description in "Electronic Representation of Chaucer Manuscripts: Possibilities and Limitations," in *Computer-Based Chaucer Studies,* ed. I. Lancashire, CCH Working Papers 3 (Toronto: University of Toronto, 1993), 1–16. McGillivray's approach puts into practice the "scribal profile" transcription advocated by Angus Macintosh in "Towards an Inventory of Middle English Scribes," *Neuphilologisches Mitteilungen* 76 (1975): 218–35.
19. This was done for pages of early printed Bibles by PIXE (Particle Induced X-Ray Emission) testing: see R. N. Schwab, T. A. Cahill, B. H. Kusko, and D. L. Wise, "Cyclotron Analysis of the Ink in the Forty-Two-Line Bible," *Papers of the Bibliographical Society of America* 77, no. 3 (1983): 283–315. This article reports the work of scientists based at the Crocker Nuclear Laboratory at the University of California, Davis, using the cyclotron beam "for the rapid, non-destructive, and inexpensive chemical analysis of inks in printed and manuscript books" (286). Particularly remarkable was their discovery of the correspondence of the ingredients of the ink of the early Gutenberg Bibles with those known to be present in contemporary oil paint mixes. This suggests that Gutenberg may have drawn the recipe for his ink from oil painting (303–4). A successor to the PIXE work is currently under development in the Department of Nuclear Physics in the University of Oxford, where Raik Jarjis has devised a technique for considerably sharper focus of the proton beam that produces the X-ray emissions and is testing the technique on Islamic medical manuscripts.
20. Heinz R. Pagels, *Perfect Symmetry* (London: Penguin, 1992), 194–97.
21. The first CD-ROM will contain digital monochrome images (black-and-white only) of the manuscript pages, derived from microfilm by scanning A4-size paper prints from the microfilms with a flatbed scanner at resolutions of between 150 and 200 dots per inch. At an average image size of 250 kilobytes, we will be able to accommodate comfortably the twelve hundred manuscript pages containing the *Wife of Bath's Prologue* on a single CD-ROM. These images will be adequate for viewing alongside our transcriptions but will fall short of our aim of providing the highest possible quality facsimiles. We intend to achieve these best facsimiles in the "single-manuscript" CD-ROMs that will follow: these will contain, beside our complete transcript of the manuscript, a full photographic record of the whole manuscript taken with a digital camera direct from the manuscript in 24-bit color at around 300-dot-per-inch resolu-

tion. With compression, these images will be around 1 megabyte in size, so that a full manuscript of around five hundred pages may fit on a single 650-megabyte CD-ROM.

22. M. J. Warren, *The Complete King Lear, 1608–1623* (Berkeley and Los Angeles: University of California Press, 1989). But even Warren admits that the editor cannot help but be present in the text, as he found himself having to order the text with the parallel texts placed first: "Thus I who wish to avoid editing as far as possible find myself, incongruously enough, placing my version before the historical documents" (vii).
23. "Guidelines for Transcription of the Manuscripts of the *Wife of Bath's Prologue*," in *"The Canterbury Tales" Project*, Occasional Papers, vol. 1, ed. N. F. Blake and P. M. W. Robinson (Oxford: Office for Humanities Communication, 1993), 21.
24. Thus, Wells and Taylor's description of the "unattainable" ideal of editors: "By editing Shakespeare, they essay to un-edit him, to compensate for the deficiencies and biases of previous intermediaries who were less informed or less careful or less interested or less dis-interested" (*William Shakespeare: A Textual Companion* [Oxford: Clarendon Press, 1987], 6).

Editing English Renaissance Electronic Texts

Ian Lancashire

INTRODUCTION

Renaissance Electronic Texts (RET) are diplomatic editions of individual books and manuscripts, issued freely on the Internet with an introduction and an apparatus consisting of tags. RET employs SGML (Standard Generalized Markup Language) and optionally COCOA-style (Count and Concordance generation on Atlas) tags to record both the printer's or the scribe's book (title page, table of contents, running titles, foliation and pagination, catchwords, signatures, and colophons) and within the book, the author's text. The series retains original spelling, often (but not invariably) representing archaic letters, contracted or curtailed forms, marks of abbreviation, ligatured typeface, and typographical errors. These experimental editions give combinable and rapidly searchable volumes from the library that an English Renaissance writer might have had.

While editing Renaissance dictionaries, reference works like the Elizabethan homilies (1623), and literary books such as Shakespeare's sonnets,[1] I met with methodological problems for which solutions were not obvious. First, many pieces of type, letterforms, and brevigraphs common in Renaissance printing and writing appear neither in ASCII nor in current International Standards Organization (ISO) character sets. I thus had to identify and encode a basic Renaissance character set. Second, although SGML gives a sound syntax for tagging, and SGML guidelines such as those of the Text Encoding Initiative (TEI)[2] are indispensable reference works in learning how to tag *texts,* I had to devise my own scholarly tag set for *books*. Care also has had to be taken to devise a SGML document-type definition (DTD) that can parse these tags without imposing an anachronistic interpretation on them, one not of the age of More, Shakespeare, and Milton. Third, I learned about usability testing. Electronic texts lean on the programs employed with them. Only after trial and error does an editor find the right software tools. UNIX-based text utilities and programming languages, however, enabled me to make, encode, manage, and read a large personal electronic-text library. It would have done little good if I had made editions that could not be browsed and analyzed with readily available programs. Sometimes complexities led me to overencode, to the point that the editions were unreadable. Usability begs for a minimal tag set.

I learned something more fundamental: the value of editing a closed set of electronic texts, selected and encoded for a specific need. One name for purpose-driven, closed electronic-text collections is corpora. I am working on three of them. RET editions, the first, are experiments in computerizing volumes in a Renaissance working or reference library. The second is instructional: the Toronto *Representative Poetry* Corpus, works by English poets and critics from the Middle Ages to the late nineteenth century that were studied in literature (and criticism) courses at my university during this century.[3] The third is research oriented: the Early Modern English Dictionaries Corpus, selected bilingual and monolingual dictionaries and specialized glossaries from 1530 to 1660.

To make corpora, an editor must transform paper books as well as transcribe them. Corpora differ from collections by being "virtual" constructs implemented by software operating on the editor's texts, tagged so as to carry some purpose. Encoding in RET editions makes possible comparative studies of many books, or parts of them, and enables us to see the interconnectedness of their thought and styles. The *Representative Poetry* Corpus, an anthology of taught English poetry, gives students and teachers a place to begin their reading as well as a front end for (providing hypertextual links to) electronic versions of the original books or manuscripts from which the poems were taken. The third corpus grew from my research into word meaning. It questions whether Renaissance writers recognized the existence of referential definitions, philosophical abstractions by which most dictionaries since the time of Samuel Johnson define words. The English Renaissance seems to have understood a word's meaning instead in terms of its equivalence with other words (English synonyms, or translations into other languages), its connotations or associations, its etymology, and especially its denotations of things in the world.[4] Early modern English dictionaries and glossaries become a corpus when transformed into a virtual Renaissance English lexicon, one that might conceivably be understood by those alive before English-only dictionaries were available and long before assumptions, which grew in the seventeenth century, that words, not just things, could be defined philosophically.

In this paper I will discuss these three closed electronic corpora.

RENAISSANCE ELECTRONIC TEXTS

Character Sets

A Renaissance compositor's type box, and scripts such as secretary and italic, offer many characters beyond those that the ISO now recognizes in its official character sets. Early modern English characters such as yogh, alternate long *s,* alternate secretary *r* (shaped like *2* with hooked left descender), the hyphen when used to indicate censorship of a letter or group of letters, the capitulum (like a capital *C* with a vertical stroke through the center), and flourishes occur often enough to need attention in editing early texts electronically. Renaissance English also offers many kinds of brevigraphs, which consist either of combinations of abbreviating mark and baseline character, or of otherwise unfamiliar shapes themselves on the baseline. Unusual letterforms or nonalphabetic characters are usually rendered as what are called SGML entities in TEI-conformant documents, or they take unique codes that are recorded in what TEI guidelines describe as a special writing-system declaration. (An entity reference is a unique ASCII code beginning with an ampersand, ending with a semicolon, and containing an arbitrary name for the character in question; e.g., *&* for the ampersand & itself. A TEI writing-system declaration explains unique character codes and can relate them to equivalent entity references.) TEI recommends using entity references throughout. TEI represents abbreviations, such as brevigraphs, by enclosing them in *<expan abbrev=yyy>xxx</expan>* or *<abbrev expan= xxx>yyy</abbrev>* tags. Abbreviated characters may appear as entities within the *<expan>* tag—the *yyy* value following the *abbrev* attribute, where *xxx* stands for the expanded abbreviation—or as *yyy,* unexpanded text tagged with an *<abbrev>* tag.

However, many characters and brevigraphs found in the Renaissance have no ISO-defined entity reference. Those that do often cannot be displayed in the software used by most people today. If standard ISO entity references existed, and if they could be displayed by conventional software, it would make sense to use them. Yet available software does not interpret the entities to produce the shape of the character on the screen. Figure 1 shows an excerpt from a manuscript written in a hand supposed to be Shakespeare's.[5] A transcription that uses entity references for special characters would then be as follows:

<handShift new=D style=elizsecr>

. . . .

but ry&s1;e again&s1;t god , what do yo&u^; to yo&ur^; &s1;owles
in doing this , o de&s1;perat <del rend=overstrike>ar</del> as you are.
wa&s1;h your foule mynds w&t^; teares and tho&s1;e &s1;ame hand&es;
that yo&u^; lyke rebells lyft again&s1;t the peace
lift vp for peace

The TEI <*handShift*> tag identifies the script as Elizabethan secretary. This tag causes the alphabet of any subsequent text to be interpreted as generic secretary forms (e.g., long *h* in the MS form *this*), but we still need entities to distinguish alternative secretary forms for a given letter (e.g., long *s* from short *s*), to record brevigraphs for *with* and swash *es*, and to identify deletions like *ar*. The resulting text is almost unreadable. For the time being, another character representation is needed.

RET encoding guidelines employ two pairs of delimiters to surround character codes. Braces delimit special letterforms and nonalphabetical characters, and vertical bars delimit abbreviations like brevigraphs. The two slim delimiter pairs interfere minimally with reading and seldom occur in Renaissance texts. (Where braces appear, they are represented within braces, e.g., *{{}}*.)

but ry{s}e again{s}t god , what do yo{u} to yo|^r| {s}owles
in doing this , o de{s}perat <del rend=overstrike>ar</del> as you are.
wa{s}h your foule mynds|wt| teares and tho{s}e {s}ame hand|es|
that yo{u} lyke rebells lyft again{s}t the peace
lift vp for peace

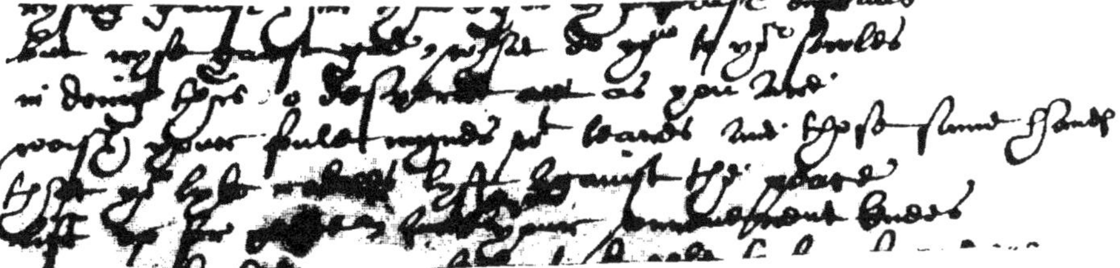

Fig. 1. Hand D in "The Booke of Sir Thomas Moore"

A RET-style transcription can be read more easily than a transcription using entity references. Braces surround raised or superscript letters and long *s*, as well as print ligatures such as *{ct}*, *{ffi}*, and *{{s}t}*. Vertical bars surround unexpanded contractions, of which well over one hundred can be easily found. In general, the syntax for these character codes is simple. Accents precede the letters to which they are attached; thus *é* and *ç* are rendered *{'e}* and *{,c}*, and *õ* (*o* tittle, a mark of abbreviation often for *on* or *om*) is *|~o|*. Punctuation or forms employed in an unusual way, such as a colon used as a word separator character, or an intentional space, just go within braces (*{:}* and *{ }*) to alert the reader to a special significance. A form that no ASCII character resembles would receive a code that abbreviates the name of the form, for example, *{sm}* for section mark §, and *{P}* for paragraphus ¶.

The RET inventory of the Renaissance character set is not detailed enough to study manuscript letterforms, for which each form would have to be encoded for the shape, position, and direction of all constituent strokes. It instead assigns a unique character code to every generic form that was arguably recognized by educated readers in the period. No list of such generic forms exists, as far as I know. Renaissance writers themselves are also ambiguous on what their alphabet is. For instance, *A Newe Booke of Copies* lists fifty-three single or combination forms in the secretary hand, in "alphabetic order," from *a* to *&* but has *j* only in the ligatured combination *ij* (roman 2), and *u* not at all, except perhaps as the two joined minims that appear between *ll* and six joined minims, and four joined minims and *o*.[6] Are we to conclude that in 1574 the ampersand was the last item of the English alphabet and that a form comprising two joined minims made up the letter *n* only and did not even deserve mention as an alternate (medial) writing of the letter *u*/*v*? Or are we to believe that people did not think about the letters of a generic alphabet, abstracted from their rendering in one hand or another? Typically, tagging raises unanswerable questions like this. The more intractability governs problems in tagging, the less optimistic we can be about a standard writing system for the period.

Tag Sets

Tagging has no end. Individual characters or words may be encoded for as many features or attributes as an editor can dream of. Letters and words can be tagged for author, damage, font, hand, dictionary lemma, etymology, length, meaning, meter, morphology, part of speech, position, pronunciation, scribe or compositor, syntactic role, translations, and so on. Words in combination may be tagged as grammatical phrases, sentences, paragraphs, and sections, and for speakers and functions. Given that tags characterizing streams of text can relate them to almost anything and that, hypertextually, tags can link these streams, short or long, to an on-line image or document anywhere in the world, an editor has to set limits for how much tagging should be done. A minimalist tag set is needed.

RET editions use only as many tags as are needed to tell readers and their text-processing software five things:

> how to separate functionally different kinds of text (e.g., a heading from a main paragraph, and a speech prefix from dialogue);
>
> how to locate words and passages (i.e., by means of a reference system, such as numbers for pages and lines);
>
> what word-level features of text potentially affect meaning (e.g., language, font, damage, possible scribal or compositor error, status of word as a proper or place name);
>
> who wrote, spoke, performed, and edited each part of the text (e.g., the printer-publisher-scribe, the author, the speaker, etc.); and
>
> the address of any electronic version of a work (where available) directly referenced by the text.

Each kind of tag has practical value for viewing or analyzing text. The first and the fourth ensure that readers can retrieve subsets of all occurrences of a pattern. Anyone looking for the name *Lear* in dialogue may want to filter out, for example, speech prefixes. The second keys the electronic text to its printed source so that it may be quoted. The third permits a reader to interpret the retrieved text by presenting uncontroversial features of the text without which misunderstanding might arise. The last makes possible the reader's browsing of a complete electronic library.

RET guidelines describe five sets of tags (global, feature, structural, word level, and hypertextual) in both SGML and COCOA[7] syntax. Global tags give bibliographical information: in COCOA format they appear at the beginning of the text, and in SGML format they appear in a summary file like the TEI header. Feature tags characterize discrete parts of a text, viewed separately from the whole. They include such things as title page, ornament, preface, incipit, speech prefix, canto number, column, catchword, quotation, font, and errata. Structural tags define units of text and place them in a sequence or in a hierarchy. For example, the structural tags *<pmdv4 type=line n=3>*, *<pmdv3 type=octave n=1>*, *<pmdv2 type =stanza n=12>*, and *<pmdv1 type=canto n=4>* might describe four nested types of poetic unit: for example, the third verse-line inside the first octave, itself within the twelfth stanza of the fourth canto. Such numbered tags define their own hierarchical relations clearly enough, but SGML enables parsers to recognize and act on these hierarchies. TEI guidelines define the basic textual structure as flat—in it the *<body>* of a text is always preceded by a *<front>* and followed by a *<back>*—but each of these three tags may also subdivide into numbered or unnumbered divisional tags. Word-level tags encode specific features of words, such as spelling, lemma, and part of speech. Finally, the HTML (Hypertext Markup Language) *<a>* or "anchor" tags allow readers easily to follow the references in one text (*<a href=yyy>*) to their sources in another text (*<a name=xxx>*).

RET draws on TEI guidelines for many tags. Some RET-only tags like *<bookseller>*, *<price>*, and *<error>* and *<correct>* within *<errata>* are minor, but others depart conceptually from the purposes of the TEI. These explicitly do "not address the encoding of physical description of textual witnesses: the materials of the carrier, the medium of the inscribing instrument, the layout of the inscription upon the material, the organization of the carrier materials themselves (as quiring, collation, etc.), authorial instructions or scribal markup, etc."[8] TEI tends to see text as structured by authors. It does not recognize a printer's or a scribe's bibliographical matter as structural, but only as a collection of elements that may or may not have anything to do with any other element in the text. Accordingly the TEI *fw* (form work) tag, which has two main attributes, *type* (e.g., header, footer, pagination, signature, and catchword) and *place* (e.g., top, bottom, left, and right), falls within the required TEI structural tags, *front,* *body,* and *back,* rather than subsuming them.[9] The form-work tag is thus flat, without hierarchical relations. In contrast, RET recognizes two overlapping structures in Renaissance works: textual and bibliographical. RET codes *ttdv1, ttdv2,* and so on (which are modeled on the optional TEI *div0, div1,* etc., tags) represent the text structure, and RET book-structure codes *bkdv1, bkdv2, bkdv3, bkdv4,* and *bkdv5* identify repeating units in the making of the book itself. These units are commonly the line of type (tagged *bkdv5 type=l n=x*), repeating on each page; the page (tagged *bkdv4 type=p n=x*), occurring one or more times on the inner or the outer side of the form; the inner or outer form (tagged *bkdv3 type=f n=x*), followed by the form or sheet (tagged *bkdv2 type=f n=x*), and finally the gathering into which these sheets are collected (tagged *bkdv1 type=g n=x*). These five units are truly nested: a book consists of gatherings, each gathering comprises one or more sheets (or forms), every sheet consists of two sides that during printing are called the inner and the outer form, each side has multiple pages, and all pages are a stack of lines. However, if we strictly obeyed the order of pages as they appeared in the forms, they would be out of sequence with the pages as we read them in the author's text.

Renaissance electronic editions should record the contributions of all parties to an original print or manuscript work. Authors are not alone responsible for its contents. The title page contains the name and address of those who made the book into gatherings and forms, as specified in the signatures, which label a bibliographical structure different from front, body, and back. The printer, not the author, makes title page, running titles, catchwords, pagination, colophon, woodcuts or engravings, and sometimes a preface or an epistle to the readers. The table of contents belongs jointly to the author and the press because the table correlates logical structure, the title of the chapters or parts chosen by the author, with page numbers, which are purely a reflection of how the printer put together the physical book. The errata page may be shared: it lists instructions that match a printer's bibliographical coordinates (page and line numbers, often) with changes in text arising from proofreading that may be done by either printer or author, or both. Errata correspond to a computer batch list of search-and-replace commands; as such, they belong to another nonsequential bibliographical structure. TEI recommends that a reference system specify "at least the page boundaries of the source text,"[10] and of course it recognizes the line number also. Yet page boundaries and line boundaries are part of a bibliographical structure that extends outward to the inner and outer form, the sheet, and the gathering or quire. There is perhaps an inconsistency in TEI here.

Textual structure can often only be identified once bibliographical structures affecting textual transmission are understood.[11] Textual criticism in Shakespeare studies, for example, has pioneered applying compositor analysis to finding the "best text." It has shown that compositors make systematic unauthorized changes to an author's text. These include general alterations in spelling to save time and paper (i.e., by the use of shortened forms), the introduction of abbreviations or rewordings that enable a compositor to justify individual lines of verse, and press styles of capitalization and punctuation. Bibliographical structure directly affects the author's text because these compositors do not behave uniformly but impose their individual styles to different degrees. A marked-up book or manuscript will often be parceled out to several compositors operating simultaneously under instructions of a master printer. The units of work in this division of labor are bibliographical in nature, for example, what can be printed on an inner or an outer form (on which only some pages from a sequential group appear, and at that in a nonsequential order). It follows that English Renaissance books and manuscripts, as pieces of material culture, cannot be tagged in a way that is both faithful to their origins and conforms to the 1994 TEI document-type definition.

Usability and Editorial Tools

Unlike books, electronic texts are created without the means to use them. I can read Renaissance books five centuries after their making, but some electronic texts that I wrote in the early 1980s are now unusable because they are tied to a technology no longer available. There is no point in making RET editions if they cannot last. The only way to ensure their long life is to publish them, without restrictions that may limit their circulation, on the most widely available operating systems in a form accessible to the greatest number of people and easily importable into the most stable text-processing software on that system. Usability considerations, then, make RET texts common ASCII files, encoded with SGML (an ISO standard) and published freely on the Internet in a form suitable for browsing on the World Wide Web or for downloading to personal computers for analysis with software running on different commercial operating systems.

To be World Wide Web–browsable at present, RET editions must be encoded with HTML tags. This is an SGML scheme with a very simple document-type definition, one devised only to permit on-line browsing (within a text and among texts) and printing. For the most part, HTML represents the least-demanding DTD for general texts. Its SGML tags may be automatically added to any encoded RET text. There is also a RET-specific DTD, on the other hand, for readers who want to read through the glasses of a full SGML parser; it is unusable for most people. Anyone interested in processing RET editions on other text-analysis software can do so, but the onus is on the user to transform the text and its tag set into what this software expects. For example, personal-computer software like Oxford Concordance Program and TACT (Text-Analysis Computing Tools) expect COCOA-like tags, but WordCruncher requires its own encoding, one that can best be applied by the person using it.

Making usable RET editions can be managed well under UNIX with its superbly crafted editors, text utilities, and simple programming tools. Popular DOS word-processing programs fare unreliably with very large files—for example, the tagged Elizabethan homilies run to over 2.3 megabytes—and tend to work best with texts to which many invisible formatting characters have been added. UNIX-based editor "emacs" and utilities like "grep," "sed," and "tr" are not subject to memory problems, use only ASCII files, and have first-rate pattern-matching and search-and-place functions.[12] Files on institutional UNIX hosts also are not as vulnerable to corruption and loss as on personal computers maintained by an editor.

Outside of "emacs," the UNIX programming language Perl is my most valued tool.[13] With it, in a short time, I learned how to write small programs to reformat text, transform tag sets in multiple files, assign line numbers to tags, extract tagging information from files to make other HTML files that index the contents of electronic texts, and enable others to interrogate the library. I can write a program and repeatedly test it on a file until I am satisfied. This testing process gives me an opportunity to do more than fix syntax and logic errors in programs that would execute intended tasks. Perl allows me to experiment with different ways of tagging and searching texts and to discover other ways to bend programming to the needs of editing.

SPECIAL PURPOSES AND THE USABLE CORPUS

Corpus linguistics is the computer-based analysis of representative encoded texts or partial texts for the purposes of studying language both diachronically and synchronically. Electronic editing in this field has been going on since 1963, when Henry Kučera, W. Nelson Francis, Randolph Quirk, and others met to formulate a proposal for the Brown University Corpus of American English, the first representative computerized database of modern English, one million words built from five hundred two-thousand-word samples.[14] This seminal research venture in the history of the English language led to other English corpora, such as LOB (Lancaster-Oslo-Bergen) and London-Lund corpora, as well as three very large projects in development now, DCI (the Data Collection Initiative of the Association for Computational Linguistics), ICE (the International Corpus of English) and BNC (the British National Corpus). After word-class tagging and the encoding of syntactic structures, these corpora are processed statistically to give profiles that have been successfully applied in many ways, such as machine translation, lexicography (e.g., the revision of the second edition of the *OED* and the writing of the COBUILD [Collins Birmingham University International Language Database] dictionary), and the preparation of second-language teaching materials. One specialized new corpus from Helsinki contains 1.5 million words from four hundred text samples from the eighth century to about 1720 and so covers the early modern English period.[15] Corpus editors over the past thirty years thus represent a valuable and, for English literature studies, almost untapped source of knowledge about electronic editing. Perhaps the most important thing they have to teach editors of electronic texts relates to viable purpose and closure. Editing without specific, realizable goals will only satisfy the collecting instinct. Scholarly electronic editing, like corpus linguistics, focuses on a limited number of texts, encoded for specific purposes that can be satisfied promptly.

Sustained reading is not a viable use for electronic literary texts. Eyesight, convenience for notetaking and comparison, and portability make printed books the preferred medium for scholarly study. Matti Rissanen of the Helsinki Corpus notes that "text corpora should never be allowed to alienate scholars—particularly, young scholars—from the study and love of original texts,"[16] by which is meant the manuscripts and printed books that are the foundation of all work in literature departments. Electronic editions properly supplement physical books, not replace them, but both have well-known advantages. We can rapidly search larger electronic texts than can be searched manually, dynamically transform texts into other forms (collations, concordances, etc.), and count textual features. Electronic-text technology also enables us to print or consult copies of rare books and manuscripts without damaging them and to make on-demand course textbooks virtually free to students. These seem to me to be generic viable purposes of scholarly electronic editing today.

The experience of corpus linguists also tells us that, because realizing viable goals depends on access to resources outside the project in the marketplace, editors must anticipate how they will handle the limitations of those tools and the general standards that their makers follow. Editing texts electronically does little good if they are encoded as databases that cannot be read. Corpus linguists thus publish corpora in a form, ASCII text, that can be interrogated by many kinds of programs. Although the Helsinki Corpus adds, to the ASCII text, various COCOA-style tags required by software like the Oxford Concordance Program and TACT, it is clear that the developers, as they analyze the corpus, often treat the tags exactly the same as they do the rest of the text. Hence virtually any browser with pattern-matching functions will do for most operations.

My electronic corpora are closed because of their specific purposes and because of a realistic appreciation of what is possible. The English Renaissance offers vast collections of books, manuscripts, and records that can be made machine readable. The revised *Short-Title Catalogue* lists over twenty-six thousand texts from the beginnings of printing in 1475 to 1640, and many more thousands of books from the Wing catalog, beginning in 1640, would also fall within the Renaissance. It has taken 350 years even to itemize and locate the different printed works in the period. How impractical would it be, then, to imagine that most could be converted to searchable electronic text.

The Toronto *Representative Poetry* Corpus

The instructional corpus includes selected works by those English poets and critics from the Middle Ages to the late nineteenth century who were commonly studied in literature courses at my university. The core poets are those found in *Representative Poetry,* a classroom textbook edited by members of the Department of English at the University of Toronto and published by the University of Toronto Press from 1912 to 1967.[17] Each generation of teachers in this fifty-five-year period selected authors, and works by those authors, that met contemporary needs of the discipline of literary studies. William John Alexander and W. H. Clawson produced the first edition in 1912, 425 pages of fourteen eighteenth- and nineteenth-century poets, from Pope to Morris. The second edition of 1916 made room for material by authors from Wyatt to Dryden, and for the first time by Blake and Coleridge, by removing *In Memoriam*. Further editions in 1920, 1923, and 1928 added Canadian (but not American) poets. After Alexander's retirement, R. S. Knox took over and produced a completely revised and enlarged two-volume (sixth) edition in 1935 that began with Middle English and continued to the end of the nineteenth century. This was reissued, revised in details, from 1941 to 1956. The final (and seventh) edition came out from 1962 to 1967 in three volumes, edited by F. E. L. Priestley and F. D. Hoeniger. This dropped Middle English poets and started again with Wyatt, but it considerably changed the selection of works. Editing tasks were parceled out to different faculty. For example, Hoeniger undertook sixteenth-century poets except for Spenser (whom Millar Maclure addressed), A. S. P. Woodhouse and Hugh MacCallum took Milton, Northrop Frye edited Smart and Blake, Kathleen Coburn and R. S. Woof did Coleridge, and Marshall McLuhan attended to Tennyson. The differences between the sixth and seventh editions tell us much about changes that had taken place to the discipline of English in that period. For instance, the 1950 reissue offered selections from about sixty Renaissance poets, but by 1962 that number had halved, and the remaining poets received much more space (especially Spenser and Milton).

The selections from the 150 poets across all editions of *Representative Poetry* reflect the collective judgment of three generations of teachers with widely different critical perspectives. To their works, I am adding three things: selections from neglected poets, especially women; full texts of important works that my predecessors would no doubt have wished to have; and critical and biographical commentaries on poetry and poets from those periods. Unlike other electronic corpora of English poetry, *Representative Poetry* was and is being shaped by teachers to describe what in English poetry is most worth reading. The Toronto corpus thus has two purposes. It allows present-day students and researchers to search many important texts of major English poets over six centuries to locate important themes, phrases, and words, both in the poetry itself and in an intertext with contemporary criticism by the poets and by others on the poets, and to test theories of stylistic variation. Yet this corpus also allows us to study the curriculum and critical preoccupations of a fairly typical (if Canadian) English department for the first half of the twentieth century. It is a tool in the study of aesthetic taste.

The Early Modern English Dictionaries Corpus

The Early Modern English Dictionaries Corpus (EMEDC) project now includes a dozen of over fifty bilingual and English-only dictionaries and glossaries published in England between 1530 and 1660 (see table 1, in

TABLE 1. Bilingual and English-only Dictionaries and Glossaries Published in England, 1530–1660

Date	Author	Title	Editions	*STC/Wing*	Language	Type	Lemmas	E-Text
1530	**John Palsgrave**	***Lesclarcissement***	**1**	**19166**	**ef**	**bi**	**23,000**	**EMEDC**
1538	**Sir Thomas Elyot**	***Dictionary***	**6(–1559)**	**7659**	**le**	**bi**	**26,000**	**EMEDC**
1543	Joannes de Vigo, tr. B. Traheron	*Chirurgerye* [JS]	4(–1586)	24720	le	me	426	
1547	William Salesbury	*Dictionary*	1	21616	we	bi	4,400	
1548	William Turner	*Names of Herbes*	1	24359	Gledf	bo	408	
1550	**Richard Sherry**	***Treatise of Schemes and Tropes***	**1**	**22428**	**el**	**rh**	**128**	**OUP**
1550	**William Thomas**	***Principal Rules***	**3(–1567)**	**24020**	**ie**	**bi**	**9,000**	**EMEDC**
1551	Robert Record	*Pathway to Knowledg* [JS]	3(–1602)	20812	eGl	ma	113	
1555	**Richard Sherry**	***Treatise of . . . Grammer and Rhetorike***	**1**	**22429**	**el**	**rh**	**156**	**EMEDC**
1561	Palingenius, tr. Barnabe Googe	*Zodiake of Life* [JS]	5(1560–87)	19149	e	a	129	
1567	Thomas Harman	*Caueat for Commen Cursetors*	5(–1592)	12787	e	c	117	
1570	Peter Levens	*Manipulus Vocabulorum*	1	15532	e	ri	9,000	
1571	Leonard Digges	*Pantometria* [JS]	2(–1591)	6858	e	ma	104	
1575	George Tuberville	*Noble Arte of Venerie* [JS]	2(–1611)	24328	e	h	187	
1577	Henry Peacham	*Garden of Eloquence* [JS]	2(–1593)	19497	e	rh	195	
1579	**Edmund Spenser**	***Shepheardes Calender***	**7(–1617)**	**23089**	**e**	**ee**	**503**	**OUP**
1582	Stephen Batman	*Batman upon Bartholome* [JS]	3(1495–)	1538	e	g	147	
1582	Richard Mulcaster	*First Part of the Elementarie*	1	18250	e	g	8,000	
1584	de Salluste & du Bartas, tr. T. Hudson	*Historie of Judith* [JS]	1	21671	e	g	116	
1587	**Thomas Thomas**	***Dictionarium***	**14(–1644)**	**24008**	**le**	**bi**	**37,000**	**EMEDC**
1588	Edward Bulkeley	*Answere* [JS]	1	4024	e	bb	152	
1589	**George Puttenham**	***Arte of English Poesie* [JS]**	**2(1589)**	**20519**	**e**	**rh**	**256**	**OUP**
1594	Paul Greaves	*Grammatica Anglicana* [JS]	1	12208	e	ee	121	

1596	**Edmund Coote**	***English Schoole-maister* [JS]**	**49(–1700)**	**5711**	**e**	**g**	**1,368**	**EMEDC**
1597	John Gerard	*Herball* [JS]	3(–1634)	11750	e	bo	191	
1598	Robert Barret	*Moderne Warres* [JS]	1	1500	defGis	w	114	
1598	John Rastell	*Termes of the Lawes* [JS]	2(ca. 1523–1641)	20710	fe	l	466	
1598	Christoph Wirsung, tr. Jacob Mosan	*Praxis Medicinae* [JS]	4(–1611)	25862	el	me	574	
1599	Angel Day	*English Secretary* [JS]	9(1586–1635)	6404	e	rh	125	
1599	Osward Gaebelkhover, tr. A. M.	*Boock of Physicke* [JS]	1	11513	e	me	113	
1599	**John Minsheu**	***Dictionarie in Spanish and English***	**3(1591–1623)**	**19620**	**se**	**bi**	**18,000**	**EMED**
1601	Pliny, tr. P. Holland	*Historie of the World* [JS]	4(–1635)	20029	e	me	280	
1602	Chaucer, ed. Thomas Speght	*Workes* [JS]	5(1594–1602)	5080	MEe	ee	2,706	
1603	Plutarch, tr. Philimon Holland	*Morals* [JS]	1	20063	e	a	402	
1604	**Robert Cawdrey**	***Table Alphabeticall* [JS]**	**4(–1617)**	**4884**	**e**	**g**	**2,543**	**R. Siemens**
1605	Richard Rowlands or Verstegan	*Antiquities* [JS]	2(–1634)	21361	ASe	ee	917	
1607	John Cowell	*Interpreter* [JS]	6(–1684)	5900	e	l	2,330	
1608	Thomas James	*Against . . . Begging Friars* [JS]	1	25589	e	g	126	
1608	Thomas Dekker	*Belman of London* [JS]	6(1608–40)	6481	e	c	115	
1608	de Salluste & du Bartas, tr. J. Sylvester	*Devine Weekes and Workes* [JS]	8(1605–33)	21650	e	g	851	
1610	Samuel Rid	*Martin Mark-all* [JS]	1	21028.5	e	c	136	
1611	**Randle Cotgrave**	***Dictionarie***	**12(–1673)**	**5830**	**fe**	**bi**	**50,000**	**EMEDC**
1611	John Florio	*Queen Anna's World*	2(1598–)	11099	ie	bi	70,000	
1616	**John Bullokar**	***Expositor***	**14(–1698)**	**4083**	**e**	**g**	**4,249**	**EMEDC**
1617	John Minsheu	*Vocabularium Hispanicolatinum*	5(–1627)	17944	es	bi	28,300	

(continued)

TABLE 1. (*Continued*)

Date	Author	Title	Editions	*STC/Wing*	Language	Type	Lemmas	E-Text
1617	John Woodall	*Surgions Mate*	2(–1639)	25962	e	sc	125	
1623	**Henry Cockeram**	***English Dictionarie* [JS]**	**12(–1670)**	**5461**	**e**	**g**	**5,836**	**EMEDC**
1627	John Smith	*Sea Grammar*	5(–1699)	22794	e	se	850	
1635	John Swan	*Speculum Mundi* [JS]	1	23516	e	bo	110	
1640	Philomuseus (J. Gough?)	*Academy of Complements* [JS]	3(1640)	19882.5	e	g	472	
1644	**Henry Manwayring**	***Seaman's Dictionary***		**M 551**	**e**	**se**	**575**	**.Howard-Hill**
1650	Michael Sendivogius, tr. John French	*New Light of Achymie*		S 2506	e	sc	700	
1656	**Thomas Blount**	***Glossographia***	**6(–1681)**	**B 3334**	**e**	**g**	**10,000**	**EMEDC**
1657	Anonymous	*Physical Dictionary*		P 2143	e	sc	1,900	
1658	Edward Phillips	*New World*	7(–1700)	P 2068	e	g	12,700	
1659	William Somner	*Dict. Saxonico-Latino-Anglicum*		S 4663	eAS	ee	20,400	

which texts now in electronic form are in boldface). This is a representative subset of over 170 works, existing in five hundred different editions or issues from the beginning of printing to the Restoration in 1660.[18] The EMEDC, available locally at Toronto in a *Pat* database, has 210,000 entries. Some have been edited by others for different reasons, but together they have the potential to be an on-line virtual dictionary database of Renaissance English. Specifically, such a corpus could serve the student of literature in the age of Shakespeare as well as the makers of the new *Oxford English Dictionary*, who lack a period dictionary for the Renaissance comparable to the *Dictionary of Old English* and the *Middle English Dictionary*.[19] Elsewhere I have analyzed several dictionaries for what new information they have to contribute to the *OED* and to the annotation of contemporary literary works.[20] My purpose is not just to collect certain electronic texts. In themselves they cannot be employed for the specific purpose that has led me to edit them. The actual corpus is a transformation of these texts, not found in any file or files but created as needed, on the fly, in response to a researcher's on-line request.

The first English dictionary appeared in *The English Schoole-maister*, published by Edmund Coote in 1596 for young people in schools.[21] It listed and explained 1,368 hard words, often Latinate in form. Coote evidently paid attention to Richard Mulcaster's *Elementarie* (1582), which lists about 8,000 core English words for educational purposes and suggests that schoolmasters routinely teach English vocabulary. Robert Cawdrey published the first stand-alone dictionary of English hard words only in 1604. His 2,543 entries led to similar English-only dictionaries by John Bullokar (1616; 4,249 words) and Henry Cockeram (1623; 5,836 words), but although these went through many more editions, they did not cover a reasonably full English vocabulary. It remained for Thomas Blount in his 10,000-entry *Glossographia* (1656) and Edward Phillips's somewhat larger *New World* (1658) to produce lexicons of the kind Mulcaster had in mind. So it was that no one possessed an English-language dictionary until the very end of the Renaissance period and that—until the beginning of the reign of James I, just five years before Shakespeare retired—very few even conceived such a language reference work. For the past three centuries, writers have relied routinely on huge dictionaries, but Renaissance authors worked throughout their careers without any English dictionary at all. Yet they wrote literature such that Samuel Johnson willingly spent several decades of his life on a historical dictionary that tried to define the words they used. The makers of the *Oxford English Dictionary* did likewise, for Shakespeare is its most-cited author. If immense works like the *OED* not only exist but are now being revised, what reason is there for making a virtual Renaissance English dictionary, particularly if the period offers but few and even then very late exemplars?

An English dictionary of the age of Shakespeare, if faithful to the understanding of lexical meaning then, would be unlike Johnson's dictionary and the *OED* because it would lack referential definition, or what is called "fixed word-senses." Categorical referential meaning lends words themselves the abstract conceptual attributes of the things for which they are signs. These attributes are "the general class (category) and . . . those relevant (distinctive, criterial) features that differentiate the given *referent* ('thing, concept being defined') from other members of the same class."[22] Renaissance writers evidently did not think words had philosophical meaning as such but that they just denoted, pointed to, or were signs for things in the world.[23] Only *things* in the world could be logically defined by class or category, and then by criterial features. Thus the Renaissance spawned immense encyclopedic volumes—Gerard's *Herball* (1597) is a good example—that pictured and verbally described those things to which words pointed. When speaking about the various *senses* of a word, Renaissance writers mean, literally, those different sense experiences, or perceptions, to which that word was conventionally applied as a sign. The very absence of a Renaissance dictionary of the kind Johnson wrote is consistent with this interpretation of how the period understood language.

Very large bilingual dictionaries existed in England, long before Coote's, but their lexicographers did not transfer to words those logical definitions appropriate then to things. French-English, Latin-English, Italian-English, Spanish-English, and polyglot dictionaries by men like John Palsgrave, Sir Thomas Elyot, Thomas Cooper, Thomas Thomas, Randle Cotgrave, John Florio, and John Minsheu had a sizable share of the bookseller's market from the beginning. These lexicons, however, "explained" foreign words by means of various English equivalences or translations, a method of definition (still respected and widely used today) that defers explanation by substituting other signs with the same or comparable denotations. None of these works gives referential definitions. The English-only, so-called hard-word dictionaries of the period, from Robert Cawdrey's in 1604 to Edward Phillips's *New World* in 1658, treat lexical explanation as if it meant giving synonyms or paraphrases, that is, equivalent expressions in English. That is, unilingual English dictionaries in the Renaissance behave like bilingual dictionaries, as if translating from a hard subset of English into an easier subset.

What are the implications of this interpretation of how Shakespeare and his contemporaries understood words? One is that Renaissance words in themselves articulate little of how they relate to or denote the world. If so, we have lost much of the sixteenth- and seventeenth-century England its words denoted, except in the material culture it has left behind—woodcuts, engravings, paintings, sculptures, buildings, tools, and artifacts. A dictionary capable of recovering Renaissance "word senses" should include illustrations of these things and logical definitions (or descriptions) of those things in contemporary works. Another is that we need to depend on situating the senses of an English word by reference to equivalent expressions not only in English but in other languages at that time. Without pictures to label a word, we have to rely on synonyms, comparable expressions, and translations to explain words. Etymological reference books, like John Minsheu's *Ductor Linguas* (1617), are probably too idiosyncratic to be used as evidence of what the general English speaker and writer of the time thought.

The Early Modern English Dictionaries Corpus should arguably encompass English-only glossaries with more than one hundred entries, English-only hard-word dictionaries, and bilingual dictionaries by lexicographers who denote plenty of space to English explanations of foreign lemmas. Most of the small glossaries have been carefully mined by Jürgen Schäfer for additions to the *OED* already: see works marked by "[JS]" in table 1.[24] They cover many specialized subjects: botany, canting, food, hunting, law, mathematics, medicine, mining, rhetoric, science, sailing, theology, and war. To ensure linguistic diversity across time and language, the corpus aims to include two chronologically separated works for each of French (Palsgrave 1530, and Cotgrave 1611), Italian (William Thomas 1550, and Florio 1598), and Latin (Elyot 1538 and Thomas Thomas 1587), and one each for Welsh (Salesbury) and Spanish (Minsheu 1617). These are rich with English equivalences, illustrative quotations, proverbs, and phrases. Other works with limited English text, like polyglot dictionaries such as Minsheu's *Ductor Linguas,* may be omitted initially. Some books are excluded for reasons of manageability: Thomas Cooper's great Latin-English *Thesaurus* (1565), the different lexicographical traditions offered in Latin by *Promptorium Parvulorum* (1499) and in French by John Baret (1573), grammars, and phrase books by men like Nicholas Udall and John Florio are all rich sources for an English lexicon. A subset is enough to discover how useful a corpus of this kind might be.

Anticipating how the corpus will have to be used, and encoding it accordingly, constrains an editor. For instance, there are various structures for dictionary entries across these texts, but each must appear—in a virtual Renaissance dictionary database of use to English researchers—to have the same form. This structure begins with an English (not other-language) headword, followed by foreign-language equivalents, its inflections and gender, illustrative quotations, English synonyms, usage statements, and sometimes elaborate descriptions of which things in the world the headword denotes. Yet most bilingual dictionaries reverse this directionality, putting the other-language term in headword position and the English equivalents after it. Researchers in English will value the relation of the English synonyms or equivalents to one another more than their relation to the other-language headword. Using the printed texts of huge dictionaries like Cotgrave is difficult for English researchers because they have to read through the entire book to locate all instances of any given English word.

If texts share the same tag set for all dictionary entries and their parts (headword, gender, inflection, explanation, illustrative quotation, translation of that quotation, and usage label), retrieval software will be able to treat quite differently organized dictionaries uniformly, as if they were the same. Yet each text retains its integrity for study individually by researchers interested mainly in its other, non-English language. For example, consider the following entries from Elyot's Latin-English, Cawdrey's English hard-word, Cotgrave's French-English, Florio's Italian-English, and Cockeram's English hard-word dictionaries. They all include the English word *player,* but it occurs in explanations of a non-English word (*<explan>*), in translations of illustrative phrases in the other language (*<egttr>*), and in the headword itself (*<form n=1>*).

> *<ttdv2 lemma="actor" lang=l>* *<form n=1>*Actor,*</form>* *<explan>*whiche dothe the dede. Also in the lawe the plaintife, complaynant, or demandaunt. Also a player of enterludes. Also a mannes factour or baylyffe, that hathe the charge of his busynesse. *</explan>*[25]
>
> *<ttdv2 lemma="actor" lang=e>* *<form n=1>Actor.</form>* *<explan>*A stage player, or one doing a thing.*</explan>*[26]
>
> *<ttdv2 lemma="joueur" lang=f>* *<form n=1>*Iou{:e}ur:*</form>* *<gen>*m.*</gen>* *<explan>*A player, gamester; dallier, sporter. *</explan>*[27]

<ttdv3 type=phrase><egt n=1> Iou{:e}ur d' esp{'e}e.*</egt> <egttr n=1>*A Fencer.*</egttr>*

<ttdv3 type=phrase><egt n=1> Iou{:e}ur de farces.*</egt> <egttr n=1>*A Comedian, Stage-player, or common Player.*</egttr>*

<ttdv3 type=phrase><egt n=1> Iou{:e}ur de Moralitez.*</egt> <egttr n=1>*An Entrelude-player; also, a Buffoone, or professed Ieaster.*</egttr>*

<ttdv3 type=phrase><egt n=1> Iou{:e}ur de passe passe.*</egt> <egttr n=1>*A Iugler.*</egttr>*

<ttdv3 type=phrase><egt n=1> Il n'est ieu qu' {'a} iou{:e}urs: *</egt> <usg type=dialect>*Prov.*</usg> <egttr n=1>*There is no playing with any that cannot play.*</egttr>*

*<ttdv2 lemma="attore" lang=i> <form n=1>*Attore,*</form> <explan>*a cha{ll}enger or prouoker in any combat or quarre{ll}, an a{ct}or, a doer, a demandant, a plaintife, an accu{s}er, a pleader, an atturney, a fa{ct}or, a player in a comedie, a bailife in husbandrie.*</explan>*[28]

*<ttdv2 lemma="player" lang=e><form n=1>*a Player of Tragedies.*</form> <explan>*Tragedian.*</explan>*[29]

To transform these entries into a virtual Renaissance dictionary entry for the word *player,* we have to reverse the directionality of all but one entry. To exemplify a method for doing so, I wrote a small Perl program. It processes the dictionaries to produce an HTML-tagged report suitable for browsing on the World Wide Web. The report is a definition list where each sought-after keyword (e.g., *player*) takes the *<dt>* (word to be defined) tag and all dictionary entries containing it follow, in order, nested within a *<dd>* (definition) tag. To make the list clearer, all nested entries are formatted as a numbered (*<ol>*) HTML list. Here is the beginning of a report for this word (the examples come from Elyot).

<body>

<dl>

*<dt><em>*player*</em>*

<dd><ol>

*<li><ttdv2 lemma="actor" lang=l><form no=1>*Actor, *</form>*

<explan>whiche dothe the dede. Also in the lawe the plaintife, complaynant, or demandaunt. Also a <em>player</em> of enterludes. Also a mannes factour or baylyffe, that hathe the charge of his busynesse.</explan>

<li><ttdv2 lemma="choraules" lang=l><form no=1>Choraules, </form> <explan> <em>players</em> on the sayde Instrumentes.</explan>

<li><ttdv2 lemma="chorus" lang=l><form no=1>Chorus,</form> <explan>the company of
<em>players</em> or dauncers. also a quyar.</explan>

<li><ttdv2 lemma="comoedus" lang=l><form no=1>Com{oe}dus,</form> <explan>a
<em>player</em> in enterludes.</explan>

<li><ttdv2 lemma="histrio" lang=l><form no=1>Histrio, </form> <i>onis,</i> <explan>a <em>player</em> in enterludes and stage players.</explan>

<li><ttdv2 lemma="histrionicus" lang=l><form no=1>Histrionicus,</form> <i>ca,cum,</i> <explan>pertaining to
<em>players.</em></explan>

. . . . . .

</ol>

</dd>

</dl>

This report is only "virtually" (that is, by means of computer-based transformation, implicitly) an English Renaissance dictionary, and it cannot be read without having to interpret each lexicographer's method for writing entries—expertise that cannot be automated. In most dictionaries, each word of the explanation denotes one of the same things in the world, one of the word's "senses" (its manifestations to human senses, mentally or experientially), as the headword denotes. For example, one of Elyot's Latinists would say "Comoedus," and an English speaker "player in enterludes," in naming one and the same person, perceived or conceived. The terms were functionally identical signs for Elyot in the 1530s. Because a Latin headword sometimes may denote two or more different things in the world, however, Elyot did not always equate the various units of the explanation *with one another*. That is, "Histrio" may denote what both "player in enterludes" and "stage players" do, but Elyot is not saying that these two English expressions are equivalent (although the conjunction "and" suggests they may be). English here may have two signs, and Latin only one, for two different things. The Latin headword "actor," in contrast, denotes four clearly different kinds of people, only one of which acts in plays. That Elyot uses periods to separate the four equivalent English phrases in this explanation implies that the English phrases could not be employed interchangeably. Plaintiffs thus were only accidentally the same as interlude players. From these six entries, Elyot tells us that "players" were certainly "in" and "of" interludes, had the group name "company," and were associated with (but not necessarily the same as) instrumentalists, dancers, and stage players. Whatever other Latin dictionaries may indicate, at least Elyot about 1538 would always have identified "histriones" with players of interludes and stage plays, never with musicians or other entertainers.

Metalexicography studies the notational systems of lexicographers like Elyot. These schemes differ unpredictably and may not always be internally consistent. Cawdrey allows for multiple senses in the postheadword explanation, but not Cockeram: his entry admits no ambiguity. Consider Randle Cotgrave's complex entry for *Ioüeur* and its intelligent notation. He lists phrases with a given headword under that headword entry but also shows that headwords used alone, and used in combination with other words, may denote quite different, even unrelated, things in the world. If (as seems) a semicolon in the postheadword position in one of his entries normally separates two English expressions that do not denote the same thing, and a comma normally links two expressions that signify (are signs for) the same thing, the word *ioüeur* alone means someone who plays games and engages in sports but never an actor in an interlude or play. The word *ioüeur* in its theatrical sense is always signaled by a following prepositional phrase with *de*. Cotgrave's scruples in distinguishing equivalents give us useful insights into English too. He equates "Enterlude-player" with "Ioüeur de Moralitez" but not with "Ioüeur de farces." The actor of farces is equated with "A Comedian, Stage-player, or common Player" instead. In 1611, Cotgrave gives us grounds for distinguishing English interludes, by reason of their moral purpose, from other plays, and for viewing common or stage players and comedians as being professionally distinct from interluders (who may have enjoyed a higher standing).

This is an interpretation. The Early Modern English Dictionaries Corpus itself is only "virtually" the basis for a Renaissance English dictionary. It is made to *appear* to be one, by computer-based transformations, although it need never actually *exist* as such. These transformations make interpretation possible; they do not actually explain Renaissance word meaning. An editor first selects, enters, and edits the texts. Next, because of the specific purposes of the corpus, the editor devises displays—transformations of the data—that allow for an analysis during which these purposes can be met. With software operating on properly encoded texts, an editor can identify the boundaries and constituent parts of entries, extract them, and reformat them into such displays so as (for instance) to reverse a dictionary's directionality.

CONCLUSION

Scholarly electronic-text editing is best driven by specific purposes. For Renaissance studies, one broad specific purpose is to create electronic copies of its original books and manuscripts so as to permit us to study them for the ideas and information they offer, and for the ways these things interrelate with other works of the period. This goal requires an editor to enter the complete book, to respect everything in it. RET has this specific purpose. My other two goals in electronic editing are *(a)* to produce a teaching library of Renaissance poets, including RET books and manuscripts, hypertextually interconnected to show the main literary, philosophical, and political principles at work informing authors when they wrote, and the public when they read, and *(b)* to make a lexicographical corpus of original sixteenth- and seventeenth-century glossaries and dictionaries that students of that literature can use to interpret the meaning of words and phrases in it in a way that respects their historicity. These two purposes go hand in hand: the second enables the researcher to comment on the first.

Editors who try their hand at electronic editing of this kind need new skills. One is to encode texts in ways that follow current international standards for encoding syntax (SGML) but that otherwise derive their tag content from the editor's own understanding of the edited books. Another editorial essential skill is to reshape these electronic texts into corpora. Utilities programmers call them *filters,* an image that does not do justice to what they find can transform individual works into something with a unity born of critical purpose. Editors thus write programs to turn their scholarly editions into critical corpora. I think that corpus creation is one of the newer objectives of scholarly electronic editing. In the near future, editorial theory and practice should consider what these computer-based transforms of electronic editions are. One of the first corpus-making tools, of course, is an SGML document-type definition, which transforms text and tags into an interpreted structure.

NOTES

1. Ian Lancashire, *The Elizabethan Homilies 1623,* vers. 1, Renaissance Electronic Texts 1 (Toronto: Centre for Computing in the Humanities, forthcoming); Hardy M. Cook and Ian Lancashire, eds., *Shake-speares Sonnets, 1609,* vers. 1, Renaissance Electronic Texts 2 (Toronto: Centre for Computing in the Humanities, 1994); and Lancashire, *Encoding Guidelines,* vers. 1, Renaissance Electronic Texts SS 1 (Toronto: Centre for Computing in the Humanities, 1994). Available on the World Wide Web at http://library.utoronto.ca/www/utel/ret/ret.html.
2. *Guidelines for Electronic Text Encoding and Interchange,* ed. C. M. Sperberg-McQueen and Lou Burnard (Chicago: Text Encoding Initiative, Association for Computers and the Humanities, Association for Computational Linguistics, and Association for Literary and Linguistic Computing), April 8, 1994.
3. *Representative Poetry, Prepared by Members of the Department of English at the University of Toronto,* 3d ed., ed. F. E. L. Priestley and F. D. Hoeniger (Toronto: University of Toronto Press, 1962–63). Available on the World Wide Web at http://library.utoronto.ca/www/utel/utel.html, and in COCOA-encoding in Ian Lancashire, John Bradley, Willard McCarty, Michael Stairs, and T. R. Wooldridge, *Using* TACT *with Electronic Texts: A Guide to* Text-Analysis Computing Tools (New York: MLA, 1996).
4. Ian Lancashire, "The Early Modern English Renaissance Dictionaries Corpus," in *English Language Corpora: Design, Analysis, and Exploitation,* ed. Jan Aarts, Pieter de Haan, and Nelleke Oostdijk (Amsterdam: Rodopi, 1993), 11–24; "The Early Modern English Renaissance Dictionaries Corpus: An Update," in *Corpora across the Centuries: Proceedings of the First International Colloquium on English Diachronic Corpora,* ed. Merja Kytö, Matti Rissanen, and Susan Wright (Amsterdam and Atlanta: Rodopi, 1994): 143–49; and "Early English Bilingual Dictionary Databases, 1530–1659," in *Early Dictionary Databases,* ed. Ian Lancashire and R. W. Wooldridge, CCH Working Papers 4 (Toronto: Centre for Computing in the Humanities, 1994), 75–90.
5. Anthony G. Petti, *English Literary Hands from Chaucer to Dryden* (London: E. Arnold, 1977), 86–87.
6. *A Newe Booke of Copies, 1574,* ed. Berthold Wolpe (London: Oxford University Press, 1962), plate 19.
7. So-called from early concordance software written at Oxford. See my *Human-*

ities Computing Yearbook 1989–90: A Comprehensive Guide to Software and Other Resources (Oxford: Clarendon Press, 1991), 486–88, 495–96.

8. *Guidelines,* 557.
9. *Guidelines,* 995–96.
10. *Guidelines,* 184.
11. Jerome J. McGann, *A Critique of Modern Text Criticism* (Chicago: University of Chicago Press, 1983), 114.
12. Richard M. Stallman, *GNU Emacs Manual,* 9th ed., vers. 19 (Cambridge, Mass.: Free Software Foundation, August 1993); and Dale Dougherty, *Sed and Awk* (Sebastopol, Calif.: O'Reilly and Associates, 1990).
13. Randal L. Schwartz, *Learning Perl* (Sebastopol, Calif.: O'Reilly and Associates, 1993); and Larry Wall and Randal L. Schwartz, *Programming Perl* (Sebastopol, Calif.: O'Reilly and Associates, 1991).
14. Randolph Quirk, "On Corpus Principles and Design," in *Directions in Corpus Linguistics: Proceedings of Nobel Symposium 82 Stockholm, 4–8 August 1991,* ed. Jan Svartvik (Berlin and New York: Mouton de Gruyter, 1992), 459–60.
15. Matti Rissanen, "The Diachronic Corpus as a Window to the History of English," in Svartvik, *Directions in Corpus Linguistics.*
16. Rissanen, "Diachronic Corpus," 202.
17. Robin S. Harris, *English Studies at Toronto: A History* (Toronto: University of Toronto, 1988), 64–66.
18. R. C. Alston, *The English Dictionary,* vol. 5, *A Bibliography of the English Language from the Invention of Printing to the Year 1800* (Leeds: E. J. Arnold and Sons, 1966); and Gabrielle Stein, *The English Dictionary before Cawdrey* (Tübingen: Niemeyer, 1985). Some texts on my list have already been put in electronic form by the North American Reading Program for the new *Oxford English Dictionary* (directed by Jeffery Triggs) and by Raymond Siemens, T. H. Howard-Hill, and contributors to the Oxford Text Archive.
19. Richard W. Bailey, "Progress toward a Dictionary of Early Modern English, 1475–1700," in *Proceedings of the Second International Roundtable on Historical Lexicography,* ed. W. Pijnenburg and F. de Tollenaare (Dordrecht: Foris, 1980).
20. Lancashire, "English Renaissance Dictionaries Corpus."
21. See table 1 for *Short-Title Catalogue* numbers to these and subsequently mentioned dictionaries.
22. Morton Benson, Evelyn Benson, and Robert Ilson, *Lexicographic Description of English* (Philadelphia: John Benjamins, 1986), 204.
23. Lancashire, "Early English Bilingual Dictionary Databases, 1530–1659."
24. Jürgen Schäfer, *Early Modern English Lexicography,* 2 vols. (Oxford: Clarendon Press, 1989).
25. Thomas Elyot, *The Dictionary of Syr Thomas Eliot Knyght* (London: T. Bertheleti, 1538).
26. Robert Cawdrey, *A Table Alphabeticall, conteyning and teaching the true writing, and vnderstanding of hard vsuall English wordes* (London: I. R. for Edmund Weauer, 1604). (Electronic copy courtesy of Raymond Siemens)

27. Randle Cotgrave, *A Dictionarie of the French and English Tongues* (London: Adam Islip, 1611).
28. John Florio, *Queen Anna's New World of Words, Or Dictionarie of the Italian and English Tongues* (London: M. Bradwood for E. Blount and W. Barret, 1611).
29. H[enry]. C[ockeram]., *The English Dictionarie: or, An Interpreter of Hard English Words* (London: N. Butter, 1623).

The Rossetti Archive and Image-Based Electronic Editing

Jerome McGann

A PROBLEM OF IMAGE

From a traditional scholar's point of view, an ideal scholarly edition of a literary work would marry the respective virtues of facsimile editing and critical editing. A good facsimile edition gives a meticulous reproduction of some single text or textual subset of all textually relevant documents. A good critical edition reproduces (in coded and abbreviated form) the complete set of textually relevant documents in an order that exposes their structural and historical relations.[1] In either case, the editing is grounded in primary textual materials, since all agree on the absolute value of these materials (in both a semantic and a documentary point of view).

These two editorial procedures have always been pursued separately for one simple but profound reason: the editing of the documents has been (perforce) executed within the limits of a book format. This means that scholarly analysis will function at the same level as the material to be studied. The critical edition aspires to a higher level of study, but its paper-based format checks the flight of that aspiration.[2]

The emergence of electronic texts, and in particular the more recent development of image-editing technology, has completely altered the traditional situation, as Peter Robinson recently suggested: "One can now conceive an electronic edition . . . in which the texts are linked both to manuscript images and transcriptions and to dictionaries, concordances, and indices by links that fashion themselves anew" according to need.[3]

This remark forecasts a marriage of facsimile and critical editing. As Robinson immediately adds, however, while there has been much talk *about* such editions in recent years, "as yet, no such edition has actually appeared" (285). The problem lies in the scholar's need to work closely with original materials, which in an electronic environment means working with digitized images. To this point in time such images have not been able to be "read" electronically.

As Robinson implies in his discussion, projects of this kind have to date been structured around a core set of character-based electronic texts. If original documentary materials are present, they are either translated out of their original archival state into character-based machine-readable forms, or they appear on the computer screen as nonreadable images. The user may be allowed to "see" various original documents—facsimile images can be called up and annotated—but these materials are not integrated into the computing matrix. In this respect such projects follow the pattern established by earlier editors who translate original documents into modernized typographical equivalents. As with computerized editions, these ("critical") editions drastically alter and manipulate the original documents for various analytic purposes.

So to this point, if a computer-based editorial project has linked images, they function as simple illustrations. Until the Rossetti Archive, no project was undertaken with the intention to incorporate imaged materials into the full computational apparatus (not only on-the-fly hypertext linking, but full electronic search and analysis of the database).

Two difficulties are raised against the development of an image-based electronic edition like the Rossetti Archive. One is a philosophical objection, the other is a technical problem.

The philosophical objection is implicit in the long-standing tension (in editorial theory) between documentary and critical editing, and in traditional distinctions made by scholarly editors between what is considered "textually significant" and what is not. (The traditional distinction between "substantives" and "accidentals" replicates this larger set of assumptions.) T. H. Howard-Hill's recent formulation is entirely normative:

> The editor seeks to stabilise the text within the context of its unstable transmissional history. He jettisons the accidents of multiple historical-determinate forms for the necessary accidents of his own historically-defined form of text, the critical edition. It supplies a text momentarily purged and refreshed at a particular moment in history.[4]

This comment is part of Howard-Hill's general critique of recent scholarly efforts to theorize the critical editing of printed *works* (as opposed to linguistic *texts*). Howard-Hill's rejection of these efforts stems from his clear understanding of the limits of the codex as an engine for textual analysis. Howard-Hill contests the idea "that a book is a text" (33) because he understands the limits of the codex form as an instrument for the critical analysis of other codex forms. The limit, in Howard-Hill's view, forces the critical editor to deal with "texts" rather than whole documents or books.

This traditional editor abstracts his attention from the document in order to secure a critical focus on a complex transmissional situation. The scholar thus works under the horizon of the question of textual relevance: in practical terms, what will editors choose to *edit,* what will they "jettison"? For facsimile editors, all originary textual features—documentary design features, for example—are so significant that they will sacrifice the full power of critical editing in order to preserve as much "truth of material fact" as possible. Critical editors, by contrast, choose to give up varying degrees of textual detail and documentary fact in order to acquire an analytical power over the textual condition they wish to study.

This long-standing differential has resurfaced in contemporary discussions of electronic textuality. More to the point for the Rossetti Archive project, the philosophical problem assumed practical form when I began trying to develop a formal markup structure for the archive. These efforts naturally began with a study of the Text Encoding Initiative (TEI) guidelines for electronic text markup, and specifically with SGML (Standard Generalized Markup Language). It was clear to me from the beginning that these formal schemes would be shaping much of our work in the Rossetti Archive, and that we would want to model our markup structure in TEI and SGML terms.

But it was equally apparent that SGML and especially the TEI guidelines were taking a strongly linguistic approach toward textual documents. In doing so, they implicitly distinguish "trivial aspects of the text" from significant ones.[5] This distinction reinstalls the idea that the physical features of documents, and in particular page design, are relatively nonsignificant so far as the informational and expressive aspects of the texts are concerned.

From a traditional literary scholar's point of view, SGML markup limits itself in several important ways. Most significant, it does not adequately recognize the radical difference between an aesthetic and an informational textual structure. This limitation appears most problematic in the case of poetical works (verse or prose), but it comes to the fore whenever a literary work seeks to exploit the aesthetic potential of text. At the physical limit of text, for example, SGML provides only elementary markup structure for the bibliographical codes that shape documents.[6] At the opposite end of the textual horizon, SGML has not sought to formalize either more abstract levels of documentary information, or the conceptual content of the verbal or pictorial features of documents. (As we shall see, there is nothing as such in the TEI approach or in the formal character of SGML markup that would exclude either of these bodies of information from the markup system.)

The practical objection to image-based editing centers in the electronic structure of the digital image. The information reconstituted in electronic images cannot be searched and analyzed—at least not in the way that electronic texts can be searched and analyzed. Computerized operations can be carried out only on images that have been artificially created (as is done by various CAD [computer-aied design] programs), but not on facsimile images of original documents.

The philosophical objection is grounded in axiomatics and cannot, in a certain sense, be "disproven." One can only say that many traditional textual scholars, in particular literary scholars, do not see documentary information as "trivial." Facsimile editing has a long and distinguished history precisely because readers and scholars appreciate the informational and aesthetic importance of original and authorial documents. In many cases—they are far from unusual—literary works consciously exploit their apparitional and design features.[7] Character-based electronic texts (to date) tend to homogenize or even erase these textual elements, which is one of their distinctive weaknesses when they operate on paper-based materials. On the other hand, because computerized environments can store and connect large numbers of documents, they can be extremely powerful instruments from a traditional scholar's point of view. Every documentary state of a literary work is unique and therefore historically (and aesthetically) significant; and many documentary states are manifestly nontrivial by any measure of judgment. The more nonabbreviated documents an edition can include, the more useful the edition will be.

In an important sense, then, there is a (reciprocal and positive) philosophical urgency toward scholarly editions that can incorporate as much facsimile material as possible into their analytic apparatus. That inertia underscores the importance of including digitized images in the computational database. The Rossetti Archive was begun with the express purpose of addressing and, so far as possible, overcoming the practical difficulties that digital images raise for computerized scholarly editions of literary works.

THE CHOICE OF ROSSETTI

From its inception in 1992, the Rossetti Archive was conceived as a theoretical exploration of the general structure of handmade and machine-generated documents, on one hand; and, on the other, of the methodology of representing such materials in an electronically based "critical" format. The exploration was undertaken as a practical task: to build a complete hypermedia "edition" of all the writings and pictures of the late-nineteenth-century English poet and painter Dante Gabriel Rossetti (1828–82). The project aims to design a model for scholarly editing that can exploit as fully as possible the powers of electronic textuality. The archive is to be a practical illustration of a general model for computerized scholarly editing and data management.

Rossetti was chosen for this project because his works lend themselves perfectly to the development of the editorial model here envisioned. His work forces one to address the broadest range of design problems. The surviving documents are rich and numerous, the materials are exceedingly complex. The extreme instability and transformational character of Rossetti's works—especially apparent features of the textual materials—cannot easily be represented, much less analyzed, within a typographical format. For example, Rossetti typically worked and reworked his poems and pictures in the minutest fashion: dozens of authorized textual states survive for most of his works, many carrying complex revisions and alterations; and these revised documents stand in often labyrinthine patterns of relation with each other. Constructing a codex-based critical edition even of Rossetti's poetry alone is therefore a daunting, perhaps an impossible, task. It is not without reason that even great scholars like Paull Baum hesitated to undertake such a job.[8]

Furthermore, loose interactive relations exist between various works in the two broad media that Rossetti used (textual and visual); and his important corpus of translations from "Dante and His Circle" have additional intimate filiations with his original written and pictorial work. Most important of all, Rossetti's textual work was executed with a profound consciousness of the expressive character of documentary materials. In his meticulous concern for every facet of the typographical and bibliographical features of his textual works, Rossetti showed his understanding that a text's communicative horizon extends far beyond the semantic order of things. Indeed, his famous "double work of art"—those remarkable ensembles of poem and picture typified by works like "Introductory Sonnet" and "The Blessed Damozel"—dramatize Rossetti's effort to redefine our view of the structure of communicating artifacts.[9]

In this he directly follows the work of his master, William Blake. Unlike the latter, however, Rossetti meant to show that a radically expanded approach to the vehicles of communication could be carried out entirely within the order of traditional (mechanical and commercial) book and text production. Indeed, because his approach to document production is nonidiosyncratic, his work lends itself to the broad theoretical ambitions of this project.

The resources of computerization, and especially recent developments in "windowized" environments, hypermedia, and graphics technology, have made it possible to build a scholarly edition that would be adequate to the complexity of a body of work like Rossetti's. Four broad sets of problems have had to be addressed: design of the database structure; methods and tools for the creation, storage, and editorial management of the digital images; choice of search-and-analysis engines and hypermedia programs; and decisions about methods of distributing or "publishing" the archive.

This paper will not take up all of those matters. Rather, I will be concentrating on the issue of database design, and on the models that we developed from the imperative we initially laid down: to include digital images in the computational field. What emerged was a set of procedures—a set of file structures—for adapting the general logical form of SGML markup. These specially designed SGML files, among other things, expose digital images to traditional kinds of computational operations (search and analysis as well as hypertext linking).

ADAPTING SGML DESIGN TO THE ROSSETTI ARCHIVE

Because SGML is an open-ended grammar for descriptive markup, it can be modified to include far more information in the formal markup structure than is provided in the TEI guidelines. Thus modified, SGML becomes a flexible tool for building a database model for a full critical presentation of literary and pictorial works as they exist in their original documentary forms.

SGML is a text markup system designed for processing by computer applications. It standardizes the markup of electronic text with a set of defined tags that are embedded in the text to denote features of its physical appearance and its substantive content.

SGML markup, originally designed to aid document portability, is equally well suited to identify formally (for search-and-analysis operations) grammatical and substantive features of linguistic text. We realized very early in our thought about the Rossetti Archive that SGML might be adapted to mark up documents for important physical and/or visual features that the standard SGML markup does not deal with: for example, for the iconography of pictures as well as for information about their media and physical characteristics; or, in the case of text, for information about page design and layout, typography, and all the so-called paratextual features of linguistic text that have been so important for so many writers. We also realized that a formal markup scheme could be designed that would open the database for more abstract computational operations than are permitted in the current TEI orientation toward document analysis.

From the viewpoint of the Rossetti Archive, the TEI guidelines have been shaped by a (linguistic) view of "text" that corresponds to the view theorized by critical editors (like Howard-Hill) who work in paper-based formats. In this respect the *actual* guidelines may not have fully realized their own theoretical grounds. By freeing us from the limits of paper-based editing, electronic textuality makes the marriage of facsimile and critical editing a practical goal. One can finally imagine the construction of a critical framework for analyzing bibliographical as well as linguistic codes—that is, for analyzing the total literary work: not simply the linguistic text, but the entire book or published object. Literary scholars are particularly aware that "text" is an aesthetic as well as an informational environment, and hence that an ideal critical edition would incorporate the totality of the documentary work into its analytic field. For every textual feature of a document is potentially exploitable for expressive purposes. In this frame of reference, SGML markup (and the TEI guidelines) unnecessarily restrict and normalize our view of the information in literary and aesthetic documents.

The Rossetti Archive is a response to this situation. One of its primary goals is to design a set of specialized DTDs (see immediately below) that will be widely applicable to the electronic editing of literary works.

Specifically, we set out to design three kinds of formal structures: one for every textual document (whether printed or manuscript or composite); one for every pictorial document (painting, drawing, design); and one for every "work" (the term signifying that abstract entity, usually identified by a conventionally accepted title, that subsumes a number of individual documents bearing the same name or title, whether textual or pictorial or both). In the Rossetti Archive these are the RADs (Rossetti Archive documents), the RAPs (Rossetti Archive pictures), and the RAWs (Rossetti Archive works).

Each of these three entities represents an effort to give a formally explicit description of all those features of documents and works that scholars have come to consider fundamental for critical analysis and interpretation. The formal description is set forth in a DTD (document-type definition). The DTD is constructed as a set of logical descriptions for each tagged feature of the document.[10] Software like Pat and Lector then allow a computer to read and display the information coded in these descriptions.

So the RADs and the RAWs, for example, formalize matters that are organized in bibliographies, concordances, dictionaries, and different types of encyclopedias, as well as various kinds of critical and historical information generated by scholars. The RAPs provide the same sort of analysis for pictorial materials.

To construct these tools we subject all of the archive's original materials (manuscripts, printed texts, pictures) to a rigorous formal analysis. The analyses produce the various fields and subfields of information that are codified in the SGML structure. When the archive is completely operational, these fields will be organized in searchable indices.

At present, the search-and-display tools are the Pat and Lector programs familiar to anyone who uses the on-line *OED*. Because Pat and Lector impose certain inconvenient restrictions (both copyright and technical), the archive may well switch to other tools in the future. However that may be, the search model provided by Pat and Lector has allowed us to develop the design of the database and test its workability, which we are now doing. So the archive will offer the user an index of searchable fields for studying and relating its various materials.

One further component of the project should be mentioned. We have built a special piece of software, an Image Annotation Tool, that will augment the power of the archive to study its basic digitized materials. This tool is a flexible image-editor that permits various manipulations of the archive's image files. It also allows the images to be directly linked to related textual materials, and to have specific information in the images—specific physical locations and points—hypertextually linked to any part of the archive as a whole.

This tool may be imagined as an electronic overlay that allows one to map the terrain of an electronic document (whether textual or pictorial document). Once the document is thus mapped, "hot buttons" can be attached to the electronic overlay that identify any of the document's features and allow one to connect those features to other parts of the archive. The overlay can thus allow one to annotate the document at specifically localizable points, to pull out and blow up desired features and areas, and to relate these aspects of the document to other documents in the archive.

The tool was developed for use in conjunction with our modified SGML markup system. The SGML markup defines the archive's understanding of the formal features of its materials.

The Image Annotation Tool allows the archive's user to focus attention upon specific features of the graphic images, to access information about those features, and to connect those features to specific features of other graphic images.

AN EXPERIMENT WITH DESIGN: THE NETSCAPE/MOSAIC BROWSER

We are constructing software filters that permit the database to generate on-the-fly organizations of the database information. At the moment these filters are being designed only for delivering the archive's (SGML) database to appropriate locations in the World Wide Web's Netscape or Mosaic browser.[11] The design of these filters will guide us in making filters for transporting the archive to other environments.

The Web filters allow on-the-fly output of information from the archive's basic files. The filters select fields of information from the database and organize them for presentation by the Netscape or Mosaic client. The hypermedia structure of the Web then becomes an instrument for organizing further complex searches and comparative studies of the archive's materials. (Let it be said here that we are working *with*—we are not tied *to*—the Netscape or Mosaic client. It proves extremely useful as a vehicle for experimenting with hypermedia design and presentation, as well as with filtering-design problems.)

The general structure we have built organizes the Rossetti Archive into an introductory and a full archive. The latter—to which I shall confine myself here—has the following basic set of (horizontally structured) directories:

Paintings, Drawings, and Designs; Poems; Prose Works and Fragments; Manuscripts; Rossetti Letters; Periodicals; Other Books; Other Pictures. Each of these directories has further sets of nested subdirectories, and the whole is interconnected by cross-links. The subdirectories consist of a general introduction (fig. 1), an index (fig. 2), an introduction to a specific document (fig. 3), the text of the document (fig. 4), and a set of critical annotations on the document (fig. 5). The text of the document has an icon hotlinked to a digital image of the document itself.

As the illustrations show, specific information in the archive's files is preselected by the filters and sent to the relevant Web pages. The archive's basic files contain far more information about its materials, however. This additional information is accessed through the Pat/Lector index of marked SGML fields.

The vertical organization of the hypertext structure created by Mosaic, which is HTML (Hypertext Markup Language) based, is thus built in three broad levels: level A, a general introduction to any particular work

The Rossetti Archive: The Poems

Rossetti's *Juvenilia* comprises a fairly substantial body of poems, dramas, prose tales, and translations written in the 1830s and early 1840s. All of this work is invested with heavily romantic, not to say gothic, preoccupations. Much has not survived.

The important poetical work begins suddenly in 1847, the year he composed the earliest version of one of his masterpieces, "The Blessed Damozel", as well as a number of other significant works like "My Sister's Sleep". It seems very likely that the mature and finished character of these poems was achieved because of the discipline Rossetti acquired at that time translating Dante and the poets of the early *stil novist* circle. These translations -- perhaps begun as early as 1845 -- plunged Rossetti into a deep involvement with Europe's most significant body of love poetry .

The years 1847–49 produced a remarkable body of writing in original poetry, translation, and prose as well. In 1850, however, his work in painting became his chief interest. Although he continued to write (largely poetry) through the 1850s and 60s, the period is dominated by his pictorial work.

Rossetti did publish one book in this period -- his first book: the collection of his translations called *The Early Italian Poets* (1861). An advertisement at the back of this book announced the imminent publication of a collection of original poetry, *Dante at Verona, and Other Poems*, but this work never appeared. The death of Rossetti's wife was a major factor in preventing this project.

In the late 1860s, however, Rossetti turned back to his poetry. The years 1868–1872 were devoted to the composition of much new original poetry and the recovery/revision of his earlier poetry as well. This work centered in the production of Rossetti's 1870 volume of *Poems*, upon which he expended himself in the most painstaking way. The volume was designed by Rossetti from cover to cover and contained the first book version of his masterwork, the sonnet-sequence "The House of Life". The latter was revised and augmented in a major way throughout the 1870s. Also, in 1874 Rossetti issued a revised edition of his 1861 collection of translations, this time under the title *Dante and his Circle*. A new edition of the *Poems* was issued in 1881.

Rossetti continued to revise his poems and to produce new work throughout the 1870s. In 1882 he brought out a volume of that included a much expanded text of "The House of Life", as well as some new poems, including a group of new narrative poems.

Rossetti died in 1882. Four years later his brother William Michael published the first of his series of editions, *The Collected Works of Dante Gabriel Rossetti* in two volumes. This work, which contained many unpublished writings, was repeatedly revised and augmented over the next twenty-five years, until it achieved its culminant form in the one volume *The Works of Dante Gabriel Rossetti* in 1911.

For access to specific poems click on the INDEX icon above. That icon will also take you to indexes for all the other materials in the archive.

Fig. 1

The Rossetti Archive: Index of Poems

This Index lists all of Rossetti's poems in alphabetical order by title. A chronological index is also available. This chronological index arranges the poems by the following groups: (a) Poems 1835–1851; (b) Poems 1852–1866; (c) Poems 1867–1871; (d) Poems 1872–1882.

- Index: The Paintings, Drawings, and Designs
- Index: The Prose Works and Fragments
- Index: The Translations
- Index: The Manuscripts
- Index: Rossetti's Letters
- Index: Periodicals
- Index: Other Books
- Index: Other Pictures

INDEX: THE POEMS

- **The Blessed Damozel**
- **Dantis Tenebrae. (In Memory of my Father.)**
- **For an Allegorical Dance of Women By Andrea Mantegna. (In the Louvre.)**
- **The House of Life**
- **Introductory Sonnet [to *The House of Life*]**
- **Mary's Girlhood**
- **On the 'Vita Nuova' of Dante**
- **Poems (1870)**
- **Sonnets for Pictures**

Fig. 2

(e.g., "The Blessed Damozel"); level B, a general introduction to every documentary state of each work; level C, the text of the documents. Each of these levels comes with its own scholarly apparatus of materials, including notes and commentaries as well as hypertext links to related materials. So far as Netscape or Mosaic is concerned, the filters work in the following way. One set of filters selects information from the RAW and sends it to level A; another set selects data from the RADs and passes it on to level B and/or to level C.

Note that in all this structure there is no "copytext" or "basic text" or "reading text." Every textual document is readable; the student makes the choice, not the editor or the archive's compiler. The latter will of course provide informed commentary—his or her own or others'—on the historical relation and status of the various texts. This commentary is not designed to promote any particular approach to the study of the documents, however, but simply to lay out what is known about them, and hence to supply students with information that promotes informed judgments and decisions.

Rossetti Archive: The Poems

The Blessed Damozel

Written originally in 1847, this famous poem went through a great many revisions and changes. Through all these changes, the poem remained DGR's most important (evolving) textual interpretation of his Dantescan inheritance. In the mid–1870s Rossetti began a series of paintings and studies that culminated in his painting of the same title. The pictures are themselves "readings" of their precursive texts, and the whole composite body of texts and images makes up a closely integrated network of materials; it is a network, moreover, that stands as an index of DGR's essential artistic ideals and practises.

DOCUMENTS

`Manuscripts`

- Pierpont Morgan Manuscript
- Princeton Manuscript Fragment

`Printed Texts`

- **The Germ** Text (1850)
- **The Oxford and Cambridge Magazine** Text (1856)
- **The Crayon** Text (1858)
- **The New Path** Text (1863)

- **Poems** (1870)
  - First Trial Book (Privately Printed, 1869)
  - Second Trial Book (Privately Printed, 1869)
  - Proof, First Edition
  - First Edition

- **Poems. A New Edition** (1881)
  - First Edition

COMMENTARIES

- Textual History
- Printing History
- Historical
- Literary
- Pictorial
- Autobiographical
- Bibliography

Fig. 3

 Princeton MS

TEXT

```
Around her, lovers, newly met
   'Mid deathless love's acclaims,
Spoke evermore among themselves
   Their rapturous new names;
And the souls mounting up to God
   Went by her like thin flames.
```

Fig. 4

Document:

"The Blessed Damozel", stanza 7 manuscript fragment (1872)

This is the text for the sixth (1872) edition of Rossetti's *Poems*, first published in 1870.

Page Information:

- **title:** *untitled*
- **MS type:** *fair copy*
- **location:** *Troxell Collection, Princeton U. Library*
- **MS annotations:** *Instead of verse 7 of "The Blessed Damozel" [Rossetti's note to the printer written at the top of the manuscript]; Autograph of D G Rossetti [William Michael Rossetti's annotation added below MS text]*
- **note:** *This text was also printed in the 1873 Tauchnitz edition of Rossetti's Poems.*

Read the text.

Fig. 5

THE ORDER OF THINGS: EXAMPLES OF RADS AND RAWS

Preliminary DTDs for all the materials in the Rossetti Archive were designed in 1992–93. (For those interested, the DTD for the RADs is given as appendix 1.) In 1993–94 we began testing the DTDs for the RADs and the RAWs. These tests exposed various kinds of weaknesses in the original design of the DTDs, which underwent a process of revision (now nearly completed).

The most complex of the DTDs, and the one most pertinent to the work of literary scholars, is the RAD, which formalizes information relevant to the study of literary manuscripts and printed texts (or composites of the two). I give here excerpts from the marked-up electronic files of three of the archive's RADs. (Excerpts only are given because the full RAD in each of these cases is far too long to reproduce here.) The first is from the RAD for the manuscript of "The House of Life" owned by the Fitzwilliam Museum (appendix 2). The second and third represent equivalent parts of two different copies of the first trialbook of the 1869–70 *Poems:* the Princeton University Library's copy (appendix 3), and the copy in the British Library (appendix 4).[12]

The templates show the SGML fields that are open to electronic search. Every textual document in the archive is formally organized according to the fields defined in the DTD of which these templates are partial representations. The archive provides an index of these fields as well as a mechanism (at the moment, Pat/Lector) by which they can be searched and cross-field analyses executed.[13]

If texts of independent works are contained within larger works—as is the case in each of the RAD examples given here—the more comprehensive document is marked so that the textual instances of the embedded works can be accessed and searched. So the archive does not have to prepare independent RADs for (say) any of the 1869–70 texts of "The Blessed Damozel." Similarly, the 1850 *Germ* text of "The Blessed Damozel" does not have an independent RAD; the archive prepares a RAD for the entirety of the *Germ,* and the comprehensive RAD integrates the embedded works in the archive's computational structure. But an independent RAD *is* prepared for the Morgan Library manuscript of "The Blessed Damozel" since that manuscript is an integral document.

In contrast to the RADs, which organize information about all the textual documents in the archive, the RAW files organize information about the archive's various works, that is, those abstract totalities that comprise all the documentary states of a named textual and/or pictorial unit. The RAW holds information applicable to all the documentary states of the work. It includes various kinds of comparative information, and its embedded references to other materials are hotlinked to those other parts of the archive that contain those materials.

These RAD and RAW files encode information about the archive's basic resources, that is, the original manuscript and printed documents and the secondary information related to those documents. The information is either intrinsic to the documents or has been developed to explain the documents. The explanatory information may be either positive (commentaries and glosses, for example), or it may be relational (links to other documents or bodies of information).

CONCLUSION

The Rossetti Archive thus develops a computerized model for studying texts whose original physical condition is an essential feature of their textuality. The archive will be a collection of digitized images (electronic facsimiles, 24-bit color as needed) of every manuscript, proof, printed text, painting, and drawing by Rossetti. All of these materials—about fifteen thousand digital images in the initial phase of the project—will be hypertextually connected to each other and to a related set of critical materials (notes and commentaries); and the whole structure will be open to full electronic search and analysis. It is a research tool that integrates critical editing, facsimile editing, and electronic editing in a single network of scholarly operations.

APPENDICES

Appendix 1. The Rossetti Archive DTD for a RAD File

```
<!--This is the DTD for the Rossetti Archive document (rad) structure-->
<!--revised:  6 Oct 94 to add titlePage tags (seg)-->
<!--revised:  9 Mar 95 to add r attr to l, lg and lv (seg)-->
<!--revised: 25 Apr 95 to add gap and orn.lb tags (seg)-->
<!--revised:  4 May 95 to add addSpan and delSpan tags (seg)-->
<!--revised: 25 May 95 to add sup and sub tags (seg)-->
<!--revised:  1 Jun 95 to add lineNotes structure to workHeader-->
<!--             and div0 to front and back-->
```

```
<!--revised: 14 Jun 95 to add group option to rad for serials-->
<!--revised: 15 Jun 95 to add contemporaryCrit structure to commentaries-->
<!--             and periodical tag to reference -->
<!--revised: 26 Jun 95 to add part attribute to line tag-->
<!--             and title to pageNote tag-->
<!--revised: 24 Jul 95 to add author tag to workHeader tag-->
<!--revised:  1 Aug 95 to add label and p tags to item tag-->
<!--revised: 30 Aug 95 to allow the add and del tags within title-->
<!--revised: 15 Jan 96 to change commentaries to generic sections
            and "." style name to Caps style
            and rad to header and text (including group)-->

<!--= = = = = = = = = = = = = = = = = = = = = = = = = = = = =-->

<!ENTITY % pnotes ' pageHeader | pageNote | msAdds '>
<!ENTITY % pg ' page | epage '>
<!ENTITY % renderings ' b | c | i | sc | sub | sup | u '>
<!ENTITY % floats 'bibl | cit | ornLb | omit | %pg; | %pnotes; |
            %renderings; '>
<!ENTITY % low ' add | addSpan | del | delSpan | gap | l | lg | lv |
            note | p | phrase | scribe | %floats; '>

<!--Global attributes-->
<!ENTITY % global 'id ID #IMPLIED n CDATA #IMPLIED
            rend CDATA #IMPLIED lang CDATA #IMPLIED'>

<!ELEMENT add  - -  (#PCDATA)  >
<!ELEMENT addSpan  - -  (#PCDATA) +(%low;)  >
<!ATTLIST addSpan
            extent CDATA #IMPLIED  >
<!ELEMENT assign  - -  (#PCDATA)  >
<!ELEMENT author  - -  (#PCDATA)  >
<!ELEMENT authorization  - -  (#PCDATA)  >
<!ELEMENT authorline  - -  (#PCDATA)  >
<!ELEMENT b  - -  (#PCDATA)  >
<!ELEMENT back  - -  (div0 | %low;)+ +(%floats;)>
<!ELEMENT bibl  - -  (#PCDATA | (title | author | imprint | city | date |
                     periodical | resp)+)>
<!ELEMENT biblioSig  - -  (#PCDATA)  >
<!ELEMENT binding  - -  (cover,endpapers?, note*)>
<!ELEMENT body  - -  (div0 | work)+ +(%floats;)>
<!ELEMENT c  - -  (#PCDATA)  >
<!ELEMENT cit  - -  (quote, bibl?)  >
<!ELEMENT citnStruct  - -  (title+,author+,(imprint | msProd), scribe*,
                           corrector*, provenance, physicalDesc)>
<!ELEMENT city  - -  (#PCDATA)  >
```

```
<!ELEMENT collation  - -  (#PCDATA)  >
<!ELEMENT columns  - -  (#PCDATA)  >
<!ELEMENT commentary  - -  (#PCDATA)  >
<!ELEMENT commentaries  - -  (head, section+)  >
<!ATTLIST commentaries
          type  (intro | textHistComp | textHistRev | prodHist | receptHist |
                icon | printHist | pictorial | historical | literary | translation |
                autobio | biblio ) intro #REQUIRED  >
<!ELEMENT corrector  - -  (#PCDATA)  >
<!ELEMENT cover  - -  (#PCDATA)  >
<!ELEMENT date  - -  (#PCDATA)  >
<!ELEMENT del  - -  (#PCDATA)  >
<!ELEMENT delSpan  - -  (#PCDATA) +(%low;)  >
<!ATTLIST delSpan
          extent CDATA #IMPLIED  >
<!ELEMENT desc  - -  (#PCDATA)  >
<!ELEMENT divHeader  - -  (title, authorline?, author?, note*, commentary?,
                          lineNotes?)  >
<!ELEMENT div0  - -  (divHeader?, epigraph*,
                 ( p | lg | div1 )+)  +(list)>
<!ATTLIST div0
          type  CDATA #REQUIRED
          n     CDATA #REQUIRED
          title  CDATA #REQUIRED
          workCode CDATA #IMPLIED  >
<!ELEMENT div1  - -  (divHeader?, epigraph*, (p | lg | div2)+)  +(list)>
<!ATTLIST div1
          type  CDATA #REQUIRED
          n     CDATA #REQUIRED
          title  CDATA #REQUIRED
          workCode CDATA #IMPLIED  >
<!ELEMENT div2  - -  (divHeader?, epigraph*, (p | lg | div3)+)  >
<!ATTLIST div2
          type  CDATA #REQUIRED
          n     CDATA #REQUIRED
          title  CDATA #REQUIRED
          workCode CDATA #IMPLIED  >
<!ELEMENT div3  - -  (divHeader?, epigraph*, (p | lg | div4)+)  >
<!ATTLIST div3
          type  CDATA #REQUIRED
          n     CDATA #REQUIRED
          title  CDATA #REQUIRED
          workCode CDATA #IMPLIED  >
<!ELEMENT div4  - -  (divHeader?, title?, note*, epigraph*, (p | lg)+)  >
<!ATTLIST div4
          type  CDATA #REQUIRED
```

```
            n       CDATA #REQUIRED
            title   CDATA #REQUIRED
            workCode CDATA #IMPLIED   >
<!ELEMENT docAuthor   - -   (#PCDATA)   >
<!ELEMENT docDate   - -   (#PCDATA)   >
<!ATTLIST docDate
            value CDATA #IMPLIED   >
<!ELEMENT docEdition   - -   (#PCDATA)   >
<!ELEMENT docImprint   - -   (#PCDATA)   >
<!ELEMENT docTitle   - -   (titlePart+)   >
<!ELEMENT edition   - -   (#PCDATA)   >
<!ELEMENT editionStmt   - -   (edition)   >
<!ELEMENT encodingDesc   - -   (#PCDATA)   >
<!ELEMENT endpapers   - -   (#PCDATA)   >
<!ELEMENT epage -o EMPTY   >
<!ELEMENT epigraph   - -   (#PCDATA) +(l | p)   >
<!ELEMENT extent   - -   (#PCDATA)   >
<!ELEMENT fileDesc   - -   (titleStmt, editionStmt, extent, publicationSt!
                            seriesStmt, notesStmt, sourceDesc)   >
<!ELEMENT font   - -   (#PCDATA)   >
<!ELEMENT front   - -   (titlePage | div0 | %low;)+  +(%floats;)>
<!ELEMENT funder   - -   (#PCDATA)   >
<!ELEMENT gap -o EMPTY   >
<!ATTLIST gap
            desc CDATA #IMPLIED
            extent CDATA #IMPLIED   >
<!ELEMENT gloss   - -   (#PCDATA)   >
<!ELEMENT group   - -   (text | group)+   >
<!ATTLIST group
            %global;   >
<!ELEMENT head   - -   (#PCDATA)   >
<!ATTLIST head
            %global;   >
<!ELEMENT i   - -   (#PCDATA)   >
<!ELEMENT imprint   - -   (publisher, printer, city, date, edition?, prePub?,
                           pagination, printing?, issue?, authorization,
                           collation, note*)   >
<!ELEMENT imprimatur   - -   (#PCDATA)   >
<!ELEMENT issue   - -   (#PCDATA)   >
<!ELEMENT item   - -   (#PCDATA)   >
<!ATTLIST item
            %global;   >
<!ELEMENT iteml   - -   (label, p*)   >
<!ATTLIST iteml
            %global;   >
<!ELEMENT l -o (#PCDATA) +(%low;)   >
```

```
<!ATTLIST l %global;
            indent  CDATA #IMPLIED
            part    (Y | N | I | M | F) N
            r       CDATA #IMPLIED  >
<!ELEMENT label  - -  (#PCDATA)  >
<!ELEMENT length  - -  (#PCDATA)  >
<!ELEMENT lg  - -  (l+)  >
<!ATTLIST lg
            n      CDATA #IMPLIED
            r      CDATA #IMPLIED
            type   CDATA #IMPLIED>
<!ELEMENT lineNotes  - -  (lines+)  >
<!ELEMENT lines  - -  (gloss*, textual*)  >
<!ATTLIST lines
            %global;  >
<!ELEMENT list  - -  ((head?, item*, iteml*) | list)+  >
<!ELEMENT location  - -  (#PCDATA)  >
<!ELEMENT lv -o (#PCDATA) +(%low;)  >
<!ATTLIST lv %global;
            indent  CDATA #IMPLIED
            r       CDATA #IMPLIED  >
<!ELEMENT margin  - -  (#PCDATA)  >
<!ATTLIST margin
            type  (top | bottom | right | left) #REQUIRED>
<!ELEMENT msAdds  - -  (trans?, desc?) +(%low;)  >
<!ATTLIST msAdds
            type  (sig | add | assign | note | prtrdir | other)
                             #REQUIRED>
<!ELEMENT msProd  - -  (date, type, assign?, collation, note*)>
<!ELEMENT name  - -  (#PCDATA)  >
<!ELEMENT note  - -  (#PCDATA) +(%renderings;)  >
<!ELEMENT notesStmt  - -  (#PCDATA)  >
<!ELEMENT number  - -  (#PCDATA)  >
<!ELEMENT omit -o EMPTY  >
<!ATTLIST omit
            extent  CDATA #REQUIRED
            reason  CDATA #REQUIRED  >
<!ELEMENT ornament  - -  (#PCDATA)  >
<!ELEMENT ornLb  - -  (#PCDATA)  >
<!ELEMENT p  - -  (#PCDATA) +(%low;)>
<!ATTLIST p
            indent  CDATA #IMPLIED  >
<!ELEMENT page -o EMPTY  >
<!ATTLIST page
            n       CDATA #REQUIRED
            image   CDATA #REQUIRED  >
```

```
<!ELEMENT pageHeader  - -  (ornament?, techNotes?, biblioSig?, note*)>
<!ELEMENT pageLines  - -  (number, length)  >
<!—PgNote was just (#PCDATA) - changed 13 Oct to following to incorp
                              title  - ->
<!ELEMENT pageNote  - -  (title?, (%low;)+)  >
<!ATTLIST pageNote
          place    (f | e | l | r | t ) #IMPLIED
          anchor   (y | n) #IMPLIED
          resp     (au | ed) #IMPLIED
          target   IDREF #IMPLIED  >
<!ELEMENT pagination  - -  (#PCDATA)  >
<!ELEMENT paper  - -  (#PCDATA)  >
<!ELEMENT periodical  - -  (title, issue)  >
<!ELEMENT phrase  - -  (#PCDATA)  >
<!ATTLIST phrase
          %global;  >
<!ELEMENT physicalDesc  - -  (binding?, typography?, paper+,
                              watermark?, size?, note*)  >
<!ELEMENT point  - -  (#PCDATA)  >
<!ELEMENT prePub  - -  (#PCDATA)  >
<!ATTLIST prePub
          type  CDATA #IMPLIED  >
<!ELEMENT principal  - -  (role+, name+)  >
<!ELEMENT printer  - -  (#PCDATA)  >
<!ELEMENT profileDesc  - -  (workCode, commentaries)  >
<!ELEMENT provenance  - -  (location, recNum, note?)  >
<!ELEMENT publicationStmt  - -  (#PCDATA)  >
<!ELEMENT publisher  - -  (#PCDATA)  >
<!ELEMENT quote  - -  (#PCDATA)  >
<!ELEMENT rad  - -  (radHeader, text)  >
<!ATTLIST rad
          type  (book | proof.page | proof.galley | trialbook | pamphlet |
                private.printing | MS.draft | MS.copy | MS.corrected.copy |
                MS.printer | MS.faircopy | MS.faircorr | MS.notebk |
                translation | extract | criticism | serial | letter | review)
                #REQUIRED
          id    CDATA #REQUIRED>
<!ELEMENT radHeader  - -  (fileDesc, encodingDesc, profileDesc,
                          revisionDesc) +(%renderings;)  >
<!ELEMENT recNum  - -  (#PCDATA)  >
<!ELEMENT resp  - -  (role+,name+)  >
<!ELEMENT revisionDesc  - -  (#PCDATA)  >
<!ELEMENT role  - -  (#PCDATA)  >
<!ELEMENT sc  - -  (#PCDATA)  >
<!ELEMENT sub  - -  (#PCDATA)  >
<!ELEMENT sup  - -  (#PCDATA)  >
<!ELEMENT scribe  - -  (#PCDATA)  >
```

```
<!ELEMENT section  - -  (head, %low;+)  >
<!ELEMENT seriesStmt  - -  (titleSeries, principal, resp+, sponsor+,
                           funder+)  >
<!ELEMENT size  - -  (#PCDATA)  >
<!ELEMENT sourceDesc  - -  (citnStruct)  >
<!ELEMENT sponsor  - -  (#PCDATA)  >
<!ELEMENT techNotes  - -  (#PCDATA)  >
<!ELEMENT textual  - -  (#PCDATA)  >
<!ELEMENT text  - -  (front?, (body | group), back?)  >
<!ELEMENT title  - -  (#PCDATA) +(add & del)  >
<!ATTLIST title
          %global;  >
<!ELEMENT titleSeries  - -  (#PCDATA)  >
<!ELEMENT titlePage  - -  (docTitle, docAuthor?, docEdition?, docImprint?,
                         docDate?)  >
<!ATTLIST titlePage
          type  CDATA #IMPLIED  >
<!ELEMENT titlePart  - -  (#PCDATA)  >
<!ATTLIST titlePart
          type  (main | submain) #REQUIRED  >
<!ELEMENT titleStmt  - -  (title, author, principal, resp+, sponsor+,
                         funder+)  >
<!ELEMENT trans  - -  (#PCDATA)  >
<!ELEMENT trimsize  - -  (#PCDATA)  >
<!ELEMENT type  - -  (#PCDATA)  >
<!ELEMENT typeface  - -  (point, font)  >
<!ELEMENT typography  - -  (typeface+, pageLines+, columns?, margin*,
                           note*)  >
<!ELEMENT u  - -  (#PCDATA)  >
<!ELEMENT watermark  - -  (#PCDATA)  >
<!ELEMENT workCode  - -  (#PCDATA)  >
<!--end of rad DTD-->
```

Appendix 2. The Rossetti Archive RAD for Fitzwilliam MS of "The House of Life" (Excerpt)

```
<!DOCTYPE rad SYSTEM '/home/jjm2f/DTD.plus/rad.dtd' [
<!ENTITY % OTAents system "/home/jjm2f/DTD.plus/unixlat0.dtd">

  %OTAents; ]>
<rad type="manuscript" id="fiz44-69ms">
<radHeader>
  <fileDesc>
    <titleStmt>
      <title>The House of Life, Fitzwilliam Manuscript </title>
```

```
    <author>DGR</author>
    <principal><role>editor and project manager</role>
      <name>Mcgann, Jerome</name></principal>
    <resp><role>systems analyst</role>
      <name>Staples, Thornton</name></resp>
    <resp><role>consultant</role>
      <name>Price-Wilkin, John</name></resp>
    <sponsor>Institute for Advanced Technology in the Humanities,
      University of Virginia</sponsor>
    <funder>funded in part by an equipment grant from International
      Business Machines Corporation</funder>
  </titleStmt>
  <editionStmt>
    <edition>1</edition>
  </editionStmt>
  <extent></extent>
  <publicationStmt>
    published by the Institute for Advanced Technology in the Humanities
    (this information can be more elaborate and tagged)
  </publicationStmt>
  <seriesStmt>
    <title.series>Archive of the Complete Works of Dante Gabriel Rossetti
      </title.series>
    <principal><role>editor and project manager</role>
      <name>Mcgann, Jerome</name></principal>
    <resp><role>systems analyst</role>
      <name>Staples, Thornton</name></resp>
    <resp><role>consultant</role>
      <name>Price-Wilkin, John</name></resp>
    <sponsor>Institute for Advanced Technology in the Humanities,
      University of Virginia</sponsor>
    <funder>funded in part by an equipment grant from International
      Business Machines Corporation</funder>
  </seriesStmt>
  <notesStmt>
    This is where notes about the electronic edition would occur.
  </notesStmt>
  <sourceDesc>
    <citn.struct>
      <title>The House of Life Sonnets./ Dante Gabriel Rossetti M.S.
        </title>
      <author>DGR</author>
      <msProd>
        <date>This text of DGR's "House of Life" sonnets is a composite
construction. It consists mostly of original DGR MSS (draft and fair copy
both) as well as copies made by May Morris and by Charles Fairfax Murray.
Murray pasted the DGR and May Morris copies into a notebook sometime
```

after 1883 (the notebook consists of paper watermarked 1883 and 1884), probably in the mid-1880s. Murray's copies of several sonnets are written on the notebook pages, while the DGR and May Morris copies are pasted in, usually on the stubs of notebook pages that have been cut away. The May Morris copies date from the period when DGR was preparing press copy of the 1881 volume of <i>Ballads and Sonnets</i>.
<p>Thus the text represents a process of construction that extends over many years. The notebook contains autograph MSS that were written as early as the late 1840s and as late as 1881. The book is a conscious attempt by Murray to reconstruct a MS text of "The House of Life" sonnets out of the MSS that Murray had in his possession. Most had been given to him by DGR in 1869–70, when Murray helped DGR see the 1870 <i>Poems</i> volume through the press. But Murray received the May Morris copies after 1881—perhaps from Morris, perhaps from DGR.</date>

<type>Various, some draft, some fair copy, not all DGR holographs. Of the latter, virtually all are gathered here from several notebooks of the kind that DGR typically used for his poetry. The texts of individual sonnets are on notebook leaves that were torn or cut away from these notebooks. Analysis of the paper reveals that four distinct notebooks were involved: 1. A notebook that contained a group of DGR holographs as well as the May Morris copies. The DGR holographs date from 1871–1880 while the Morris copies were made in 1880–81, when the 1881 <i>Ballads and Sonnets</i> volume was going through press. Included here are the texts on the following pages of the Murray MS:

1. A notebook containing transcripts written in 1880–81, all DGR holograph. All are from paper watermarked "J. Allen & Sons/ Super Fine". This comprises the following pages from the Murray MS: leaves 1–7, 9–10, 12, 31–33, 38, 42, 46, 49, 51, 68, 81, 103, 106, 110.
2. A different notebook of texts containing DGR transcripts made between 1870–1881. This notebook originally contained both DGR holographs as well as all of the May Morris copies made in 1880–81. The paper is watermarked "J. Allen & Sons/ Super Fine". This comprises the following pages from the Murray MS: leaves 9, 16–18, 21–22, 24–25, 27, 29, 34–37, 39–40, 47–48, 50, 62–63, 65–67, 69–72, 74–75, 78, 80, 89(?), 90, 91, 93, 97–98, 107, 11–112, 114.
3. A notebook, all DGR holographs, containing texts written and transcribed mostly in 1869. The paper is watermarked "B & H/ Superfine/ Kent". These texts comprise the following pages of the Murray MS: 44–45, 57–61, 76–77, 82, 87–88, 92, 94–95, 102, 104, 108, 113.
4. A notebook containing DGR holographs of (mostly) early poems. Paper unwatermarked; the transcripts are early, dating from the 1850s. The Murray MS pages corresponding to these texts are: leaves 8, 19, 55–56, 79, 83, 85, 86, 109, 117.

<p>In addition, four other groups of poems can be distinguished by their paper. The first three are DGR copies, the fourth is the group of texts copied

```
by Murray: (a). Leaves 54, 73, 84 (transcripts date from 1880–81); (b). Leaves
11, 14, 64, 99, 105 (all transcripts from 1869–70); (c). Leaves 13(?), 20, 23,
41, 43(?)—all from 1880–81; (d). Leaves 15, 26, 30, 52–53, 96, 100,
115–116, 118–119 (Murray's fair copies).
<p>The May Morris copies and DGR's fair copy holographs of post-1870
poems may well have been used in the printing of the 1881 volume <i>Ballads
and Sonnets</i>.</type>
        <assign></assign>
        <collation>6 initial blank leaves, 119 numbered leaves comprising the
          text, five final blank leaves</collation>
        <note></note>
      </msProd>
      <scribe>DGR; May Morris; Charles Fairfax Murray</scribe>
      <corrector>DGR</corrector>
      <provenance>
        <location>Fitzwilliam Museum</location>
        <note>The MSS were given to Charles Fairfax Murray by DGR; the
          volume was acquired by the Fitwilliam Museum from the Sotheby's
          sale of some of Murray's library in 1919.</note>
      <physicalDesc>
        <binding>
          <cover>green leather</cover>
          <endpapers>marbled paper</endpapers>
        </binding>
        <paper>9x8 inch leaves (for the Murray notebook), but with various
          sizes for the individual MSS pasted into the notebook</paper>
        <watermark>J. Whatman, dated 1883 and 1884 (for the Murray
          notebook), and with various other watermarks on individual MSS
          pasted into the notebook</watermark>
        <note>For sizes of individual MS leaves see the page notes for the
          particular leaves.</note>
      </physicalDesc>
    </citn.struct>
  </sourceDesc>
</fileDesc>
<encodingDesc>
</encodingDesc>
<profileDesc>
  <workCode>44-1869_fizms</workCode>
  <commentaries>
    <intro>This bound notebook volume of 119 leaves has various manuscript
and two printed (proof) texts either written directly on the notebook leaves or
(as separate small pieces of paper) pasted on the notebook sheets. All are in the
approximate order of the sonnets as they appeared in the 1881 volume
<i>Ballads and Sonnets</i>. Most of the manuscripts are holograph, but
there are copies by May Morris and by Charles Fairfax Murray, who put the
volume together after DGR's death in the mid-1880s. The manuscripts are
```

typically pasted on the recto pages, with the opposite versos of the previous leaves being left blank. But often these blank leaves have a manuscript or other material.
<p>The earliest MSS are holograph and date from the late 1840s. Other holographs comprise three distinct groups: one from 1869–70, another from 1870–73, and a third from 1880–81. The May Morris copies were made in 1880–81 and the Murray copies were made when the volume was constructed by him into a MS text of "The House of Life" sonnet sequence based on the 1881 text (but including sonnet 6a ("Nuptial Sleep")which was not included in the 1881 sequence.</intro>

<textual.history>

<composition>The manuscripts date from many different periods. The earliest MSS are holograph and date from the late 1840s. Other holographs comprise three distinct groups: one from 1869–70, another from 1870–73, and a third from 1880–81. The May Morris copies were made in 1880–81 and the Charles Fairfax Murray copies were made when the volume was constructed by him (in the mid-1880s) from the MSS in his possession. Many of the MSS were acquired by Murray when he was making copies of the poems for DGR in the fall of 1869. Later, in 1880, DGR worked with May Morris as copiest to construct a printer's copy for the 1881 text of "The House of Life" as it appeared in his <i>Ballad and Sonnets</i> volume. The pagination (1–119) is uniformly given in small arabic numerals (upper right corner of each recto page); these appear to have been added by Murray. Many of the individual sonnet manuscripts bear other numbers which indicate DGR's efforts to define an order for the sonnets in the different printings of 1869, 1870, and 1881. Some of these numbers are by Charles Fairfax Murray, and others appear to be by the printers as they tried to keep up with DGR's evolving and changing order for the sonnets.</composition>

<revision>The MS volume has numerous levels of revision that correspond to the heteroglot character of the MSS comprising the volume. Some date back to the 1840s, some are as late as 1881, and many others fall at various points in between those termini.</revision >

</textual.history>
<reception.history></reception.history>
<printing.history>This MS has never been printed.
</printing.history>
<pictorial></pictorial>
<historical>
</historical>
<literary>
</literary>
<translation></translation>
<autobiographical>
</autobiographical>
<bibliographic>
</bibliographic>
</commentaries>

```
    </profileDesc>
  <revisionDesc>
  </revisionDesc>
</radHeader>
  <front>
  <page n="1" image="fiz44-69_1">
<scribe>DGR</scribe>
  <pageHeader>
    <note>holograph; size: 22.2x16.2cm</note>
  </pageHeader>
<titlePage>
    <docTitle>
      <titlePart type="Main">
The House of Life</titlePart>
<titlePart type="submain">Part I.</titlePart>
<titlePart type="submain">Youth and Change</titlePart>
<titlePart type="submain">Part II.</titlePart>
<titlePart type="submain">Change and Fate</titlePart>
</docTitle>
</titlePage>
  <epage>
  <page n="2" image="fiz44-69_2">
<scribe>DGR</scribe>
  <pageHeader>
    <note>Holograph; size: 22.2x16.7cm. The first six lines, cancelled by
      DGR, comprise the opening part of an introductory note that concluded
      with the words "quicken it" ; the next passage, which is the last four
      lines of the text, comprises a late addition.</note>
  </pageHeader>
  <div type="advertisement">
<l n="1">In reprinting the fragmentary series of the
<l n="2"><q>House of Life,</q> it seemed a more harmonious
<l n="3">arrangement to exclude lyrics and
<l n="4">retain sonnets only. A further number
<l n="5">of these is now added, in great measure
<l n="6">the work of earlier years.
<l n="7">To speak in the first person is <u>often</u>
<l n="8">to speak most vividly; but these
<l n="9">emotional poems are in no sense
<l n="10"><q>occasional</q>. The <q>Life</q> involved is
<l n="11">life representative, as associated
<l n="12">with love and death, with aspiration & forboding,
<l n="13">or with ideal art and beauty.
<l n="12–13a"><del>with hope, love, and death</del>
<l n="14>Whether the recorded moment
<l n="15">exist in the region of fact or of
```

```
<l n="16">thought is a question indifferent
<l n="17">to the Muse, so long only as her
<l n="18">touch can quicken it.
<l n="19">The present full series of the<q>House of Life</q> consists
<l n="20">of sonnets only. It
<l n="20a" indent="1"><del>, since Of these it Among these</del>
<l n="21">will be evident that many   now first added were
<l n="21a" indent="2"><add></add>
<l n="22">the work of earlier years.
        <note>The last four lines are a draft text with running corrections in
          this line.</note>
  </div>
  <epage>
</front>
<body>
  <page n="3" image="fiz44-69_3">
    <msAdds type="prtrdir">
      <trans>This to be used as introductory and printed in italics</trans>
      <desc>Marginal directions to the printer, written at top</desc>
    </msAdds>
      <scribe>May Morris</scribe>
  <pageHeader>
    <note>May Morris transcript with DGR's corrections and additions; size:
      22.2x17.3cm</note>
  </pageHeader>
<div0 type="sonnet" title="Introductory Sonnet" workCode="1-1880">
      <divHeader><del>The Sonnet</del>
        <note>The title in the MS is originally "The Sonnet", but this is here
          cancelled and the sonnet was not printed with a specific title by
          DGR; the title "Introductory Sonnet" was added later when WMR
          collected DGR's work and it has become traditional.</note>
      </divHeader>
      <lg type="octave">
<l n="1">A Sonnet is a moment's monument,-
<l n="2"> Memorial from the Soul's eternity
<l n="2a" indent="2"><del>thy</del>
<l n="3"> To one dead deathless hour. Look that it be,
<l n="4">Whether for lutral rite or dire portent,
<l n="5">Of its own arduous fulness reverent:
<lv n="5a" indent="2"><del>intricate</del>
<l n="6"> Carve it in ivory or in ebony,
<l n="7"> As Day or Night prevail; and let Time see
<l n="8">Its flowering crest impearled and orient.
        </lg>
        <lg type="sestet">
<l n="9">A sonnet is a coin, its face reveals
```

```
<l n="9a" indent="2"><del>whose</del>
<l n="10"> The soul,- its converse, to what Power 'tis due:-
<l n="10a"><del>Thy soul, its rear-type</del>
<l n="11">Whether for tribute to the august appeals
<l n="11a" indent="1"><del>in</del>
<l n="12"> Of Life, or dower in Love's high retinue,
<l n="13">It serve; or, 'mid the dark wharf's' cavernous breath,
<l n="13a" indent="2"><del>world's</del>
<l n="14">In Charon's palm it pay the toll to Death.
          </lg>
<lv n="1">rear-foil mintage
<lv n="2">converse mint-type
 <note>these are possible alternative readings, written below the poem</note>
        </div0>
        <epage>
   <page n="4" image="fiz44-69__4">
     <scribe>May Morris</scribe>
   <pageHeader>
     <note>Section heading in DGR's holograph (written later at the top of
       the page); text of the sonnet copied by May Morris, with DGR's
       corrections; size: 22.2x17.6cm</note>
   </pageHeader>
   <div0 type="section" title="Part I. Youth and Change" n="I"
     workCode="">
 <l n=section title>Part I. Youth and Change
   <div1 type="sonnet" title="Love Enthroned" workCode="1-1871">
     <divHeader>
       <title>Sonnet I. Love Enthroned</title>
     </divHeader>
     <lg type="octave">
 <l n="1">I marked all kindred Powers the heart finds fair:&mdash;
 <l n="2"> Truth, with awed lips; and Hope, with eyes upcast;
 <l n="3"> And Fame, whose loud wings fan the ashen past
 <l n="4">To signal-fires, Oblivion's flight to scare;
 <l n="5">And Youth, with still some single golden hair
 <l n="5a" indent=1><del>some bright spray of woman's</del>
 <l n=6> Unto his shoulder clinging, since the last
 <l n=6a><del>Yet to</del>
 <l n=7> Embrace wherein two sweet arms held him fast;
 <l n=8>And Life, still wreathing flowers for Death to wear.</lg>
 <lg type="sestet">
 <l n=9>Love's throne was not with these; but far above
 <l n=10> All passionate wind of welcome and farewell
 <l n=11>He sat in breathless bowers they dream not of;
 <l n=11a indent 2><del>dreamed</del>
 <l n=12> Though Truth foreknow Love's heart, and Hope foretell,
 <l n=13> And Fame be for Love's sake desirable,
```

```
<l n=14>And Youth be dear, and Life be sweet to Love. </lg>
        </lg>
    </div>
    <epage>
```

Appendix 3. The Rossetti Archive RAD for the British Library Copy of the First Trialbook (Excerpt)

```
<front>
<div type="bookplate">
<page n="[0]" image="1-1870_blTB1_bookplate">
<pageHeader>
  <ornament>bookplate: T. J. Wise bookplate</ornament>
  <note>This is the endpaper of the bound volume housing the document.
    </note>
</pageHeader>
</div>
<epage>
<page n="[i]" image="1-1870_blTB1_title">
<pageHeader>
<note>blank page</note>
</pageHeader>
<epage>
<page n="[ii]" image="1-1870_blTB1_title">
<titlePage>
  <docTitle>
<titlePart type="main">POEMS.</titlePart>
<titlePart type="submain">Privately Printed.</titlePart>
</docTitle>
</titlePage>
<epage>
<page n="[iii]" image="1-1870_blTB1_advertisement">
<pageHeader>
<note>blank page</note>
</pageHeader>
<epage>
<page n="[iv]" image="1-1870_blTB1_advertisement">
<div type="Advertisement">
<p> Most of these poems were written between 1847 and 1853; and are here
printed, if not without revision, yet generally much in their original state. They
are a few among a good many then written, but of the others I have now no
complete copies. The "Sonnets and Songs" are chiefly more recent work.]
<c>D. G. R.</c> 1869.</p>
</div>
<epage>
<page n="[v]" image="1-1870_blTB1_1">
```

```
<pageHeader>
<note>blank page</note>
</pageHeader>
<epage>
</front>
<body>
<page n="1" image="1-1870_blTB1_1">
<pageHeader>
  <biblioSig>B1</biblioSig>
  <note>Page numbering is at center bottom. This page is actually the first of
    the volume's three sections. The section would eventually be headed
    "POEMS" on a separate half-title.</note>
</pageHeader>
<div0 type="section" workCode="44c-1869">

<divHeader>
<title><c>POEMS.</c></title>
</divHeader>

<div1 type="ballad" workCode="30-1869" title="Troy Town">
  <divHeader>
  <title id="PN1"><c>Troy Town</c>*</title>
  </divHeader>
<lg n="1" r="2" type="septet">
<l n=1 r="8">Helen knelt at Venus' shrine,
<l n=2 r="9" indent="1">      (<i>O Troy Town!</i>)
<l n=3 r="10">Saying, &lsquo;A little gift is mine,
<l n=4 r="11">A little gift for a heart's desire.
<l n=5 r="12">Hear me speak and make me a sign!
<l n=6 r="13" indent="1">      (<i>O Troy's down,</i>
<l n=7 r="14" indent="1">      <i>Tall Troy's on fire!</i>)
</lg>

<lg n="2" r="3" type="septet">
<l n=8 r="15">&lsquo;Look, I bring thee a carven cup;
<l n=9 r="16"indent="1">      (<i>O Troy Town!</i>)
<l n=10 r="17">See it here as I hold it up,&mdash;
<l n=11 r="18">Shaped it is to the heart's desire,
<l n=12 r="19">Fit to fill when the gods would sup.
<l n=13 r="20" indent="1">      (<i>O Troy's down,</i>
<l n=14 r="21" indent="1">      <i>Tall Troy's on fire!</i>)
</lg>
<pageNote place="f" target="PN1" anchor="y" resp="au">
<p>*Herodotus says that Helen dedicated to Venus a cup made in the likeness
  of her own bosom.</p></pageNote>
<epage>
<page n="2" image="1-1870_blTB1_3">
```

```
<pageHeader>
<note>Here begins the page numbering here at center top.</note>
</pageHeader>
<lg n=“3” r=“4” type=“septet”>
<l n=15 r=“22”>&lsquo;It was moulded like my breast;
<l n=16 r=“23” indent=“1”>      (<i>O Troy Town!</i>)
<l n=17 r=“24”>He that sees it may not rest,
<l n=18 r=“25”>Rest at all for his heart’s desire,
<l n=19 r=“26”>O give ear to my heart’s behest!
<l n=20 r=“27” indent=“1”>      (<i>O Troy’s down,</i>
   <l n=21 r=“28” indent=“1”>      <i>Tall Troy’s on fire!</i>)
   </lg>

<lg n=“4” r=“5” type=“septet”>
<l n=22 r=“29”>&lsquo;See my breast, how like it is;
<l n=23 r=“30” indent=“1”>      (<i>O Troy Town!</i>)
<l n=24 r=“31”>See it bare for the air to kiss!
<l n=25 r=“32”>Is the cup to thy heart’s desire?
<l n=26 r=“33”>O for the breast, O make it his!
<l n=27 r=“34” indent=“1”>      (<i>O Troy’s down,</i>
<l n=28 r=“35” indent=“1”>      <i>Tall Troy’s on fire!</i>)
</lg>

<lg n=“5” r=“6” type=“septet”>
<l n=29 r=“36”>&lsquo;Yea, for my bosom here I sue;
<l n=30 r=“37” indent=“1”>      (<i>O Troy Town!</i>)
<l n=31 r=“38”>Thou must give it where ’tis due,
<l n=32 r=“39”>Give it there to the heart’s desire.
<l n=33 r=“40”>Whom do I give my bosom to?
<l n=34 r=“41” indent=“1”>      (<i>O Troy’s down,</i>
<l n=35 r=“42” indent=“1”>      <i>Tall Troy’s on fire!</i>)
</lg>

<lg n=“6” r=“7” type=“septet”>
<l n=36 r=“43”>&lsquo;Each twin breast is an apple sweet!
<l n=37 r=“44” indent=“1”>      (<i>O Troy Town!</i>)
<l n=38 r=“45”>Once an apple stirred the beat
<l n=39 r=“46”>Of thy heart with the heart’s desire:&mdash;
<l n=40 r=“47”>Say, who brought it then to thy feet?
<l n=41 r=“48” indent=“1”>      (<i>O Troy’s down,</i>
<l n=42 r=“49” indent=“1”>      <i>Tall Troy’s on fire!</i>)
</lg>

<epage>
<page n=“3” image=“1-1870__blTB1__3”>
<lg n=“7” r=“8” type=“septet”>
```

```
<l n=43 r="50">&lsquo;They that claimed it then were three:
<l n=44 r="51" indent="1">      (<i>O Troy Town!</i>)
<l n=45 r="52">For thy sake two hearts did he
<l n=46 r="53">Make forlorn of the heart's desire.
<l n=47 r="54">Do for him as he did for thee!
<l n=48 r="55" indent="1">      (<i>O Troy's down,</i>
<l n=49 r="56" indent="1">      <i>Tall Troy's on fire!</i>)
</lg>

<lg n="8" r="9" type="septet">
<l n=50 r="57">&lsquo;Mine are apples grown to the south,
<l n=51 r="58" indent="1">      (<i>O Troy Town!</i>)
<l n=52 r="59">Grown to taste in the days of drouth,
<l n=53 r="60">Taste and waste to the heart's desire:
<l n=54 r="61">Mine are apples meet for his mouth!&rsquo;
<l n=55 r="62" indent="1">      (<i>O Troy's down,</i>
<l n=56 r="63" indent="1">      <i>Tall Troy's on fire!</i>)
</lg>

<lg n="9" r="10" type="septet">
<l n=57 r="64">Venus looked on Helen's gift,
<l n=58 r="65" indent="1">      (<i>O Troy Town!</i>)
<l n=59 r="66">Looked and smiled with subtle drift,
<l n=60 r="67">Saw the work of her heart's desire:&mdash;
<l n=61 r="68">&lsquo;There thou kneel'st for Love to lift!&rsquo;
<l n=62 r="69" indent="1">      (<i>O Troy's down,</i>
<l n=63 r="70" indent="1">      <i>Tall Troy's on fire!</i>)
</lg>

<lg n="10" r="11" type="septet">
<l n=64 r="71">Venus looked in Helen's face,
<l n=65 r="72" indent="1">      (<i>O Troy Town!</i>)
<l n=66 r="73">Knew far off an hour and place,
<l n=67 r="74">And fire lit from the heart's desire;
<l n=68 r="75">Laughed and said, &lsquo;Thy gift hath grace!&rsquo;
<l n=69 r="76" indent="1">      (<i>O Troy's down,</i>
<l n=70 r="77" indent="1">      <i>Tall Troy's on fire!</i>)
</lg>

<epage>
<page n="4" image="1-1870__blTB1__5">
<lg n="11" r="12" type="septet">
<l n=71 r="78">Cupid looked on Helen's breast,
<l n=72 r="79" indent="1">      (<i>O Troy Town!</i>)
<l n=73 r="80">Saw the heart within its nest,
<l n=74 r="81">Saw the flame of the heart's desire;
```

```
<l n=75 r=“82”>There his arrow stood confess'd.
<l n=76 r=“83” indent=“1”>      (<i>O Troy’s down,</i>
<l n=77 r=“84” indent=“1”>      <i>Tall Troy’s on fire!</i>)
</lg>

<lg n=“12” r=“13” type=“septet”>
<l n=78 r=“85”>Cupid took another dart,
<l n=79 r=“86” indent=“1”>      (<i>O Troy Town!</i>)
<l n=80 r=“87”>Fledged it for another heart,
<l n=81 r=“88”>Winged the shaft with the heart’s desire,
<l n=82 r=“89”>Drew the string and said, &lsquo;Depart!&rsquo;
<l n=83 r=“90” indent=“1”>      (<i>O Troy’s down,</i>
<l n=84 r=“91” indent=“1”>      <i>Tall Troy’s on fire!</i>)
</lg>

<lg n=“13” r=“14” type=“septet”>
<l n=85 r=“92”>Paris turned upon his bed,
<l n=86 r=“93” indent=“1”>      (<i>O Troy Town!</i>)
<l n=87 r=“94”>Turned upon his bed and said,
<l n=88 r=“95”>Dead at heart with the heart’s desire,&mdash;
<l n=89 r=“96”>O to clasp her golden head!
<l n=90 r=“97” indent=“1”>      (<i>O Troy’s down,</i>
<l n=91 r=“98” indent=“1”>      <i>Tall Troy’s on fire!</i>)
</lg>
</div1>
<epage>
```

Appendix 4. The Rossetti Archive RAD for the Princeton Copy of the First Trialbook (Excerpt)

```
<front>
<page n=“[0]” image=“1-1870_TroxTB1_cover1”>
<pageHeader>
  <ornament>bookplate: John A. Spoor</ornament>
  <note>This is the endpaper of the bound volume housing the document.
    </note>
</pageHeader>
<epage>
<page n=“[00]” image=“1-1870_TroxTB1_cover1”>
<pageHeader>
  <ornament>Ornamented initials of Janet Camp Troxell</ornament>
  <note>This is the coversheet of the bound volume housing the document.
    </note>
</pageHeader>
```

```
<sc>Princeton</sc>
<sc>University Library</sc>
<sc>The</sc>
<i>Rossetti Collection</i>
<sc>of Janet Camp</sc>
<sc>Troxell</sc>
<epage>
<page n="[i]" image="1-1870_TroxTB1_title">
<pageHeader>
<note>blank page</note>
</pageHeader>
<epage>
<page n="[ii]" image="1-1870_TroxTB1_title">
<titlePage>
  <docTitle>
<titlePart type="main">POEMS.</titlePart>
<titlePart type="submain">Privately Printed.</titlePart>
</docTitle>
</titlePage>
<epage>
<page n="[iii]" image="1-1870_TroxTB1_advertisement">
<pageHeader>
<note>blank page</note>
</pageHeader>
<epage>
<page n="[iv]" image="1-1870_TroxTB1_advertisement">
<div type="Advertisement">
<p> Most of these poems were written between 1847 and 1853; and are here
printed, if not without revision, yet generally much in their original state. They
are a few among a good many then written, but of the others I have now no
complete copies. The "Sonnets and Songs" are chiefly more recent work.]
<c>D. G. R.</c> 1869.</p>
</div>
<epage>
<page n="[v]" image="1-1870_TroxTB1_1">
<pageHeader>
<note>blank page</note>
</pageHeader>
<epage>
</front>
<body>
<page n="1" image="1-1870_TroxTB1_1">
<pageHeader>
  <note>Page numbering is at center top. This page is actually the first of the
volume's three sections. It would eventually be headed "POEMS" and have a
half title page.</note>
</pageHeader>
```

```
<div0 type=“section” workCode=“44c-1869” title=“Poems.”>
<div1 type=“ballad” workCode=“30-1869” title=“Troy Town.” >
  <divHeader>
  <title><c>TROY TOWN.</c></title>
  </divHeader>
<lg n=“1” type=“septet”>
<l n=“1”><sc>Heavenborn Helen</sc>, Sparta’s queen,
<l indent=“1” n=“2”>      (<i>O Troy Town!</i>)
<l n=“3”>Had two breasts of heavenly sheen,
<l n=“4”>The sun and moon of the heart’s desire:
<l n=“5”>All Love’s lordship lay between.
<l indent=“1” n=“6”>      (<i>O Troy’s down,</i>
<l indent=“1” n=“7”>      <i>Tall Troy’s on fire!</i>)
</lg>


<lg n=“2” type=“septet”>
<l n=“8”>Helen knelt at Venus’ shrine,
<l indent=“1” n=“9”>      (<i>O Troy Town!</i>)
<l n=“10”>Saying, &lsquo;A little gift is mine,
<l n=“11”>A little gift for a heart’s desire.
<l n=“12”>Hear me speak and make me a sign!
<l indent=“1” n=“13”>      (<i>O Troy’s down,</i>
<l indent=“1” n=“14”>      <i>Tall Troy’s on fire!</i>)
</lg>


<lg n=“3” type=“septet”>
<l n=“15”>&lsquo;Look, I bring thee a carven cup;
<l indent=“1” n=“16”>      (<i>O Troy Town!</i>)
<l n=“17”>See it here as I hold it up,&mdash;
<l n=“18”>Shaped it is to the heart’s desire,
<l n=“19”>Fit to fill when the gods would sup.
<l indent=“1” n=“20”>      (<i>O Troy’s down,</i>
<l indent=“1” n=“21”>      <i>Tall Troy’s on fire!</i>)
</lg>
<epage>
<page n=“2” image=“1-1870_TroxTB1_3”>
<lg n=“4” type=“septet”>
<l n=“22”>&lsquo;It was moulded like my breast;
<l indent=“1” n=“23”>      (<i>O Troy Town!</i>)
<l n=“24”>He that sees it may not rest,
<l n=“25”>Rest at all for his heart’s desire,
<l n=“26”>O give ear to my heart’s behest!
<l indent=“1” n=“27”>      (<i>O Troy’s down,</i>
<l indent=“1” n=“28”>      <i>Tall Troy’s on fire!</i>)
</lg>
```

```
<lg n=“5” type=“septet”>
<l n=“29”>&lsquo;See my breast, how like it is;
<l indent=“1” n=“30”>      (<i>O Troy Town!</i>)
<l n=“31”>See it bare for the air to kiss!
<l n=“32”>Is the cup to thy heart’s desire?
<l n=“33”>O for the breast, O make it his!
<l indent=“1” n=“34”>      (<i>O Troy’s down,</i>
<l indent=“1” n=“35”>      <i>Tall Troy’s on fire!</i>)
</lg>

<lg n=“6” type=“septet”>
<l n=“36”>&lsquo;Yea, for my bosom here I sue;
<l indent=“1” n=“37”>      (<i>O Troy Town!</i>)
<l n=“38”>Thou must give it where ’tis due,
<l n=“39”>Give it there to the heart’s desire.
<l n=“40”>Whom do I give my bosom to?
<l indent=“1” n=“41”>      (<i>O Troy’s down,</i>
<l indent=“1” n=“42”>      <i>Tall Troy’s on fire!</i>)
</lg>

<lg n=“7” type=“septet”>
<l n=“43”>&lsquo;Each twin breast is an apple sweet!
<l indent=“1” n=“44”>      (<i>O Troy Town!</i>)
<l n=“45”>Once an apple stirred the beat
<l n=“46”>Of thy heart with the heart’s desire:&mdash;
<l n=“47”>Say, who brought it then to thy feet?
<l indent=“1” n=“48”>      (<i>O Troy’s down,</i>
<l indent=“1” n=“49”>      <i>Tall Troy’s on fire!</i>)
</lg>

<epage>
<page n=“3” image=“1-1870_TroxTB1_3”>
<lg n=“8” type=“septet”>
<l n=“50”>&lsquo;They that claimed it then were three:
<l indent=“1” n=“51”>      (<i>O Troy Town!</i>)
<l n=“52”>For thy sake two hearts did he
<l n=“53”>Make forlorn of the heart’s desire.
<l n=“54”>Do for him as he did for thee!
<l indent=“1” n=“55”>      (<i>O Troy’s down,</i>
<l indent=“1” n=“56”>      <i>Tall Troy’s on fire!</i>)
</lg>

<lg n=“9” type=“septet”>
<l n=“57”>&lsquo;Mine are apples grown to the south,
<l indent=“1” n=“58”>      (<i>O Troy Town!</i>)
<l n=“59”>Grown to taste in the days of drouth,
<l n=“60”>Taste and waste to the heart’s desire:
```

```
<l n="61">Mine are apples meet for his mouth!&rsquo;
<l indent="1" n="62">      (<i>O Troy's down,</i>
<l indent="1" n="63">      <i>Tall Troy's on fire!</i>)
</lg>

<lg n="10" type="septet">
<l n="64">Venus looked on Helen's gift,
<l indent="1" n="65">      (<i>O Troy Town!</i>)
<l n="66">Looked and smiled with subtle drift,
<l n="67">Saw the work of her heart's desire:&mdash;
<l n="68">&lsquo;There thou kneel'st for Love to lift!&rsquo;
<l indent="1" n="69">      (<i>O Troy's down,</i>
<l indent="1" n="70">      <i>Tall Troy's on fire!</i>)
</lg>

<lg n="11" type="septet">
<l n="71">Venus looked in Helen's face,
<l indent="1" n="72">      (<i>O Troy Town!</i>)
<l n="73">Knew far off an hour and place,
<l n="74">And fire lit from the heart's desire;
<l n="75">Laughed and said, &lsquo;Thy gift hath grace!&rsquo;
<l indent="1" n="76">      (<i>O Troy's down,</i>
<l indent="1" n="77">      <i>Tall Troy's on fire!</i>)
</lg>

<epage>
<page n="4" image="1-1870_TroxTB1_5">
<lg n="12" type="septet">
<l n="78">Cupid looked on Helen's breast,
<l indent="1" n="79">      (<i>O Troy Town!</i>)
<l n="80">Saw the heart within its nest,
<l n="81">Saw the flame of the heart's desire;
<l n="82">There his arrow stood confess'd.
<l indent="1" n="83">      (<i>O Troy's down,</i>
<l indent="1" n="84">      <i>Tall Troy's on fire!</i>)
</lg>

<lg n="13" type="septet">
<l n="85">Cupid took another dart,
<l indent="1" n="86">      (<i>O Troy Town!</i>)
<l n="87">Fledged it for another heart,
<l n="88">Winged the shaft with the heart's desire,
<l n="89">Drew the string and said, &lsquo;Depart!&rsquo;
<l indent="1" n="90">      (<i>O Troy's down,</i>
<l indent="1" n="91">      <i>Tall Troy's on fire!</i>)
</lg>
```

```
<lg n="14" type="septet">
<l n="92">Paris turned upon his bed,
<l indent="1" n="93">      (<i>O Troy Town!</i>)
<l n="94">Turned upon his bed and said,
<l n="95">Dead at heart with the heart's desire,&mdash;
<l n="96">&lsquo;O to clasp her golden head!&rsquo;
<l indent="1" n="97">      (<i>O Troy's down,</i>
<l indent="1" n="98">      <i>Tall Troy's on fire!</i>)
</lg>
</div1>
<epage>
```

NOTES

A hypertext version of this essay is available on the World Wide Web server of the University of Virginia's Institute for Advanced Technology. This electronic version contains the entirety of the RAD file for both the Princeton and the British Library copies of the first trialbook of Rossetti's 1870 *Poems,* as well as the DTD for the Rossetti Archive's RAW files. The URL address is http://jefferson.village.virginia.edu/home, where the file is located under "Research Reports."

1. All documentary states are "textually relevant," in an absolute sense. That is to say, the perfect archive would preserve every textual instance of a work that has ever existed. But the phrase "textually relevant" more commonly refers to any text that ought to be included in a scholarly collation that means to expose the complete historical record of the work's textual emergence. Obviously great differences of opinion arise over what would constitute a complete record.
2. The electronic textual environment allows the editor to surpass this textual limit defined by the codex form (although it by no means insures that the limit will be surpassed). For an extended discussion of the theoretical ground of electronic textuality and its bearing on scholarly editing, in particular the editing of literary materials, see my essay "The Rationale of Hypertext" (preprint copy available through the "Research Reports" of the Institute for Advanced Technology in the Humanities, University of Virginia; the URL address is http://jefferson.village.virginia.edu/home). The essay will appear in print in 1995 in *The Electronic Text,* ed. Marilyn Deegan and Kathryn Sutherland (Oxford University Press).
3. "Refining Critical Editions," in George P. Landow and Paul Delany, *The Digital Word* (Cambridge: MIT Press, 1993), 285.
4. T. H. Howard-Hill, "Theory and Praxis in the Social Approach to Editing," *Text* 5 (1991): 39.
5. This is a formulation attributed to C. M. Sperberg-McQueen in a discussion of the place of digital images in an electronic editorial environment. See the *Proceedings* of the 1992 Workshop on Electronic Texts (9–10 June 1992), ed. James Daly (Washington, D.C.: Library of Congress, 1992), 69–72, esp. 71.

In a letter to me Sperberg-McQueen has sharply dissented from this representation of his views. He also points out, however, that the TEI approach was taken as a reflection of the theoretical position of "the vast majority of literary scholars," who "do not actually base much of their literary study on physical evidence." In my view this approach has forced TEI into adopting a markup practice—a linguistic and paper-based approach—that is at odds with the theoretical opportunities opened up by electronic textuality, where the limits of the codex are surpassed. In following what "the majority of scholars" now perceive as "their own needs and interests," TEI has framed its analytic instruments at the same level as the subjects it is studying. This in my opinion is to misimagine the relation of electronic to paper-based textuality.

6. For a discussion of bibliographical and textual codes (respectively), see my "Theory of Texts," *London Review of Books,* 18 February 1988, 20–21.
7. For modernist literary works, the matter is handled in depth in two recent studies: Johanna Drucker's *The Visible Word: Experimental Typography and Modern Art, 1909–1923* (Chicago: University of Chicago Press, 1994); Jerome McGann, *Black Riders: The Visible Language of Modernism* (Princeton: Princeton University Press, 1993).
8. Baum was well equipped to edit Rossetti's works, as his edition of *The House of Life* (Cambridge, Mass.: Harvard University Press, 1928) and his study of the manuscripts at Duke University show (*Dante Gabriel Rossetti: An Analytical List of Manuscripts in the Duke University Library* [Durham, N.C.: Duke University Press, 1931]). Other scholars—Janet Camp Troxell and William E. Fredeman in particular—might also have undertaken the task. The textual studies of these and other scholars indicate the extreme difficulty of constructing such an edition in a paper-based format.
9. See Maryan Wynn Ainsworth, ed., *Dante Gabriel Rossetti and the Double Work of Art* (New Haven: Yale University Art Gallery, 1976).
10. For a good introduction to SGML see Eric Van Herwijnen, *Practical SGML* (Boston: Kluwer Academic Publishers, 1994).
11. Unlike SGML, HTML (Hypertext Markup Language) is a purely presentational markup language. Its simplicity recommends it for organizing the appearance of computer documents, but it cannot support computerized operations.
12. Rossetti scholars will be interested to observe the differences between the two trialbooks' printed texts. Previous scholarship has not pointed out these differences, which indicate a printing history not previously recognized.
13. In the templates shown here, not all the marked fields are "filled in"; and of the fields that have information, not all are "complete." These examples are here to show the general design of the archive's informational structure. The data will be loaded in only when the fundamental design is finished and tested.

Electronic Hardy

Simon Gatrell

At the Modern Language Association meeting in New York at the end of 1993 Andrew Brown of Cambridge University Press trenchantly declared that scholarly critical editions in book form were dead, or at least terminally ill. To look at Cambridge's current list of such editions, one might think that reports of their demise were somewhat exaggerated, but the experience of those of us who have had anything to do with trying to publish critical editions of Thomas Hardy's fiction would tend to lend support to such a notion—indeed some of us have thought of calling in Dr. Kevorkian to put us out of our misery. The tale we could tell would be like the plot of a soap opera that has outlived its time, and very few can stomach that. But Hardy editors are educated by the fiction or poetry we work on to be resilient folk, and it seems now that instead of being just a year or two too late for publishers, and a year or two too early for government agencies, we have got the timing more or less right, and it is encouraging that others seem to think so too.

Dale Kramer and I, with the indispensable participation of Peter Shillingsburg, are proposing an electronic critical edition of Hardy's fiction to be issued by a commercial publisher on compact disc. This is an account of what we envisage potential users will be able to purchase in perhaps three years' time. (First I must say that the essay by Peter Shillingsburg which also appears in this volume should be regarded as an essential first part of the following account. His enthusiasm and wisdom have materially helped Dale and myself to see what it is we want to do and how we might do it.)

What we do not want to do is to offer merely a series of electronic texts, which at the worst could be a digitization of any old print versions contained in a text archive, or at the best could be like Chadwyck-Healey's English Poetry full-text database. What we have in mind is not something like the relatively simple packages that are already available at campus bookstores, which bundle a text of a novel with text-manipulation software like WordCruncher, and which are intended, I suppose, to enable the production of yet more thought-avoiding papers from graduate students along the lines of "look, I've found out all this information about the novel, isn't it interesting, but I haven't really the faintest idea what to do with it." There won't now even be available the apology that "oh, dear, yes, well it took so long to dig out all those interrogative clauses (or color adjectives, or verbs of motion, or whatever) that I didn't have time to work on them much."

Our editions will include, as well as at least one, but very probably two or three edited versions of the novel, and appropriate variants lists, the manuscript materials belonging to a digitized archive; will also include in machine-readable form every significant version of each text. But that material, to use an architectural metaphor, will only occupy half of the building. The other half will contain the audiovisual equivalent of (or rather improvement upon) the explanatory notes that are currently avoided (to take English examples) by most Clarendon critical editions but are part of the recent spate of Lawrence and Conrad and Fitzgerald editions from Cambridge.

I have already said that we intend to offer this material to the eager public as the product of a commercial publisher, but the alternative that many other similar projects are exploring is a network-based edition. As far as we are concerned, there are things to be said on both sides. The advantages of a network-based edition are that there is theoretically no limit to the size of the edition, and that the material in the edition can be updated whenever errors are pointed out by users, or new material surfaces. There are however (depending on the market aimed at) problems of access, both in terms of the fact that network stations are still limited in their spread across the world, and in terms of control over access. Quality control might also be a problem, though I imagine that a proliferation of networked critical editions would generate its own critical-response mechanism. If a scholarly audience were the only one aimed at, this might well be the way to go. But in the end I do not think that publication of the material on compact disc by a commercial publisher necessarily puts out of count subsequently making available all the materials on the network.

The reasons we have decided to approach a publisher with the idea are essentially two; one that we intend to aim our editions at schools quite as much as at scholars and universities, the other that there is (at least currently) more chance of effective critical response to the work if it is commercially produced and distributed in a material form.

The primary disadvantage of the CD form is the relatively limited storage space currently available on a standard compact disc. It seems highly likely, however, that by the time we are ready to produce the discs themselves, their storage capacity will have materially increased.

We have chosen *Under the Greenwood Tree* as the pilot text for several reasons: it is a good novel; it is Hardy's shortest novel; it has a relatively uncomplicated though not uninteresting textual history; and much of the necessary material is already in digital form.

It seems that entry to all the materials in the edition will most conveniently be made through the doorway of an edited text. In some ways I regret this, since the edited text, or that particular edited text, is still privileged in a way similar to the printed text in a book-form critical edition. Part of the value of the kind of edition we and others are working on is the very clear evidence it offers, in dramatic form, of textual indeterminacy; indeed, I should prefer to present users with all the materials and analysis and let them make the editorial decisions—not as an abrogation of responsibility, but as a way of forcing users to recognize the variety of viable choices open to them. But, apart from the logical requirement for an entrance text, it has been pointed out to me with some force that very few, or more likely no users, will really be prepared to do all the business of editing *Under the Greenwood Tree* for themselves. I suppose I have to agree.

An edited text, probably SGML (Standard Generalized Markup Language) encoded, will be the entrance hall that opens out to two different but interconnecting apartments, to keep up the architectural metaphor. On one side there is a suite of rooms, each containing an accurate digital transcription of a significant version of the novel, also SGML marked; in essence the raw material that has gone into the production of the edited text(s). I don't, I think, need to specify to this readership the kinds of versions involved—manuscript, English, Continental, American. For *Under the Greenwood Tree* there are ten of these chambers, any of which may be entered from the edited text or from a list of variants by a couple of mouse clicks (through what Peter Shillingsburg calls webbing)—or at least this is what we are intending, though at present there is not quite the right software available—a question I will be addressing a little later. The centerpiece of this apartment is a large—perhaps overlarge—room devoted to a digital image of the holograph manuscript.

Directed by Peter Robinson of the Oxford University Computing Service, I have recently been investigating the capacities of several different methods of capturing digital images of manuscripts. There is at present no doubt in my mind that the Kontron digital camera gives the best results. I have seen what the British Library is doing with the manuscript of *Beowulf,* and I have been assured that with further manipulation of the Kontron images even more spectacular retrievals of lost script can be achieved. One charred copy of Magna Carta has been made to reveal some script previously indecipherable even using the British Library's forensic magic light box. Peter Robinson has been convinced of the superiority of the Kontron images where his Chaucer manuscripts are concerned (and his *The Digitization of Primary Textual Sources*—a 1993 publication of the Oxford University Computing Service's Office for Humanities Communication—is an invaluable guide to the topic as a whole). I am clear that there are details in Hardy's manuscripts—particularly where erasure of pen and especially pencil marks are concerned—that would be rendered more readable using a digital camera and optical fiber backlighting than through any other currently available method, including the evidence of my own naked eyes. The color images are unimaginably superior to, for instance, those you can find now in the two volumes in the Hardy manuscript archive that Garland managed to commit themselves to publishing (*Tess of the d'Urbervilles* and *The Return of the Native,* 1986); though I never thought I would say such a thing, I would rather have an accurately exposed Kontron digital image of a manuscript leaf to study than the manuscript leaf itself, especially considering the conditions under which it is necessary to view many manuscripts. The exceptional quality of the images (almost literally superhuman) *ought to mean* that owners of manuscripts could divert all inquiries to a CD, with subsequent prevention of incremental degradation.

There will also be images of other details, such as the watermarks on the paper used, that have a bearing on the composition of the manuscript, as well as reproductions of other relevant unpublished documents such as contracts, printer's archives, and the like. It would be pleasant as well to be able to offer digital images of all of the substantive texts, but the one drawback of Kontron images is the very large amount of storage space they occupy. File compression can materially diminish the spendthrift rate, but it is possible that the rather less accurate representation available from three-chip analog video cameras or from photo CDs at less expenditure of space is the way forward. However, at least some pages and the bindings of the significant editions will be included.

The goal for this aspect of the edition, then, is that users will be able to compare multiple versions of the same paragraph or sentence or phrase by clicking on the relevant text in any version, via a menu; that users will be able to generate their own editions if any wish to do so. It is an archive resource that is infinitely manipulable and combinable. There will also be a system of guidance in the form of textual notes, which will highlight problem areas. These will differ slightly from those found in conventional editions, in that they will not have to refer blindly to the various versions whose qualities or defects are analyzed but will be able to direct the user to call up the fragments of text required for their evaluation.

Unfortunately, though, at the time of writing we do not have the appropriate software to enable the performance of these tasks in the way we would like. It seems possible, on the one hand, that by the end of 1995 some acceptable version of DynaText may be available for the Hardy edition to license; on the other hand there are other possible options, such as IBM's ToolBook, and we are also working on a package of our own. But the bottom line is that no currently available software will do all that we would like in such an interactive edition.

Up to the present Hardy editors have used Peter Shillingsburg's CASE (Computer-Assisted Scholarly Editing) collation software for projects like the Oxford University Press World's Classics texts. But DOS-based CASE will not as yet run under Windows or in a hypertext environment. There are clearly important problems to resolve in this vital area.

On the other side of the hallway will be hypermedia explanatory notes. Explanatory notes, particularly those found in many paperback versions of classic works, intended primarily for the consumption of students at schools and universities, are generally extremely limited in their usefulness, aimed at some lowest common denominator of comprehension. Where contextual information is aimed at, it is usually too brief to stimulate anything in the user other than "so what." Those of us involved in the OUP World's Classics editions of Hardy's fiction have endeavored to provide considerably more extensive annotation, with more detail and more analysis than are common; but even OUP, which has been very generous in allowing us the space, has always felt constrained to cut us back. Hypermedia will allow us to propose something quite different and considerably more worthwhile.

The proper place for and function of this kind of annotation has long been a matter of debate, and I do not have space here to enter materially into that debate. But part, at least, of the argument for establishing such annotation, as far as Hardy's work is concerned, is embodied in the series of more or less direct invitations Hardy himself offered to annotators in his prefaces, in the footnotes he added to revised editions of his fiction, in the illustrations he commissioned, and in the maps he drew to accompany his works. It is, further, hardly necessary to say that as a writer Hardy feeds off and attempts to re-create specific environments, specific cultures, specific personal and folk memories, to a degree greater than most authors.

If it may be assumed for the moment that the case for explanatory annotation is granted in this instance, what advantages does a computer-based system of notes possess? The first is very simple—there is much more space. So, for instance, there will be room to do a substantial amount of cross-referencing between Hardy's works, prose and poetry; there will be room to give adequate contexts of Hardy's significant cultural borrowings—from other literature, from painting, from music—and in the latter cases, of course, there will also be the possibility of providing visual or auditory reproductions of the pieces Hardy refers to. There will also be space for discussion of the significance of the allusion or reference. Then there is the obvious possibility of incorporating video or still images of landscapes that Hardy used as the basis for environments in his fiction. It might seem that in such a suggestion we are approaching the tourist version of Hardy, and the pictures will doubtless be very lovely. But they will also serve an essential literary function. It is very well known that when Hardy revised his novels, the largest number of changes he made was almost always to the environmental details that are an essential element in the abiding appeal of his work. To take an example from *Under the Greenwood Tree*, at the beginning of the second chapter of the novel Hardy describes the cottage belonging to the Dewy family. It is no secret that in location and design this cottage bears a very close resemblance to the one that Hardy was born in. It is slightly less well known that in four successive versions of the novel, Hardy altered the description so that at each stage it became more like his Higher Bockhampton birthplace. It is perhaps slightly less well-known yet that Hardy gave a different account of the building in his autobiography, and that the typescripts on which the autobiography was based, as well as his annotations in anecdotal volumes written by others, show how sensitive Hardy was to questions of the exact status of the cottage and through it of his parentage. All this detail can be brought together in verbal and visual form in a substantial note that might have images of the cottage as it exists, ground plans, analysis of all the texts brought together, perhaps even a virtual-reality sequence showing in visual terms how the house grew in Hardy's successive revisions. If only on a very basic level, such a note would provide enlightenment with clarity for some of us who might not be able at once to summon to mind a hipped roof, or for others who might not immediately be able to identify an espalier.

Another good example of how the potential of hypermedia can provide any reader of *Under the Greenwood Tree* with a valuable service is in the matter of dance and music. Hardy vividly evokes the significant pattern of the country dance "The Triumph" or the sound of the quire singing the carol "O Thou Man"—but he had the living performances in his head as he wrote. It is in the spirit of Hardy's intention in these passages that a video account of the dance and a performance of the carol using the appropriate forces should be included and linked to other dances, other songs in this novel, and ultimately perhaps the dances or songs present throughout his work. Such material would not attempt interpretation of Hardy's accounts—it would simply provide information available to Hardy and his contemporaries in place and time, but not to a modern audience.

On the other hand, it *has* been suggested to me that it might be going a little too far to annotate the opening paragraph of the novel:

> To dwellers in a wood, almost every species of tree has its voice as well as its feature. At the passing of the breeze the fir-trees sob and moan no less distinctly than they rock: the holly whistles as it battles with itself: the ash hisses amid its quivering: the beech rustles while its flat boughs rise and fall. And winter, which modifies the note of such trees as shed their leaves, does not destroy its individuality.

It might, I suppose, be too much to go out with one's tape recorder to Thorncombe Wood next December and record the sound of the wind through the relevant trees indeed a friend added that if I did attempt such a recording, I ought also to include the sound of my breath blowing through a comb and see how many users could identify *that* tree. The implied point is a valid one. There is a real problem of gimmickry—of doing this kind of thing just because it is possible to do it, without sufficient reference to the requirements of the text itself and the proper function of explanatory annotation. Such material is not intended to be a substitute for the text, but an enlightenment of it for readers who do not have the resources of a great library, who live thousands of miles from south-west England and more than a hundred years from the work's conception.

There are, as will be evident, still many problems to be worked out, particularly in crucial areas like design or enabling software; but there is no doubt that something approximating to what we are currently proposing will quite soon be available, if not for Hardy, then for Rossetti or Yeats or someone else. And in ten years? . . . Well, the only safe prediction that whatever is available in 1996 or 1997 will in many ways be obsolete by 2005; the basic material, however, should survive intact, if (as has always been the case) the editor's work has been done well enough.

Designing a Hypertext Edition of a Modern Poem

William H. O'Donnell and Emily A. Thrush

Hypertext offers the designer of an electronic edition the potential of meeting the specific needs of a very wide range of readers—from someone encountering the material for the first time to an intermediate student ready to explore the text in more depth to the advanced researcher with specialized interests. The list of possibilities is almost endless: explanatory annotation with several levels of detail, color images, searches, links to related texts, concordances, selectable type size, the choice of modernized or old spelling, foreign-language quotations in translation or the original language, multiple versions of the text displayed simultaneously in multiple windows as full texts or as variants from a main text. And, to step from hypertext to hypermedia,[1] audio recordings cued exactly to any requested place in the text, computer animations, and video clips. But the complexity and sheer abundance of those capabilities can be overwhelming, both for the editor and the reader. These powerful technological potentials must be articulated with considerable clarity, or else the readers of a hypertext edition will balk at being transformed, in computer jargon, to "users," and editors will refuse to accept reclassification as "application developers."

This essay first will survey some of the issues that a scholarly editor encounters when using this rich new method. A hypertext edition developed by William O'Donnell of a poem by W. B. Yeats will illustrate one instance of those design issues and the decision-making process required by them. Then, in the section written by Emily Thrush, we discuss in greater detail how this decision making can be aided by the use of research in several disciplines. The particular issue we will take up is the choice of method for marking the words that have hypertext links. While hypertext designers have speculated intuitively on how various methods of displaying these "hot words" will affect the reader, few have drawn on relevant research on how readers process text. That research, conducted primarily by linguists and psychologists, has long informed technical communicators on the design of paper and computer-displayed text. We will look at how that research can assist an editor in designing a hypertext edition that can balance simplicity of operation and visual clarity against the competing demand of providing enough information to help readers predict where each hypertext link will take them. A list of resources, prepared by Gloria A. Reece and Emily Thrush, is included.

In an ideal hypertext edition, each individual reader would pursue every link that leads to information he or she needs, without pursuing any links that would turn out to be a waste of time for that reader. That test of the functional efficiency of hypertext links can be illuminated by its utter lack of appropriateness for experimental fiction written in hypertext, for there a reader is invited to wander aimlessly, delighted by the clever design of a maze that yields interesting artistic results from even random choices of path. But in all other applications of hypertext a reader's movement through its links should be as purposeful, logical, and efficient as possible. Much discussion has been given to the problem of "navigating" a hypertext document's web of links without losing track of how to get back to a starting point in the main text. But at least as much attention needs to be given to how a reader decides whether to follow a link. This applies equally to the two general structural categories of hypertext documents. The form of hypertext editions that is most closely analogous to conventional scholarly editions is a multilayered set of notes to a main text; the reader selects from among hypertext links that have been provided by the editor. The other basic structure for hypertext is an archive of interrelated data banks that the reader consults by inventing links among information, but the reader's ability to browse within that archive is nonetheless limited by the structure of the data and by the tools provided by the editor or software designer. The layered-notes structure assumes that the reader will begin at the main text and will want to return there. Conversely, the archive of interrelated data banks allows the reader to enter from any of its data banks. My hypertext edition of W. B. Yeats's poem "Lapis Lazuli" is an example of the layered-notes structure, with the innovation of signaling the presence of hypertext links in first-level summary notes so the text of the poem itself remains free of visual clutter.[2]

The poem "Lapis Lazuli" has five stanzas, which range in length from six to sixteen lines. The hypertext edition shows one stanza at a time but could be configured to allow continuous scrolling of the entire poem. A

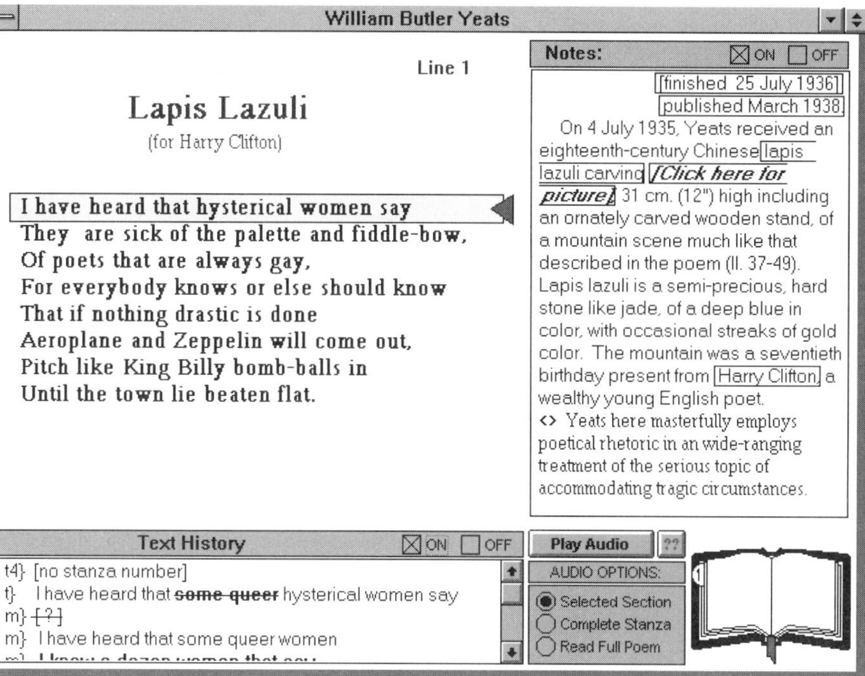

Fig. 1

reader can select simultaneous display of explanatory notes with color illustrations, a complete textual history of the published and manuscript versions, belletristic literary commentary, and an audio recording by Irish actor Cyril Cusack.[3] Figure 1 is an example of the screen layout. The reader controls the various features by clicking the mouse on "buttons" that have self-explanatory labels. The edition opens with a title screen and color portrait of Yeats and then provides a brief sequence of three "help" panels, which can be retrieved at any time. Explanatory notes and the textual history are displayed in separate windows that remain on the screen and are linked to individual lines of the poem (or small groups of lines). If a reader prefers to leave either of those features turned off, the empty window and its on/off button remains on the screen, as a reminder that those features are available. The reader selects a line by clicking the mouse while pointing anywhere on that line; the selected line is then highlighted in yellow and its line number is displayed until the reader selects another line, moves to another stanza, or clears the highlighting by clicking a second time on that line. The reader can move ahead or back one stanza at a time or can return to the start of the poem from any of the five stanzas; the program can be closed from any stanza.

An audio recording is available, without interfering with any of the other features, of Cyril Cusack reading the selected line (with any adjacent lines that comprise a single phrasing unit in the reading), or the stanza, or the entire poem. The audio playback can be stopped at any time. If the reader chooses to hear the entire poem, the screen display automatically advances stanza by stanza during the playback.

The notes window provides a concise overview of the explanatory information and belletristic comments for the selected line. Any hypertext links from this first-level notes window are signaled by "hot words," marked with an enclosing rectangle. The text of the poem itself remains free of those markings to links to additional, more detailed information. When a reader clicks on any of those hot words, the next level of annotation temporarily occupies the entire screen. That next screen often will provide several hot words that the reader may select to pursue a reference through additional levels of annotation. For example, from the main screen with line 1 selected, as shown in figure 1, a reader might choose the hot word "lapis lazuli carving," which would bring up a full screen of information (see fig. 2) that includes a mention of a Chinese court poem inscribed on the back of the

William Butler Yeats

This lapis lazuli, hard-stone mountain or boulder is 26.7 cm. (10.5") high, or 30.7 cm (12.1") including its elaborately carved wooden stand and is 18 cm. (7.1") wide. It dates from the Qian Long (Ch`ien Lung) period (1736-95) of the Qing (Ch'ing) Dynasty. On the front of the mountain are three men climbing toward a temple or tea house; pine trees are carved on the front and back of the mountain; two cranes, one flying and one standing on the ground are carved on the back of the mountain, along with the barely legible inscription, 3.7 x 3.7 cm. (1.5" x1.5"), of a Chinese court poem by Emperor Qian Long (Ch`ien Lung).

The lapis lazuli mountain, although its carving is not of exceptional skill, would have been valued in 1935 at approximately L200-L300 ($1,000-$1,500). A similar, but more skillfully carved lapis lazuli Mountain of the Immortals (24 cm. height x 33 cm. width) (9.3" x 13") with a poem by the Emperor Qian Long (Ch`ien Lung) is in the Avery Brundage Collection, Asian Art Museum of San Francisco. These hard stone carvings in jade or lapis lazuli during the Qing (Ch'ing) dynasty "were carved to represent the rocky, mountainous landscapes so dear to the poetic imagination of the Chinese," and smaller mountains "were made as interior furnishings, or should perhaps be regarded as objects for poetic contemplation. Their rocky slopes are often peopled with symbolic figures and animals drawn from the mythology of Taoism, and many are engraved also with poems."

A decal label of the British Antique Dealers' Association is on the bottom of the stone and also on the bottom of the stand; that style of label dates from 1918 or later. Harry Clifton, who gave the carving to Yeats as a seventieth birthday present, 4 July 1935, must therefore have acquired it no earlier than 1918.

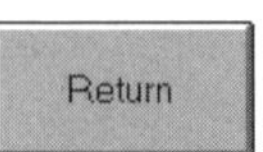

Fig. 2

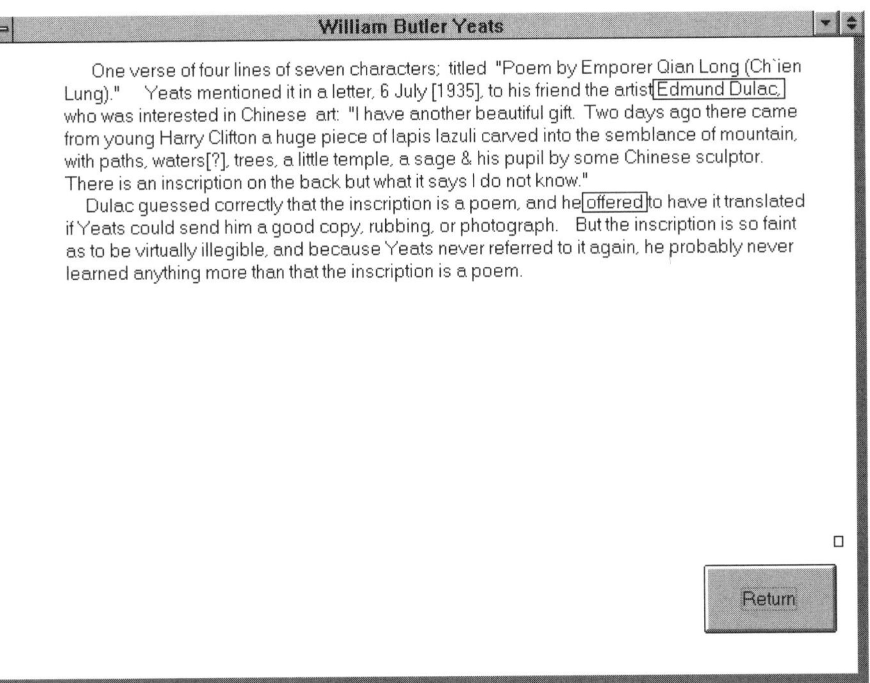
William Butler Yeats
One verse of four lines of seven characters; titled "Poem by Emporer Qian Long (Ch'ien Lung)." Yeats mentioned it in a letter, 6 July [1935], to his friend the artist Edmund Dulac, who was interested in Chinese art: "I have another beautiful gift. Two days ago there came from young Harry Clifton a huge piece of lapis lazuli carved into the semblance of mountain, with paths, waters[?], trees, a little temple, a sage & his pupil by some Chinese sculptor. There is an inscription on the back but what it says I do not know."
Dulac guessed correctly that the inscription is a poem, and he offered to have it translated if Yeats could send him a good copy, rubbing, or photograph. But the inscription is so faint as to be virtually illegible, and because Yeats never referred to it again, he probably never learned anything more than that the inscription is a poem.
Return

Fig. 3

carving. Then by clicking on "Chinese court poem," which is one of the hot words on that second screen, the reader would move to a third screen for a discussion of that poem (see fig. 3), and from that screen could select the hot word "Edmund Dulac" for information, on a fourth screen, about Yeats's friend, who offered to help get a translation of the Chinese poem. Each of those screens has a return button that takes the reader back to the immediately previous display. Some of the links are to color photographs of the lapis lazuli carving and include enhanced enlargements of details (see fig. 4) that are mentioned in the poem.

RATIONALE

This hybrid approach to hypertext annotation, by providing a selectable summary note that contains the prominently marked hot words, has several advantages over the usual hypertext method, in which words in the poem itself would be marked as hot words. Each of the available methods for directly tagging hot words in the text itself is either visually intrusive (color, italics, boldface, enclosure in a rectangle or braces, superscript numeral or symbol, etc.) or is annoyingly labor intensive (visual signal that

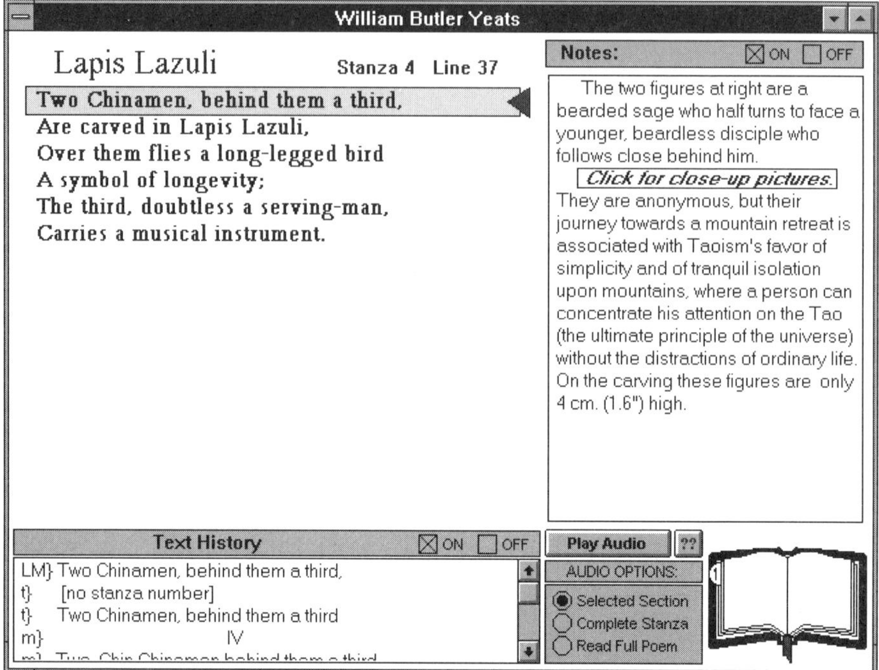

Fig. 4a

remains hidden until the reader pushes a button or points the mouse at the individual word). If a hypertext edition that uses visual tagging of hot words allows the reader the option of turning off the visual tags, the reader is faced with the unwelcome prospect of either putting up with the visual distractions or losing any convenient access to the hypertext links. Another hypertext marking system, which uses symbols in the margin to announce that there are one or more hypertext links to that line, avoids cluttering the text, but at the price of vagueness as to which word or words in that line have hypertext links. The hybrid system, with hot words in the first-level summary notes window, often is able to give the reader a more specific idea about the link marked by a hot word. Systems that rely on marking hot words directly in the main text are closely similar to printed books with superscript numbers for notes that mark the place but do not necessarily suggest what kind of information the reader is likely to find by turning to the notes at the back of the book or the bottom of the page. The hybrid approach allows the text of the poem to remain completely clean, while more clearly suggesting what annotation is available, and thus radically reducing the amount of guesswork that a reader must spend in deciding whether to pursue a hot word.

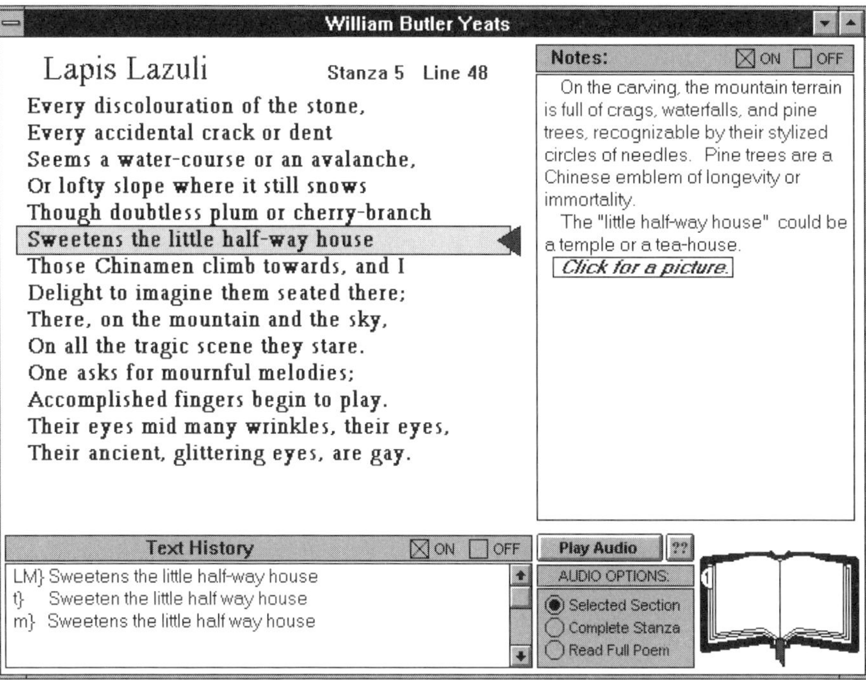

Fig. 4b

In a printed book, the notes must meet the publisher's economic limits on length, and one set of notes must serve all the readers. In a hypertext edition the editor can have much more space for notes, and, because hypertext editions can be designed to give the reader substantial control of whether to display a note, the editor can be much more flexible in meeting the needs of a wide range of readers. In a printed book each note is a forced compromise between the equally legitimate demands of readers who are or are not experts on a particular subject. The editor of a printed book tries to find a level of detail for the notes that won't be excessively annoying to either of those groups of readers. In a hypertext edition, instead of compromising on a single note, the editor can provide linked series of notes that address all relevant issues, but most of which will be seen only by individual readers who have chosen to continue following that particular line of inquiry. The hybrid approach used in the "Lapis Lazuli" hypertext edition heightens those general advantages of hypertext by providing an introductory summary note that is displayed to every reader who wants to learn something about that line, and so has turned on the notes feature and then selects that particular line by clicking on it. The

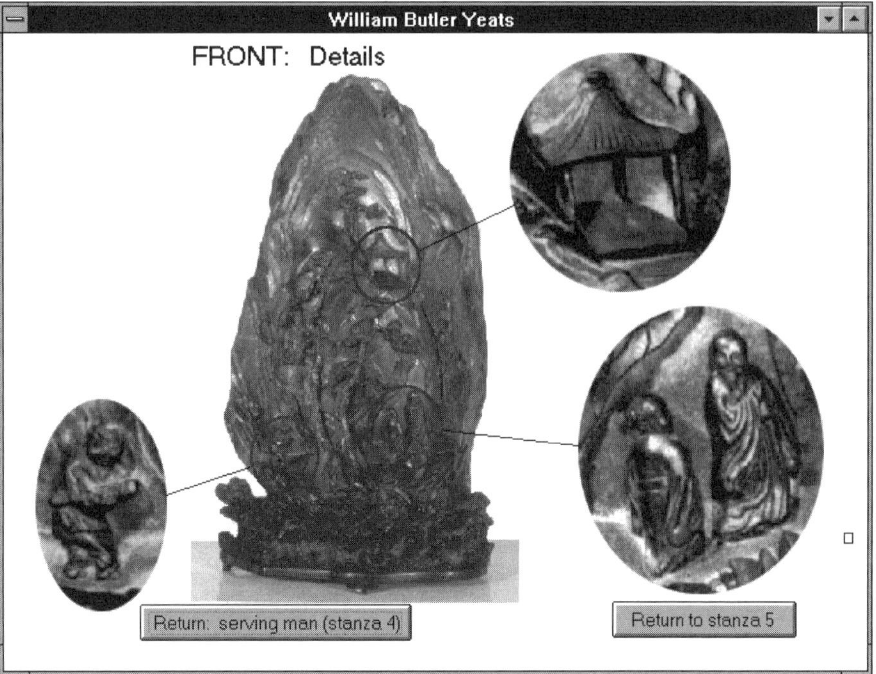

Fig. 4c

editor uses that note and/or commentary to introduce any topic that is likely to be helpful to *any* (rather than *most*) of a wide range of readers. If the structure of the annotation is effectively designed, the expert can pursue topics of interest that would be arcane to most readers, while at the same time the nonexpert reader is free to pursue topics that would be annoyingly tiresome to experts. The hypertext editor can even choose to use a portion of the first-level notes window for belletristic commentary that can enrich the reading of persons who are new to the poem. In the "Lapis Lazuli" hypertext edition those belletristic remarks are set apart from the explanatory notes by being flagged with an identifying symbol (here a diamond) and by using a slightly smaller type size.

The necessity for a hypertext editor to consider a bold range of possibilities rather than seeking a direct translation of the conventional methods of a printed edition is strikingly apparent when we consider how textual-history information can be displayed. Hypertext allows a very wide range of possibilities, of which the worst would be the densely compacted, coded apparatus used in printed texts. In the "Lapis Lazuli" edition, the textual-history window, at the bottom left of the screen in figure 1, shows in reverse chronological order all variants in published or manuscript versions of the line that the reader has selected in the main text. The reader can tell at a glance if the textual-history information for that particular line is likely to be worth additional attention. Hypertext editions could provide display of variant texts in multiple windows that automatically scroll in unison with the main text. The variant texts could be displayed either as transcriptions or as scanned images of the original documents. The textual variants could be shown with colored highlighting of revised passages and strike-throughs of canceled versions (that presentation is available in the "compare" feature in the WordPerfect word processing program). The textual-history window could show a line of text with the variant passages printed above the line, aligned with the main text. As in the CASE (Computer-Assisted Scholarly Editing) textual-collation program, which includes such a display, the reader could select which particular variant texts to include in that display. The variants could even be animated so that a reader could watch the changes occur, accompanied by a reference window that identified each variant. An ideal system would give readers several choices of the method (or simultaneous methods) of displaying the textual history. At the same time, the reader of a hypertext edition is free to turn off the display of textual history.

A hypertext edition can easily provide a reference window that automatically displays the source and date of information that is being viewed in a notes window. Other convenient features would be a notepad where the reader could annotate the text and notes, and place markers that a reader could activate. A reader should be able to print and/or copy to another file the contents of the hypertext edition. An ideal system would automatically maintain a log of what the reader has looked at and would allow the reader to mark items of interest when they are displayed. Then at the end of a session the reader could print that serial listing or store it as a computer file, either in its entirety or only items the reader selects.

The "Lapis Lazuli" hypertext edition, in which the main text is accompanied by several underlying layers of notes and other supplementary information, has a general resemblance to a book. If instead of that layered-notes structure, the edition were to be an archive of interrelated data banks, a reader would be allowed considerable initiative in browsing among those data banks, gathering related information from any combination of them. For example, a program written by Patricia Search allows an art museum curator to search and make connections among information archived under *work of art, exhibition, bibliography,* and *biography.* If that approach were applied to "Lapis Lazuli," the separate sections might be

"Lapis Lazuli" and all of Yeats's poems, explanatory annotation (with subdivisions such as definitions and biography), textual history (primary bibliography of publishing history, translations, recordings, etc.), audio track, concordances of words and of imagery, belletristic commentary, and other categories such as prosody. That archive or information matrix, within which the reader browses, is not anchored to the single linear structure of a primary text. A reader's starting point could be one of the poems but could just as easily be a verse form *(sonnet)* or biography *(Maud Gonne)* or imagery *(hair)* or chronology *(1921)*.

RESEARCH ON VISUAL ELEMENTS IN HYPERTEXT DESIGN

The importance of adhering to good document design principles in the production of paper documents is well recognized by technical writers and, intuitively, by the users of these documents. One researcher in the field has said, "The organization and format of a document may be just as important as its language. The degree to which the document is matched to the capabilities of its users and the setting of its use may affect comprehension as much as clearly written sentences."[4] Courses in document design are a standard part of degree programs in technical writing. These courses combine theoretical and practical knowledge from a variety of fields, including cognitive psychology, social psychology, psycholinguistics, rhetoric, graphic design, human factors, discourse analysis, cultural studies, and instructional design.[5]

Now many documents are being written expressly to be read from a computer screen, rather than from paper, often with little thought to visual design. Hypertext documents in particular, because they are more complex than simple word-processed files, e-mail messages, standard forms of Computer Assisted Instruction, or more traditional on-line help systems, raise complex questions about the applicability of established document design principles. An informal survey of hypertext project developers reveals that most did not take screen design principles into account as part of the development process, nor did they involve writers beyond the original production of the text in hard copy. Many rely on intuitions for designing the complex displays and linking systems of a hypertext document. Much of the help available to hypertext designers, such as Randy M. Brooks's article in *Technical Communication,*[6] consists of "helpful hints" articles that often do contain valuable tips but fail to convey the underlying theoretical principles for design that allow an individual designer to adapt the principles for a specific purpose.

REVIEW OF RESEARCH ON DOCUMENT DESIGN AND SCREEN DISPLAY

The first step in establishing a visual rhetoric for hypertext documents is to review what we know from research about paper documents and how that knowledge relates to screen design. While some research has been done specifically on computer screen displays, the rapid changes in hardware capabilities make this research outdated almost before it is published.

Ways of Showing Links

The defining characteristic of hypertext is that users follow links to see and hear elements of the document that are of interest to them. This is the primary way in which hypertext is different from other types of computer documents. Clearly, then, the ability of the user to find and follow links is a key element in the success of the document. Hypertext-authoring systems provide several different methods to indicate where links exist:

- Highlighting (or inverse text)
- Boldfacing
- Underlining
- Asterisks beside the link word(s)
- Boxes around the link word(s)
- Change in color for the link word(s)
- A change in the form of the cursor as it travels over the link word(s)
- Lists of link words, indices, glossaries, tables of contents, cross-references
- A miniversion of the graphic or moving image that is the destination of the link
- Icons or buttons to click on
- Keyboard input of search terms
- Marginal annotation or titles
- Clicking on any graphic or figure

This wide range of methods could cause confusion for users who need to read hypertext documents written with different authoring systems, but may not be a problem for users who only use one system or who do not have to switch systems frequently.

The problem for the hypertext designer is to choose among these options for optimal ways of showing the user the location of links to be followed and to help the user anticipate what is at the end of the link. While these choices may ultimately be determined by common usage, we are still at the point where the research on document design can inform the hypertext designer and make design choices easier and more appropriate.

Typographical devices. One of the most common ways of showing links is boldfacing. Document design research has shown boldfacing to be the best device for showing contrast, for emphasizing important points, and for getting the reader's attention.[7] It is often used for headings, in lists and tables, and for short items of information that are separated from the main text. However, boldfacing loses its effectiveness and its impact on the reader when used for long passages of text,[8] and, more importantly, dramatically slows reading rates because the reader's attention is drawn away from the text to the boldfaced items.[9] Italics, underlining, and text in all caps are often used for similar purposes and share the same advantages and disadvantages as boldfacing.

Since extensive use of boldfacing, highlighting, or underlining to indicate links could interfere with reading speed and comprehension, they may not be appropriate choices for hypertext documents with lengthy blocks of text. Additionally, asterisks and boxing, devices that also interfere with the smooth flow of reading, could also be predicted to hamper speed and comprehension.

Change in color. The use of color in document design is controversial. There are those who see color as distracting from the content of the text and damaging to its readability,[10] while others see color as a way of enhancing the document. Winn, for example, suggests that color can help by "directing attention, delimiting shapes and areas, clarifying complex issues, facilitating identification, and creating affect."[11] This first effect of color, directing the attention of the reader to the colored area, presents the same problem if color is used within a text to indicate links as previously discussed in regard to typographical devices. When colors are translated for display on monochrome monitors, some colors, such as blue, are distinct, but others, such as white and yellow, are not.

Cursor shape. In authoring systems such as Owl's Guide, the cursor changes shape when it passes over linked words or elements. While this allows the user to read through the text with no interference, it also requires the user to move the cursor over every line of text to find the links, a tedious process at best.

Icons or buttons outside the text. Icons or buttons outside the text do not interfere with reading speed or comprehension; however, they take up screen space, limiting the amount of text shown at any given time. This might be particularly problematic for documents that will be viewed on the smaller, standard screens.

Keyboard entry. Keyboarding is the normal way of searching databases and thus may be familiar to the user, but it may also negate some of the advantages of hypertext over more traditional database types. The use of keyboarding or menus is similarly a return to earlier, less flexible computer technologies.

Link activation. An authoring system designed specifically to write lessons in reading skills, Versatext (although not considered a hypertext-authoring tool by its publishers) presents the text first without the links indicated. By activating a choice in a pull-down menu, the user views a version of the text with the links shown in boldface. Thus, the reader can read the text without interference before beginning the process of linking to other areas. However, as previously discussed, this complicates the moving back and forth from reading text to following links.

Methods of Displaying Text

Another problem for the hypertext designer—and the user—is that many different types of information can be at the end of a link. How does the designer indicate to the user whether the link leads to a brief explanation of a term or to a major piece of primary text? In many authoring systems, the following types of displays are possible.

Overlapping windows. Familiar to users of Macintosh and PCs with Windows, overlapping windows of display gives users the freedom to bring up a number of screens simultaneously and keep them open.

Scrolling. Scrolling is the process of revealing more text at the bottom of the screen while the top rolls out of view. It means that a single block of text can be longer than the screen or window, while a frame requires that the text be written in chunks that fit inside a box. Some systems use a combination of scrolling windows and frames for different kinds of information—graphics, for example, might appear in frames, while text appears in scrolling windows.

Pop-up notes. Sometimes text is located in pop-up notes, which means that users can click on a word, box, or icon and a note will appear on the screen for as long as the user holds the mouse button down. As soon as the button is released, the message leaves the screen. The major advantage of pop-up notes is that they allow small bits of information, such as definitions for unfamiliar terms, to be accessed and disposed of quickly without losing or obscuring the text that is on the screen. But important or lengthy messages may lose their emphasis if displayed this way.

Metaphors. Hypertext designers often work on the assumption that presenting users with something that looks familiar will help them adapt to an unfamiliar technology. For this reason, many hypertext documents are based on a visual metaphor, so that they may look like a stack of file cards, or a notebook with tabs, or as much like a paper version as possible. But, as Ted Nelson has pointed out, this may be restricting the possibilities and potential of hypertext.[12] Paper documents have been restricted in design by the limitations of the medium itself, by the capabilities of printing processes, and by the expense of printing and distribution. Hypertext, on the other hand, at least holds the promise of transcending these limitations. Designs with visual metaphors may be appropriate for certain hypertext documents and their intended users. For example, hypertext applications have been developed to provide information to museum visitors, who may be unfamiliar with hypertext usage and who will work with the system only for a few minutes. This type of usage is probably facilitated by an interface design that closely resembles familiar documents. However, a hypertext system or document that is to be used by the same group of users over long periods of time can afford to take advantage of new strategies. Users will adapt to these strategies as they work with the system.

Using a metaphor may also present a space problem, especially on small screens. Many early hypertext documents displayed the text as the open pages of a book. To make the screen look three dimensional, other pages of the book are shown, as is the binding on two or three sides of the book. While this metaphor is creatively displayed, it takes up as much as three quarters of an inch at the bottom and sides of the screen, reducing the space available for the content of the document.

IMPLICATIONS FOR HYPERTEXT DESIGNERS

A software designer starting from scratch to develop an interface for a software application can use what is known about document design. But a developer using an authoring system is at the mercy of the designers of that system. We have noticed in our work with the major hypertext-authoring packages, such as HyperCard, Guide, Architext, HyperTies, KnowledgePro, ToolBook, Storyspace, and others, that most have built-in constraints on how we can display text, highlight important information, and arrange items on the screen. Frequently, the devices used by the authoring systems to display links overlap or interfere with the devices normally used to show emphasis or provide structural cues. In addition, the forms of display available in a particular authoring system may not suit the types of material we want to include in a particular hypertext. While we can sometimes choose an authoring system based on our knowledge of the contents and purpose of the document we are planning, at other times our choices are constrained by logistics of hardware, portability, and decisions already made by other designers.

DIRECTIONS FOR RESEARCH

Kostelnick suggests that there are three ways of determining guidelines for document design decisions: "(1) deductively follow conventions outlined in textbooks, (2) inductively extract principles from actual documents and contexts, or (3) consult theories and research encompassing the visual processing of texts."[13] Hypertext designers, however, are working with a technology so new that this prescription may be of little value. Drawing design principles from other types of documents, whether hard copy or on-line, may limit the promise of hypertext to open up new ways of dealing with information.

Clearly it is difficult if not impossible to develop a set of general principles that apply to materials developed for different purposes and different audiences. Research studies have been performed using a wide variety of types of documents and readers. Principles that hold for one situation may not for another. Therefore, someone interested in developing a hypertext document has to be careful about applying guidelines established through a study on a different type of document. Schriver suggests that readers read for many purposes: to learn, to enjoy, to do a task, to write, to understand, to be persuaded, to find information quickly, to compare and contrast, to learn to do, to make a decision, to assess the relevance or interestingness of a text, and to interpret and use information for a purpose other than the text's intended purpose.[14] Readers may be novices, intermediates, or experts in the subject area. All of the these factors may affect choices in document design. It may be that the different purposes for reading are facilitated by different design options. Roger Grice and Lenore Ridgway even suggest that "The shift in our view of information from a body of material to be absorbed and internalized to a set of answers to questions has already changed the way people use material and has invalidated many of the rules of writing."[15]

For all these reasons, continuing research is needed to test hypertext documents for persuasiveness, comprehensibility, memorability, and usability in particular situations with particular audiences. Only then can we begin to develop principles for hypertext and hypermedia design that are enabling rather than limiting. Future research needs to look at a number of variables that should be taken into account by the author of a hypertext document, including

The intended purpose of the document

The reasons readers have for reading the document

The reading strategies that will be used

The amount of previous experience the intended users have with similar documents

The amount of time a given user can be expected to spend learning and using the system

The method of distribution of the document and the amount of control the designer has over the display equipment that will be used

The rhetorical strategies familiar to the intended audience

The specific information needs of a population of users.

ADDITIONAL RESOURCES ON DOCUMENT AND HYPERMEDIA DESIGN

Alexander, G., and M. Walter. "A Fresh Look at SGML: The Conventional Wisdom Changes." *Seybold* (Dec. 1990): 3–6, 9–14, 16.

Basara, D., D. Burgin, G. Ryan, and K. Holtzblatt. "Contextual Inquiry: Listening and Questioning to Improve Information Design." *Society for Technical Communication 40th Annual Conference* (1993): 466.

Benson, Phillippa J. "Writing Visually: Design Considerations in Technical Publications." *Technical Communication* 32 (1985): 35–39.

Brockmann, R. John. "The Unbearable Distraction of Color." *IEEE Transactions on Professional Communication* 34 (1991): 153–59.

Burger, Jeff. "Type and Design: Designing for the Screen." *PUBLISH!* (Nov. 1992): 64–69.

Brooks, Randy M. "Principles for Effective Hypermedia Design." *Technical Communication* 40 (1993): 422–28.

Duin, Ann Hill. "How People Read: Implications for Writers." *Technical Writing Teacher* 15 (1988): 185–91.

Durst, Sherri K. "Designing a Successful Online Help System: What Works, What Doesn't." *Society for Technical Communication 39th Annual Conference* (1992): WE, 87–90.

Felker, Daniel B., et al. *Document Design: A Review of the Relevant Research.* Washington, DC: American Institutes for Research, 1980.

———. *Guidelines for Document Designers*. Washington, DC: American Institutes for Research, 1981.

Galitz, Wilbert O. *Handbook of Screen Format Design*. Wellesley, MA: QED Information Services, 1989.

Glushko, Robert. "Using Off-the-Shelf Software to Create a Hypertext Electronic Encyclopedia." *Technical Communication* 37 (1990): 28–33.

Grice, Roger A., and Lenore S. Ridgway. "Usability and Hypermedia: Toward a Set of Usability Criteria and Measures." *Technical Communication* 40 (1993): 429–37.

Hartley, James, and David H. Jonassen. "The Role of Headings in Printed and Electronic Text." In *The Technology of Text: Principles for Structuring, Designing, and Displaying Text*, edited by D. H. Jonassen, 237–63. Englewood Cliffs, NJ: Educational Technology Publications, 1985.

Keyes, Elizabeth. "Typography, Color, and Information Structure." *Technical Communication* 40 (1993): 638–54.

Kinzie, Mable B., and Richard L. Berdel. "Design and Use of Hypermedia Systems." *Educational Technology Research and Development* 38 (1988): 61–74.

Kostelnick, Charles. "Visual Rhetoric: A Reader-Oriented Approach to Graphics and Designs." *Technical Writing Teacher* 16 (1989): 77–86.

Marcus, Andrew. *Graphic Design for Electronic Documents and User Interfaces*. New York: ACM Press, 1992.

Miller, G. A. "The Magical Number Seven, Plus or Minus Two: Some Limits on Our Capacity for Processing Information." *Psychological Review* 63 (1956): 81–97. [Landmark essay.]

Nelson, Theodor H. *Literary Machines*. South Bend, IN: [self-published], 1987.

Niekamp, Walter. "An Exploratory Investigation in Factors Affecting Visual Balance." *Educational Communication and Technology Journal* 29 (1981): 37–48.

Nielson, Jakob. "The Art of Navigating Through Hypertext." *Communications of the ACM* 33 (1990): 296–310.

Nord, M. A., and B. Tanner. "Design that Delivers—Formatting Information for Print and Online Documents." In *Techniques for Technical Communicators*, edited by Carol M. Barnum and Saul Carliner, 219–52. New York: Macmillan, 1993.

Olkes, Cheryl. "Typography/Graphics." In *Document Design: A Review of the Relevant Research*, edited by Daniel B. Felker, 103–10. Washington, DC: American Institutes for Research, 1980.

Radecki, S. L. "Developing Online Help for OS/2 Applications." *Society for Technical Communication 40th Annual Conference* (1993): 434–37.

Redish, Janice C. "Reading to Learn to Do." *Technical Writing Teacher* 15 (1988): 223–33.

Rose, Andrew. "Human Factors." In *Document Design: A Review of the Relevant Research*, edited by Daniel B. Felker, 92–102. Washington, DC: American Institutes for Research, 1980.

Rubens, Paul M. "A Reader's View of Text and Graphics: Implications for Transactional Text." *Journal of Technical Writing and Communication* 1 (1986): 673–86.

Rubens, Paul M., and Robert Krull. "Application of Research on Document Design to Online Displays." *Technical Communication* 32 (1985): 29–33.

Schell, D. A. "Testing Online and Print User Documentation." *IEEE Transactions on Professional Communications* 29 (1986): 87–92.

Schriver, Karen A. 1989. "Document Design from 1980 to 1989: Challenges that Remain." *Technical Communication* 36 (1989): 316–31.

Search, Patricia. "HyperGlyphs: Using Design and Language to Define Hypermedia Navigation." *Technical Communication* 40 (1993): 414–21.

Southard, Sherry G. "Practical Considerations in Formatting Manuals." *Technical Communication* 35 (1988): 173–78.

Tinkel, Kathleen. "Classic Composition, Part Two." *Aldus Magazine* (Nov. 1993): 45–49.

———. "Mixing Faces: Putting Typefaces Together Calls for Subtle Judgments—As Well as Risk-Taking." *Aldus Magazine* (Mar./Apr. 1993): 41–46.

Williges, Beverly H., and Robert C. Williges. "Dialogue Design Considerations for Interactive Computer Systems." In *Human Factors Review*, edited by F. A. Muckler, A. S. Neal, and L. Strother, 167–208. Santa Monica, CA: Human Factors Society, 1984.

Winn, William. "Color in Document Design." *IEEE Transactions on Professional Communication* 34 (1991): 180–85.

Wise, Mary R. "Using Graphics in Software Documentation." *Technical Communication* 40 (1993): 677–81.

CONCLUSION

The continuing rapid development of equipment and software can be expected to make hypertext features ever more powerful, but also simpler to use. We can look forward to a time when software programmers, editors, and publishers will have developed a nucleus of coherent, relatively standardized techniques. Those techniques will become as familiar to readers as now are the smaller set of techniques that are required for using a printed book. But until that time, editors need to pay particularly keen attention to anticipating how the various readers will respond to a hypertext edition. After the editor has announced what features are available and has explained how to use them comes the real test of the effectiveness of a hypertext's design, when the reader begins making a series of specific, local decisions of whether to use one or more of those features at each particular point in the text. Each reader of a hypertext should be given enough information, directly and from context, to predict whether stopping to invoke one of the features will produce results that are worth the effort. The marking of hypertext links should be visually unobtrusive, while still providing enough information about what is at the other end of each link so the reader can make an informed decision.

NOTES

1. In this essay we use the general term *hypertext* as including the sound and visual elements of hypermedia.
2. The edition, which is programmed in the ToolBook (Asymetrix Corp.) hypertext-authoring language, runs in MS-Windows 3.1 on IBM-compatible computers equipped with a sound card and a VGA display with 640 × 480 pixels in 256 colors. William H. O'Donnell designed the edition; William E. Kelsey provided expertise in ToolBook OpenScript programming. It was demonstrated at the Association for Documentary Editing, Philadelphia, October

1993. The edition and a reader version of ToolBook can be compressed onto two high-density disks, one of which is almost entirely filled by the compressed audio file.

3. W. B. Yeats, *Poems,* Caedmon TC 1081, 1958.
4. Daniel B. Felker, *Guidelines for Document Designers* (Washington, D.C.: American Institutes for Research, 1981), 1–2.
5. Karen A. Schriver, "Document Design from 1980 to 1989: Challenges That Remain," *Technical Communication* 36 (1989): 316–31.
6. Randy M. Brooks, "Principles for Effective Hypermedia Design," *Technical Communication* 40 (1993): 422–28.
7. Paul M. Rubens, "A Reader's View of Text and Graphics: Implications for Transactional Text," *Journal of Technical Writing and Communication* 1 (1986): 673–86.
8. Sherry G. Southard, "Practical Considerations in Formatting Manuals," *Technical Communication* 35 (1988): 173–78.
9. Rubens, "Reader's View."
10. R. John Brockmann, "The Unbearable Distraction of Color," *IEEE Transactions on Professional Communication* 34 (1991): 153–59.
11. William Winn, "Color in Document Design," *IEEE Transactions on Professional Communication* 34 (1991): 182.
12. Theodor H. Nelson, "Literary Machines" [self-published], South Bend, Indiana, 1987.
13. Charles Kostelnick, "Visual Rhetoric: A Reader-Oriented Approach to Graphics and Designs," *Technical Writing Teacher* 16 (1989): 82.
14. Schriver, "Document Design," 322.
15. Roger A. Grice and Lenore S. Ridgway, "Usability and Hypermedia: Toward a Set of Usability Criteria and Measures," *Technical Communication* 40 (1993): 435.

Traditional Theory and Innovative Practice: The Electronic Editor as Poststructuralist Reader

Phillip E. Doss

Had I written this essay several years ago, the statements from T. E. Hulme and Ernst Cassirer that follow would have been placed at the beginning as epigraphs, without comment, and left to their juxtaposed selves to do whatever semantic work they could. But I intersperse them now with comment because I have been working in hypertext and have become accustomed (not always to better effect) to the endless opportunities hypertext provides for comment. What in print medium was allusion and worked connotatively has in electronic medium become, potentially at least, denotative, articulated reference. I will note here in general the radical hermeneutic change this portends for the way we write and read, and will note later the specific pitfalls this change offers for the textual editor.

I want to use these epigraphic statements to mark some boundaries for a discussion of textual editing in electronic environments, particularly in regard to textual-editorial considerations in the shift from print to electronic media. The statements from Hulme and Cassirer were composed, obviously, not with hypertext in mind, but rather as insights into the cognitive functions that accompany reading and writing alphabetic print. That they might be recalled here, and found relevant, should be an indication that there is a fundamental communicative process that both print and electronic media support and sustain. Hulme notes of the book:

> The covers of a book are responsible for much error. They set a limit around certain convenient groups of ideas, when there are really no limits.[1]

Hulme confirms here the often artificial closure imposed by printed, bound books. The feeling of liberation and possibility we experience in hypertext arises when we escape this convenient closure. It should be noted, however, that a similar liberation is possible, indeed Hulme himself achieved it, not through electronic media, but simply through reading more books. The literate experience is, after all, not a *singular* experience, but a process that explores possibilities through a series of intermittent, not always artificial, closures. There is a danger in these jumps and starts, however, and it has to do specifically with *the way we read:*

> This blind following of interest along long and intricate paths may indirectly approximate to the results which concentration achieves directly.[2]

And so we are oriented for the present between the limitations of the book, the sometimes artificial boundaries that it erects, and the intrinsic values that attach to those limitations. We are given in this orientation to consider not only the value of an escape from a limited referentiality but also the value of limitation itself, the value of definite boundaries, and we must consider both terms in regard to the cognitive apprehension of *forms of text*.

Certainly the value of system is nowhere more apparent than in theory, for every theory, no matter how numerous its variables nor how intricately related, depends ultimately upon the closure of an equation. Ernst Cassirer remarks upon this fundamental characteristic of theoretical thinking:

> In this system [of theoretical thinking] there are no more isolated points; all its members are reciprocally related, refer to one another, illumine and explain each other. Thus every separate event is ensnared, as it were, by invisible threads of thought, that bind it to the whole. The theoretical significance which it receives lies in the fact that it is stamped with the character of this totality.[3]

Even the tropes that Cassirer uses presage hypertext: *points* (nodes) that are rescued from their isolation by *invisible threads* (linkages) and *ensnared* and *bound* into a *totality* (web). My point here is precisely to note that this totality, which theoretical thinking represents and constructs, is constituted by associations ("threads of thought"), constituted, as it were, by a structure that creates a system. The totality of which Cassirer speaks is not the totality of all possible references, but the totality, each unto itself, of the referential systems that theoretical thinking creates. One might better get the sense of his meaning by substituting the term *logicality* for the term "totality." Theoretical systems, in order to be worthy of the attribute, are throughout logical unto themselves.[4] Such systematic logicality is no small order, as any philosopher might tell you. And if we have at our disposal a tool that seemingly creates its own systems, as hypertext does, or better yet a tool that seemingly precludes the necessity of closed systems because it offers unlimited access to *all* systems, as hypertext does, then there is the danger that we might abdicate the responsibility of our own agency:

> as soon as man employs a tool, he views it not as a mere artifact of which he is the recognized maker, but as a Being in its own right endowed with powers of its own.[5]

In its recognition of the fundamental relationship between tools and toolmakers, this insight might readily be taken as the basic tenet of poststructuralist thought. I extract it from Cassirer not because he is considered an augur of poststructuralism, but to show that the end of intellectual development has always been, even in the structuralist age from which Cassirer wrote, to develop an awareness of agency. I am concerned here, as we suffer and enjoy the radical changes that electronic media bring, that we remain aware of *continuities,* not only in regard to the telos of intellectual endeavor generally, but specifically in regard to the ways in which the textual editor might employ electronic media in the tasks before him or her. We have a tool with which we can move a step beyond the book.

HYPERTEXT AND HYPERSTRUCTURE

Artists have probably always understood the necessary relationship between medium and message simply because, whether they have been restrained or empowered by their chosen medium, they have never been released from it. As sculpture is bound to its stone or bronze or other plastic material, and defies translation into a linguistic medium, so hypertext writing is bound to an electronic environment, and defies translation to print. Only an electronic environment can make immediately available the multiple referential possibilities upon which hypertext fiction relies.[6] There is a fascination in hypertext fiction and the reviews of such fiction, with the seeming freedom readers/viewers are given to create meaning, particularly in regard to the manipulation of plot and plot outcomes. That there are multiple possibilities for the resolution of conflict in a plot is nothing new; therein lies the foundation of suspense, suspense that is achieved even within the often very rigid forms of literary genres. So the *concept* of multiple possible outcomes is not new. But that the reader might choose from among those possibilities; that is new, and it is facilitated by hypertext environments. Here again is a difference in the way we write and the expectations we bring to reading. An author in such an environment is charged with creating multiple systems, each of which will lead to a logical outcome. And a reader acquires a new freedom to choose, a new type of agency that is not without its responsibilities. Jacques Derrida notes that "the god of Leibniz . . . did not know the anguish of the choice between various possibilities."[7] Derrida notes in the same passage that the force of applied *will* simplified the process of choosing. And so the specter of the *willful* reader is raised again, whose corporeality has never really been in doubt. The free relationship of the willful reader to the electronic text certainly bears thinking upon in regard to authorial intention as an editorial orientation, though it should be noted that in the hyperfiction of multiple possible outcomes the intent of the author is not given over to the reader; it is merely made manifest in multiple forms.

In the years to come, textual editors will develop methodologies to deal with the elaborate structures of hypertext fiction. I would like to consider here, however, the situation with which a textual editor is faced as he or she attempts to transfer a work of literature from print medium to electronic medium, specifically to an electronic medium that has definite boundaries, whether conceptual or physical.[8] There is an analogy, I think, between the hyperfiction author who creates an electronic document within an electronic environment and the textual editor who constructs the framework within an electronic environment that will hold a print document and at the same time exploit the hermeneutic possibilities of the new environment.

In a hypertext environment, by virtue of its precise denotative presentation capabilities, the textual editor, to an extent unthought of in print media, holds sway over interpretative possibilities. This new power derives directly from the fact that *hyperstructure is a necessary correlate of hypertext,* and it is the textual editor who must build the hyperstructures that are the basis of hypertext editions. We must never forget the nature of this *constructedness.* Despite the semblance of natural unity in a hypertext, constituted by a semblance of totality, by a semblance of completion that derives from the seeming unlimitedness of hypertext referentiality, despite its seeming readerly parthenogenesis, a hypertext document is built, piece by piece. For evidence of the builder's agency, one need only examine the source code for the computer programs that drive hypertext, or better yet, one need only construct a hypertext document. Chaos theory tells us that complexity can obscure cause, which is to say that elaborate structure can hide agency.

In "What Is Critical Editing?" Jerome McGann makes the distinction between linguistic and bibliographic codes and argues that there are different forces that work upon each.[9] In "Monks and Giants" he argues that it is the job of the textual editor to be aware of these forces.[10] One of the implications of McGann's view is that textual criticism as a discipline positions itself to account for all of the agents that act over time upon a literary text. Hypertext lends itself to McGann's school of pervasive agency, and as a presentation tool hypertext confronts the editor with new sets of choices and concomitant sets of responsibilities in regard to these agents. Heretofore, that is, in print medium, the apparatus, and all other appurtenances of the edition, referred directly to the object text, however conceived. It was in fact from such appurtenances that a reader gained clues to the textual theoretical orientation of the textual editor. In a hypertext environment the apparatus, and all other appurtenances of the edition, must refer to the entire structure of the edition itself.[11] This is precisely because the aesthetic character of the textual editor's job is more apparent in hypertext environments than in print. The "exegesis of texts and meanings" to which McGann refers now must apply to the structure of the hypertext document itself (not only to the object text). If ever the organic metaphor was more applicable to a system than the mechanical one, it is so in the case of the structures of hypertext, since a hypertext document generates meaning with every linkage. The agent responsible for encoding these linkages (and thereby creating this "extra" meaning) is the textual editor.

Just as the epigraphs for this essay create a context in which it is to be read, or at least in which I wish it to be initially apprehended, so the associative linkages that a textual editor encodes in a hypertext document create a context. But more rigidly than epigraphs, which as I noted earlier work connotatively in their usual form, the structure of a hypertext document directs readers toward particular interpretations denotatively, i.e. by indicating that term A (node 1) is associated (linked) with term B (node

2). It is possible to conceive of connotative linkages being encoded in a hypertext document simply by increasing the size of the semantic unit that constitutes term B in this example. In common usage, however, hypertext nodes seldom consist solely of such general terms as "the nineteenth century" or "the works of Faulkner." Editors use hypertext linkages for the most part, not to allude, but to specify. It becomes incumbent upon the textual editor who encodes these denotations to anticipate and justify the interpretations they imply by justifying the linkages that give rise to them.

The associative potential of hypertext is one example of the ways in which electronic environments and poststructuralism complement each other, since the latter is founded in part upon a principle of inclusion, specifically of heretofore excluded elements, and the former provides almost limitless means for such inclusion. Any honest editor must look with a mixture of anticipation and dread upon the six hundred megabytes of tabula rasa that a compact disc provides. However, the tenets of poststructuralism do not require that we include everything. Applied to the discipline of textual editing, they do require that we declare our intentions as editors, that we recognize and elucidate our own prejudices, and that we logically justify the inclusions we choose to make. Rather than pretending to editorial invisibility, we should be straightforward in our declarations, both of the assumptions we make in regard to the forces that we believe have shaped the object text, and in regard to our expectations of reader response to the object text as we present it, and further, in regard to the structures we have created in anticipation of these responses. In this way the textual editor who works in an electronic environment becomes a poststructuralist reader.

HYPERTEXT AND RESIDUAL LINEARITY

By allowing escape from the context of a single documentary sequence, hypertext allows a reader to escape the linearity imposed by print media. This ease of escape, however, also makes it quite easy to lose track of the route of return; it becomes difficult to "back out" of a hypertext web. The vector principle tells us that having lost the direction from which we came, we have also lost the direction in which we were going. Disoriented, we are all too tempted to engage in that "blind following of interest along long and intricate paths" of which Hulme speaks. Yet this ability to follow associative linkages through myriad documents is one of the most exciting aspects of a hypertext system. What must be remembered, that is, what is incumbent upon the textual editor who constructs the pathways for these associative linkages to remember, is that in a series of hypertext "leaps" it is possible to change not only the reader's focus from one document to another, but also to change *the associative rationales that link one document to another.* A reader can become lost not only by failing to follow a logical sequence, but by failing to note a sequence of logics.

G. Thomas Tanselle argues more than once that the Center for Editions of American Authors (CEAA)[12] intended to produce editions with definitive apparatuses rather than definitive texts.[13] A definitive apparatus is one that contains all the information necessary to understand the structure by which the edition is assembled. Therefore, in theory, the edition might be deconstructed and then reconstructed according to some other principle.[14] The focus here upon a detailed explication, not of the textual material itself *but of the manner in which the material is assembled,* is relevant to the shift to electronic media specifically because the possibilities for assembling material are so greatly enhanced in electronic media.

If one subscribes, as I do, to the proposition that the linearity of print media is not wholly insidious, that, done right, it in fact promotes the concentration that Hulme argues will directly achieve the ends for which we read, then one would insist upon linearity of some sort in the hypertext editions that textual editors produce. What is possible, and in my view preferable, is a hypertext edition constructed of multiple linearities. And it is quite easy to conceive of an edition in which the primary linearity might not be the object text, but instead might be the explicative comment of the textual editor. The apparatus would in fact become narrative in form and serve as a primary text that would refer to an eclectic text (when necessary) and to the source documents from which the eclectic text (when necessary) was assembled. So conceived the apparatus would assume as its raison d'être a continual explication of the hyperstructure of the hypertext document.

What becomes important to the user of a document so constructed is the rationale by which the editor chooses and branches from a primary linearity. That rationale must be continually obvious in its presentation, either in a separate introduction, as a part of the apparatus, or, ideally, as an easily accessible "help" reference. In addition to being obvious in its presentation, the rationale should be obvious in its execution. Any hypertextual branching that occurs should be directed by the rationale established by the editor. In other words, there should be a general systematicity, based on an editorial orientation, that hovers over every associative linkage; further, those linkages should integrate smoothly. Here again is evidence of the aesthetic character of the textual editor's task. Edmund Burke argues in his aesthetic theory that there is a correlation between "smoothness" and aesthetic pleasure: "Succession and *uniformity* of parts are what constitute the artificial infinite."[15] A scholar or other user of the electronic edition will be able to traverse the linkages of any conceptual direction, that is, will be able to move easily through the "artificial infinite" of the system, if there is a uniform logic evident throughout the hypertext edition. If linkages are possible that are not based upon the editor's rationale, then a system of coding should be implemented by which the users will know when they are venturing outside of the structure imposed by the editor; users should always be made aware that they are "authoring" their own associations.

This schema may at first seem to fail to take advantage of the "free spirit" of electronic media, in that it requires a primary linearity, supported by and dominant in regard to other linearities, the entire edition consisting of a network of associations that exist in a systematic, sequential binding. To the contrary, however; it merely places the responsibility for the logic of the edition, constituted by the network of hypertextual associations, squarely upon the textual editor. Only within such a schema can the rigor of textual editing methodology that has been developed from McKerrow through Greg, Bowers, and Tanselle be maintained. And further, only if a user, particularly a scholarly user, is assured that such rigor has been employed in the construction of the edition can the free spirit of electronic media be useful, for only then can the manipulations of the edition, for whatever purpose, be said to arise from initial conditions that in their entirety constitute a verifiable proposition.[16]

In a recent work entitled *The Electronic Word: Democracy, Technology, and the Arts,* Richard Lanham argues that the advent of electronic media heralds a reinstitution of a rhetorical paideia as a method for seeking and discoursing upon types of knowledge.[17] His emphasis is upon *arrangement* as a functional constituent of rhetorical technique. He argues succinctly that electronic media facilitate arrangement; that is, multiple associative models are relatively easily constructed in electronic environments, particularly vis-à-vis print. But he goes further to argue that there is a close (and natural) fit between the functional capabilities of electronic media and the cognitive patterns of a rhetorical method. His description of rhetoric demonstrates the analogue:

> rhetoric—considered as an information system that functions economically, that allocates emphasis and attention—resembles what is now called, in many fields, a nonlinear system. That is, it is dynamic rather than static, a constantly changing emergence rather than a fixed entity; global rather than specialized into disciplines and constituent parts; a system that seeks to describe the confusion of everyday experience rather than narrowing it into a delimited, predictable field of study.[18]

There is much of Lanham's assessment with which we must agree. His description of the electronic media experience as a "bi-stable oscillation"[19] between rhetoric and philosophy, that is, between a phenomenological epistemology and a philosophically positivistic one, is exceptionally accurate for the great majority of users. However, I would point out that the unique mandate of the textual editor precludes in large measure an exploration of "the confusion of everyday experience," at least for the sake of the exploration itself. Rather, the textual editor is charged with "narrowing . . . into a delimited, predictable field" a body of material that might otherwise be either misleading or incomprehensible. When Lanham notes that for some literary professionals, "To volatilize text [which electronic media do] is to abolish the fixed 'edition' of the great work and so the authority of the great work itself,"[20] he is remarking upon a critical attitude that equates variation with literary imperfection. What electronic media do, rather than merely volatilize text, is allow the textual editor *to present variation within a context of authority,* that is, to explore the hermeneutic possibilities that variation embodies without thereby dismissing the concept of authority. This is both to take advantage of the rhetorical spirit of electronic media and, most important, to make meaningful statements that will support further discourse. Only in its initial stages does rhetoric resemble a nonlinear system. What emerges from rhetorical technique, if rhetoric is successful, is a comprehensibility based upon some type of traceable, and retraceable, logic, that is, upon some type of linearity. This is, in no disguise, argument. The pitfalls that electronic media present for textual editors consist of the myriad opportunities for digression, which if sufficiently indulged do indeed create the sort of dynamic, nonlinear, global system that is immensely gratifying perceptually, but effectively defeats analytic discourse. The answer, of course, is balance. Laurence Sterne, who demonstrated in *Tristam Shandy* that he is master of the technique, said of digressions that they "incontestably are the sunshine;—they are the life, the soul of reading."[21] But he also recognized that a digression depends upon a progression:

> I have constructed the main work and the adventitious parts of [*Tristam Shandy*] with such intersections, and have so complicated and involved the digressive and progressive movements, one wheel within another, that the whole machine, in general, has been kept a-going.[22]

A FINAL WORD ON HYPERTEXT AND ARISTOTLE

I am aware that Aristotle is not always good poststructuralist company; however, the type of hypertext document I have envisioned here reinstitutes the concept of Aristotelian argument in regard to the entire hypertext edition. As in an Aristotelian narrative, there is a straightforward, generalized statement that the edition makes. This statement is constituted by the relationships among the various aspects of the edition: object text, variants, historical material, biographical material, and any other supporting documents. But it is also constituted by the rationale established by the editor to connect and present all of these elements.

As I said at the outset, hypertext appears to free the reader, to make authors of readers in a way that is a step beyond the best hopes of print-literacy reader-response theory. Hypertext offers textual editors as well the opportunity to become "authors," not only as users but as creators of the associative linkages that constitute hypertext documents. I suggest that we might prepare ourselves for the responsibility of creating these systematic networks of associations by developing an awareness of agency in general, and a particular awareness of our own agency as textual editors. We can contribute to that awareness by becoming poststructuralist readers.

NOTES

1. T. E. Hulme, *Speculations: Essays on Humanism and the Philosophy of Art,* ed. Herbert Read, 2d ed. (London: Routledge and Kegan Paul, 1936), 224.
2. Hulme, *Speculations,* 41.
3. Ernst Cassirer, *Language and Myth,* trans. Susanne K. Langer (New York: Dover Publications, 1946), 32.
4. I presume Cassirer to use the term "theoretical" as A. J. Ayer uses the term "analytical" throughout *Language, Truth, and Logic* (New York: Dover Pub-

lications, 1946), that is, to refer to a tautological realm of logical systematicity (cf. 75ff. for a particular example).

5. Cassirer, *Language and Myth,* 59.
6. For an example of this defiance, cf. David H. Jonassen, *Hypertext/Hypermedia* (Englewood Cliffs, N.J.: Educational Technology Publications, 1989). The format of this book demonstrates how the print medium can effectively exploit paradigmatic reference, though at the expense of the semantics of the syntagm.
7. Jacques Derrida, *Writing and Difference,* trans. Alan Bass (Chicago: University of Chicago Press, 1978), 9.
8. My point here is to differentiate between a scholarly edition produced for CD-ROM and one produced for electronic publication through a network. The significance of this difference is that the former has a limited field of linkages, bounded by the material included on the CD, while the latter is limited only by the enormous number of potential linkages accessible by the network (e.g. in the World Wide Web accessible through the Internet). It should be noted, however, that conceptual limitations obtain even within a network environment (e.g., the discussion groups that adhere to particular topics).
9. Jerome J. McGann, "What Is Critical Editing?" in *The Textual Condition,* ed. Jerome J. McGann (Princeton: Princeton University Press, 1991), 52ff.
10. McGann, "What Is Critical Editing?" 191. McGann argues here in fact that textual editing as a discipline is fundamental to criticism: "Current interpretations of literary works only acquire a critical edge of significance when they are grounded in an exegesis of texts and meanings generated in the past—in an exegesis of texts and meanings gained, and perhaps also lost, over time. Such an exegesis depends for its existence on the tools and procedures of textual criticism." One can find analogies to McGann's idea of diachronic agency in Cassirer's discussion of human personality: "the mythic consciousness does not see human personality as something fixed and unchanging, but conceives every phase of a man's life as a new personality, a new self" (*Language and Myth,* 51). One might also find argument here for Hershel Parker's concept of textual versions based upon periods of creative activity. Cf. *Flawed Texts and Verbal Icons: Literary Authority in American Fiction* (Evanston, Ill.: Northwestern University Press, 1984).
11. One might notice here how, via the electronic medium, postmodern self-referentiality has made itself a constituent of textual critical methodology.
12. The Center for Scholarly Editions (CSE) succeeded the CEAA in 1976.
13. G. Thomas Tanselle, *Textual Criticism since Greg: A Chronicle, 1950–1985* (Charlottesville: University Press of Virginia, 1987), 30ff., 42.
14. Tanselle, *Textual Criticism since Greg,* 30ff.
15. Edmund Burke, *A Philosophical Enquiry into the Origin of Our Ideas of the Sublime and Beautiful,* ed. Charles W. Eliot (New York: P. F. Collier and Son, 1937), 63. Burke argued that we derive aesthetic pleasure from apprehending the infinite, and that the formal unity of a beautiful object gives the illusion of infinity.
16. I am here again using the language of A. J. Ayer, who argues that only if an assertion is in some manner a "verifiable proposition" can it be said to have

meaning. Ayer's epistemology does not refer to the limitations of the human mind, but to the limitations of the language in which we set down propositions pertaining to verifiable truth (*Language, Truth, and Logic,* 35). I would consider the generalized verifiable proposition of a scholarly edition, a critical edition, or even an archive to be something on the order of "This is the relevant material and this is the way it should be juxtaposed"; or, "This is the relevant material and this is the best text that can be assembled from it"; or "This is the legitimate extant material." In all of these instances an editor, working in whatever medium, is responsible for verifying the truth of the relevant proposition.

17. Richard A. Lanham, *The Electronic Word: Democracy, Technology, and the Arts* (Chicago: University of Chicago Press, 1993), 55.
18. Lanham, *The Electronic Word,* 61.
19. Lanham, *The Electronic Word,* 25.
20. Lanham, *The Electronic Word,* xi.
21. Laurence Sterne, *Tristam Shandy,* ed. Howard Anderson (New York: W. W. Norton, 1980), 52.
22. Sterne, *Tristam Shandy,* 52.

The Electronic Text and the Death of the Critical Edition

Charles L. Ross

In "The Death of the Author" Roland Barthes predicted that "the birth of the reader must be at the cost of the death of the Author."[1] I shall argue that the birth of the reader-as-editor must be at the cost of the death of the critical edition. I refer to the "critical edition" as promulgated by W. W. Greg and promoted by Fredson Bowers and G. Thomas Tanselle, and as institutionalized in Anglo-American editing by the Center for Editions of American Authors and its successor, the Committee for Scholarly Editions (CSE); that is, a codex book including both an eclectic text established on the principle of final authorial intention and a textual apparatus listing variants and emendations. The reading text of a critical edition, usually republished without accompanying textual apparatus, is a form of the text never seen by its author. This critical edition remains the reigning model and the chief recipient of CSE emblems.

The technology of the printed critical edition, however, has not kept pace with either literary theory or the needs of readers who want texts that reflect the processes of composition and that facilitate interpretive interactions. At present, such interaction is a hope raised but largely frustrated by the critical edition. Nevertheless, monumental printed editions, most recently of decopyrighted modernists, continue to be undertaken, absorbing the limited resources of foundations and university presses while driving publishers to strike deals with estates that may restrict, not expand, readers' resources. In recent years, for example, the Cambridge University Press has undertaken editions on Bowersian principles of the works of D. H. Lawrence, Joseph Conrad, and F. Scott Fitzgerald. That, however, is a story for a sociologist or historian of publishing, perhaps a latter-day Foucault.

My argument is simply that, in place of the critical edition's technology of presence, which aims to "restore" or "reconstruct" an author's final intentions, we need a technology of difference, by which the reader can create multiple texts. Electronic editing offers the reader a hitherto unavailable opportunity, not simply to check an editor's decisions in cases of emendation, but actually to rewrite a whole text or version on the screen of his or her personal computer.

First we must recognize that the printed critical edition is a prestructuralist form in a poststructuralist age. Consider its "spatial form." There are, as W. J. T. Mitchell has noted, a "wide variety of ways that time may be organized and represented through spatial form in literary works."[2] One way is the interplay between reading text and textual apparatus, which makes the critical edition "doubly centered."[3] Since time is inextricable from space, the alteration through emendation of a text's spatial relationships changes its temporal dimensions. As a consequence, the historical moment of the reader's engagement with the work becomes "mythic." For example, the reader of an eclectic text à la Bowers experiences elements of previously synchronic systems recombined according to a myth of the author's final intentions. (There can be different myths of authority, each interpretively constructed.) This myth of final intentions might be called the teleological imperative of the Anglo-American critical edition. An appended list of textual variants supposedly complements the mythical time of the reading text. Having been plucked from their original relationships in synchronic structures, variants are reassembled diachronically in the apparatus so as to allow the reader to "reconstruct" any of the historical versions previously disassembled—or, indeed, any other version the reader might wish to construct. It might be objected here that the variants of a single passage possesses a synchronic structure, in the sense that all versions of a work of fiction can be imagined as existing in a stack, like the layers of a cake or of an archaeological site. For the reader of a critical edition, the difficulty is to see that variants laid out chronologically should be treated synchronically. That is, the textual apparatus of a critical edition emphasizes the teleology of individual variants rather than their participation in synchronic systems or historical versions. In any case, this process of dismantling all versions of an author's work; then of reassembling a version according to the author's supposed "final" intentions; and, finally, of providing lists of variants with which the reader may *re*construct other texts of the work makes virtually impossible demands on the reader.

Editors of an Anglo-American critical edition typically encourage readers to consult the tables if they want to check a reading or perhaps reconstruct the text by emending a few readings. Examples of classes of readings may be identified to get the reader started. But the tables, in all their daunting complexity and heterogeneity, discourage anything beyond local or piecemeal changes. For example, the textual apparatus of the Cambridge edition of *The Rainbow*, occupying one-fifth of the book, mixes accidentals with substantives and doesn't distinguish between transmissive factors (e.g., revision vs. corruption).[4] As Hans Walter Gabler has observed, such lists "jumbl[e] together bulks of authorial and transmissional variants in unwieldy fragmentation" (197). Though the standard introduction of a critical edition gives a narrative of transmission, it also serves as the editor's brief for the privileged interpretation by which the text has been edited. This hermeneutic circle, together with the difficulty of using the apparatus for more than local substitutions, disguises the interpretive nature of editorial reconstructions and undermines the avowed goal of empowering readers to reconstruct alternative texts.

Consider, for example, the common practice of including readings from early manuscripts, that is, those predating the copytext, in the explanatory notes, usually with little or no commentary. Evidently the rejected or superseded variant should be kept in mind as somehow explaining the later reading that fulfilled the author's intentions. But a reader cannot judge intelligently whether an omitted variant is continuous with, or different from, its revision because the variant has been plucked from a version in which it had a holistic meaning. And neither that version nor other precopytext versions can be reconstructed from the textual apparatus. Finally, once the critical text is reprinted sans apparatus, its "doubly centered" rationale vanishes. The reader has been reduced once again to a passive consumer.

Recent trends in editing have signaled the demise of the Anglo-American critical edition and the imminent birth of electronic editing. For example, Gabler's "synoptic" text of *Ulysses*, hailed by Jerome McGann as the first "postmodern" critical text, actually reveals the printed book yearning for its electronic transformation.[5] Gabler imagines a "virtual manuscript" pieced together from multiple actual documents, whose text develops not simply through but "in the interstices, as it were, between the documents" (198—99). He then superimposes an apparatus of diacritics (brackets and sigla) on what he calls the "continuous manuscript text" so as to display synoptically its development (212).

Though theoretically an improvement on critical text and appended lists of variants, the synoptic text's visual presentation cannot fully demystify the complicated stages of composition. The synoptic presentation resembles a vertical cut through strata in an archaeological dig. This cut uncovers the "paradigmatic" or common linguistic elements of all versions but still cannot reveal the horizontal or "syntagmatic" meanings of any one unfolding text. Even if a reader masters the array of symbols on the page, he or she must proceed to piecemeal reconstructions of different versions, thereby distorting Joyce's practice of working on a scene or episode. Again, the technology of the book cannot do justice to the implied goal of simultaneously exposing compositional "levels" and permitting readerly reconstructions. The printed synoptic edition, like a printed critical edition, hampers both the editor's representation and the reader's performance.

A hypertext edition can resolve the ontological tensions within the printed critical edition. It is widely recognized that computer hypertext, in contrast to print, permits readers to perform all sorts of intertextual maneuvers—linking fictional texts in an author's oeuvre, networking texts and ancillary materials (sources, annotations, commentary), and collaborating with fellow reader/authors in the creation of texts. As George Landow observes, an editor working in hypertext can reshape authorial identity by redrawing or "blurring" the boundaries of the text.[6] The next logical step would seem to be *electronically layered texts* edited from data banks or archives by readers themselves.

Hypertext can activate the lists of variants, realizing the diachronic potential of the textual apparatus in interplay with the synchronic state of a text or version of a work. To accomplish this goal, however, there would have to be many ways of layering, each of which would be explicitly interpretive and readily altered on screen. Consider the following possibilities.

1. A version with all transmissive factors, including collaboration and possible or likely "corruptions" from the whole range of prepublication and postpublication materials (manuscripts through published editions)
2. A version emended by deleting certain transmissive factors (for example, changes made by collaborators or editors or amanuenses or compositors)

3. A version that retains revision spurred by "corruption," the author's response to "accidents" in transmission, or extemporaneous and performative readings
4. A version that expunges "revision" in sense 3 and that gives the author through the editor a second chance at the clean text the author was never presented in the first place
5. Historical versions with or without all the factors specified above.

And so on. It will become clear to readers that all the key words of the editor's trade—*corruption, collaboration,* even *fact*—are inescapably interpretive, and that what Stanley Fish claims for the scene of reading applies with even greater force to the scene of editing: "Interpretation is not the art of construing but the art of constructing. Interpreters do not decode poems: they make them."[7] It will become clear too that a text is a retrospective construction founded on "the author." According to Peter Shillingsburg, "The authorial orientation has been for thirty or more years the dominant one in American scholarly editing."[8] The trouble is that, textually speaking, authors are never more than "author-functions" invented to justify editorial decisions.[9] This remains true of even revisionist textual theories. Hans Walter Gabler, for example, displaces the author but then personifies the text: "With the eclipse of intention and authority as editorial lodestars, the sharp opposition of error and nonerror also wanes, and emendation assumes the nature of an informed and considered suggestion arising out of the potentialities of the text" (211). In any case, electronic editing won't do away with the author; on the contrary, it may even revive that oft-deconstructed concept, since it acknowledges openly the need for editors and readers to tell stories about their authors (or the "potentialities" of their texts) in a species of etiological mythmaking. We have the documents, but we can't make sense of them until we re-create their origins or authorities.

The raison d'être of hypertext editing, of course, is *interactivity.* But what sort of interactivity do we envisage? To enable editing by readers, an electronic archive must contain not only textual data marked by editors but also means for readers to substitute their own markup: to re-mark, regroup, or revalue linguistic units. Currently, hypertext allows readers to link the "linguistic code" of a text to ancillary texts, including "the bibliographical code" that, as Jerome McGann argues persuasively, is part of the meaning of any text.[10] Consider an analogy to the technology of an overhead projector, which allows a teacher to add or peel away levels of detail in a stack of transparencies. Reading a marked hypertext will resemble shuffling a stack of transparencies; the reader may choose an appropriate level of detail for the desired interpretive goal.

An electronic edition's introduction would contain instructions for creating different versions rather than a defense of a single reading text. While decentering the reading text, such editions will provide readers with an escape from the hermeneutic circle in which editors preparing documents inevitably labor. There could be *both* "default" texts based on the assumptions of the editors' "interpretive communities" *and* means for the reader to create further texts according to other assumptions. For instance, the reader would access both the paradigmatic (vertical) and syntagmatic (horizontal) levels of the text, add or delete various classes of transmissive factors, choose among variants, and thus create *a* (never *the*) text. All versions foreseen by editors or subsequently envisaged by readers will exist in a virtual electronic presence—a dialogic and polyphonic writing space.

We know that, paraphrasing Barthes, to give editing its future it is necessary to overthrow the myth of the critical edition. Yet it is important to realize what the death of the critical edition, the overturning of its myth, will *not* entail. It will not bring about the death of the author, as Barthes predicted, nor even of authorial intention as the basis of some texts or versions, nor, finally, of the book. The birth of the electronic reader will *not* be at the cost of the death of the Author. On the contrary, electronic editing will empower readers, whose interests Barthes proclaimed, to fulfill the author's intentions, which are usually multiple and always contested. Moreover, an electronic text will make the bibliographical code of texts come alive and, thereby, will enable the synergy of linguistic and bibliographical codes, presently available only to scholars in rare-book libraries, to be experienced by all readers. While preserving the bookishness of the book, electronic editing will clarify the interpretive basis of all editing of a textual archive. An electronic archive will yield a multiplicity of texts whose raisons d'être will have to be conceived anew by each reader on each (re)reading.

Electronic layering will permit readers to model and enact the theories they consider in literary and cultural studies. Readers will have a stake in the cultural products they collaboratively produce on their screens. Most liberating of all, electronic editing will forge collaborations between the hitherto distinct functions of author and reader, reader and writer, and reader and editor.

NOTES

1. Roland Barthes, "The Death of the Author," in *Image, Music, Text,* trans. Stephen Heath. (New York: Hill and Wang, 1977), 148.
2. W. J. T. Mitchell, "Spatial Form in Literature: Toward a General Theory," in *The Language of Images,* ed. W. J. T. Mitchell (Chicago: University of Chicago Press, 1980), 271–99.
3. Hans Walter Gabler, "On Textual Criticism and Editing: The Case of Joyce's *Ulysses,*" in *Palimpsest: Editorial Theory in the Humanities,* ed. George Bornstein and Ralph G. Williams (Ann Arbor: University of Michigan Press, 1993), 197.
4. D. H. Lawrence, *The Rainbow,* ed. Mark Kinkead-Weekes (Cambridge: Cambridge University Press, 1989).
5. Jerome McGann, "*Ulysses* as a Post-Modern Text: The Gabler Edition," *Criticism* 27 (1985): 283–306.
6. George Landow, *Hypertext: The Convergence of Contemporary Critical Theory and Technology* (Baltimore: Johns Hopkins University Press, 1992), 23.
7. Stanley Fish, *Is There a Text in This Class?* (Cambridge, Mass.: Harvard University Press, 1980), 327.
8. Peter Shillingsburg, *Scholarly Editing in the Computer Age: Theory and Practice,* rev. ed. (Athens: University of Georgia Press, 1986), 31.
9. Michel Foucault, "What Is an Author?" in *Contemporary Literary Criticism,* 3d ed., ed. Robert Con Davis and Ronald Schleifer (New York: Longman, 1994), 342–53.
10. Jerome McGann, *The Textual Condition* (Princeton: Princeton University Press, 1991).

Electronic Scholarship; or, Scholarly Publishing and the Public

John Unsworth

In a volume devoted largely to particular electronic projects in the humanities, I thought it might be useful to talk about the context in which this activity is taking place. I don't think we can understand the real importance of electronic scholarly editions—or our own responses to them—unless we see electronic scholarship in its larger cultural context. But that argument can't be made without at least sketching out what that context might be, so I ask you to bear with me while I do that: although it may not seem so at the outset, I eventually will come around from the general to the specific.

In many quarters of our profession, and among some of its immediate neighbors, the electronification of scholarly communication has become the occasion of more than a little anxiety over the past five or six years. This gradual but apparently inevitable change in the way we go about our business is affecting scholars and students in many different disciplines of the humanities and the sciences, as well as academic and commercial publishers, tenure committees, university administrators, MLA policymakers, private and government funding agencies, and librarians. The change that is taking place has profound implications, implications that are ethical and philosophical, economic, formal and generic, legal, and—sometimes overwhelmingly—practical and procedural.

Our responses to this change and its implications have covered the full range from despair to rejoicing, but for the most part they have focused on the local effects of the situation, rather than on understanding our circumstances as a limited and special case of a much more general shift in the culture as a whole. With few exceptions, academics have not successfully addressed the public on the more global effects of computers, networks, and electronic communication, and where they have, their discourse has generally fallen prey to the impulse to celebrate or to condemn the imagined, rather than to analyze or even extrapolate from the real. In the celebratory vein, academics and the mass market seem to have a shared interest in virtual reality, but what real analysis there has been on this topic has found it difficult to compete for public attention with the imaginary VR represented in movies, newsmagazines, and television shows—a VR that is largely vaporware and speculation. On the other hand, the elegy for vanishing values in an electronic age is a popular genre that academics and the tweedier pundits have had more or less to themselves. At another time, it would be worth discussing the public discourse on VR and its academic component, but it is the Arnoldian lament for culture in the age of the chip that is more immediately relevant to the topic at hand, because it is here that the defenders of traditional academic practices find themselves in strange collusion with both the traditional and the emergent enemies of intellectualism. I will argue that this particular resistance to change within the academy serves the interests of those who would like to see these new technologies integrated into current markets with the least possible alteration of the property system or the role of the consumer.

As an example of the academic resistance to change, I can think of no better example than Sven Birkerts. Birkerts is an academic and frequent reviewer of contemporary literature in the *New York Times Book Review* and the *Washington Post,* who writes on cultural issues in books such as *The Gutenberg Elegies* (from which I will quote in a moment), and who has found an audience in literary quarterlies like *New Letters* and *Parnassus,* in scholarly journals like the *Journal of Scholarly Publishing,* in upscale mass-market monthlies like the *New Republic* and *Harper's,*[1] and even in fashion magazines like *Mirabella.* Birkerts is an unreconstructed Platonist, untouched by the decades of deconstruction and, I suspect, unfettered by much experience with the digital age that he deplores. All of this would seem to make him a straw man, but I think there are many in the academy who share his views, and certainly there are many without who take him as a representative of the humanist perspective. In short, while he may not be an especially formidable disputant, he is a thoroughly representative one.

In an essay from *The Gutenberg Elegies* called "The Fate of Reading in an Electronic Age," Birkerts writes:

> My core fear is that we, as a culture, as a species, are becoming shallower; that we have turned from depth—from the Judeo-Chris-

> tian premise of unfathomable mystery—and are adapting ourselves to the ersatz security of a vast lateral connectedness. That we are giving up on wisdom, the struggle for which has for millennia been central to the very idea of culture, and that we are pledging instead to a faith in the web. What *is* our idea, our ideal, of wisdom these days? Who represents it? Who even invokes it? Our postmodern culture is a vast fabric of competing *isms;* we are leaderless and subject to the terrors, masked as freedoms, of an absolute relativism. It would be wrong to lay all the blame at the feet of technology, but more wrong to ignore the great transformative impact of new technological systems—to act as if it's all just business as usual.[2]

It is difficult to know where to begin with this, but perhaps the first thing to note is that, in this concluding moment of his essay, it is *fear* that is foregrounded. Specifically, Birkerts fears the decline of hierarchical Judeo-Christian mysteries and their replacement with "vast lateral connectedness." The unargued premise here is that wisdom of the mystical, private, and priestly sort "has for millennia been central to the very idea of culture"—followed by a leap to the conclusion that, in its absence, we are "leaderless" and "subject to . . . terrors, masked as freedoms." For Birkerts, the emblems of the new order are the web and the hive—symbols of instinctive and collective cultures, symbols associated with lower forms of life. Under the circumstances, the recent and very rapid deployment of the World Wide Web, that Internet-based system of vast, laterally connected hypertexts, no doubt seems to Birkerts a sign of the apocalypse, and Deleuze and Guattari's theorization of the hive its demonic scriptures.

I've begun with the end of Birkerts's essay, because this paragraph makes clear the ideological basis of his discussion: it's worth pointing out that the same ideology is the basis of the most common academic objections to scholarly work in the electronic medium. In discussions at various colleges and universities around the country, where I have gone to present the work of the Institute for Advanced Technology in the Humanities or to talk about the electronic journal *Postmodern Culture,* the same fears surface, often in strenuous arguments against the perceived technological threats of depersonalization, of inauthenticity, of subjugation to the mechanical, and perhaps most centrally, of the substitution of quantity for quality. When the subject is scholarship, the fear that predominates is the fear of pollution—the fear of losing our priestly status in the anarchic welter of unfiltered, unrefined voices. When the subject is teaching, the fear expressed is the fear of obsolescence—the fear that technology will deprive our students of the inestimable value of our presence in the classroom, or more bluntly, the fear that our presence will no longer be required. When the subject is the library, the fear expressed is the fear of disorientation—that we will lose our sense of the value of the past. In different ways, each of these core fears shares with Birkerts's own the quality of being based on the assumption that "we are becoming shallower," and that "lateral connectedness" comes at the expense of vertical distinctions. In a word, the common element is a fear that, as scholars, teachers, and human beings, we stand to lose our mysterious uniqueness—or, what comes to the same thing, that this uniqueness will no longer be honored—in the new technological landscape.

It is entirely appropriate, then, that Birkerts's essay as a whole addresses itself to Walter Benjamin's "The Work of Art in the Age of Mechanical Reproduction," and that his reading of this essay should be so . . . unique. Birkerts understands Benjamin to be objecting to the decline of the aura, and to be saddened by the replacement of that artifact of presence with the infinitely reduced authority of the infinitely reproducible. Birkerts himself wishes to extend these points in a discussion of the aura of the individual in daily life, and in particular he wants to ask "how that aura may be affected by the individual's engagement with various technologies" (108). Birkerts excuses Benjamin for not taking this step himself, explaining that this extension of his topic "may not have been as pressing for Benjamin as it is for us, because in his time the forces of mediation—the technologies abstracting and deflecting natural human interactions—had not yet attained critical mass" (109).

Of course, this is either a willful or a woeful misunderstanding of Benjamin, whose whole effort in the essay Birkerts cites is, and I quote, to "brush aside a number of outmoded concepts, such as creativity and genius, eternal value and mystery—concepts whose uncontrolled (and at present almost uncontrollable) application would lead to a processing of data in the Fascist sense."[3] Far from ignoring "the great transformative impact of new technological systems" on the lives of individuals, Benjamin undertakes to analyze this impact in a discussion that has much greater historical "depth" and practical "wisdom" than Birkerts's own. Benjamin writes,

> for the first time in world history, mechanical reproduction emancipates the work of art from its parasitical dependence on ritual. To an

> ever greater degree the work of art reproduced becomes the work of art designed for reproducibility. From a photographic negative, for example, one can make any number of prints; to ask for the "authentic" print makes no sense. But the instant the criterion of authenticity ceases to be applicable to artistic production, the total function of art is reversed. Instead of being based on ritual, it begins to be based on another practice—politics. (224)

For Benjamin, politics based on art is fascism, because it gives the masses the "right" to express themselves in place of their right to change power and property relations. Communism, for Benjamin, takes the opposite course and politicizes art, using it to demystify the "cult" in "culture" and to create broad awareness of political needs, rather than using its satisfactions as a substitute for political justice.

The conclusions that Birkerts draws from his misreading of Benjamin hinge on two unexamined logical premises: The minor premise is that the epistemological situation in which we find ourselves today, with respect to new technologies, is unique and unprecedented; the major premise is that, up until this recent crisis, human communication was essentially unmediated and therefore unproblematic. Birkerts writes:

> At any and every moment, our action, our emotional disposition, our thoughts, our will, all combine into what another person might experience as our presence. At earlier stages of history, before the advent of sense-extending technologies, human interactions were necessarily carried out face-to-face, presence-to-presence. Before the telephone and the megaphone, the furthest a voice could carry was the distance of a shout. We could say, then, that all human communication is founded in presence. There was originally no severance between the person and the communication. (111)

I don't know what, in Birkerts's opinion, intervened between grunting around the campfire and gabbing on the cellphone, but his history seems telescopically primal, to say the least. Where does writing fit in this history? Does it count (and why wouldn't it?) as a "sense-extending technology"? It's remarkable, really, that this paragraph could be written in the 1990s: whether or not one agrees with Derrida's analyses of the sign, of the metaphysics of presence, of dissemination, it is remarkable that one could simply ignore them. It's been nearly twenty-five years since "Signature

Event Context," where, in a section called "Writing and Telecommunication," Derrida argued—rather persuasively, many people thought—not only that it is wrong to think of writing as a supplement to communication in person, a supplement to presence, but further that writing, and all other forms of signification including speech, are based in the presumption of absence, and therefore are independent from the context of production and from the authority of the producer. As Derrida points out, this is the substance of Plato's indictment of writing, in the *Phaedrus,* and this is why I call Birkerts an unreconstructed Platonist, even though he seems not to recognize that the diminution of aura he thinks is a consequence of new technologies was attributed, millennia ago, to the Fall from speech into writing.

At present, though, what's more pertinent is the fact that the sort of reasoning in which Birkerts engages contributes, wittingly or not, to the marginalization of the humanities and thereby helps to clear the field for the subjugation of these new technologies to the system of power and property relations that, up until now, has characterized contemporary mass media. The discipline of the humanities, at least since the nineteenth century, has found itself in much the same position as modern art—not quite to the extent of adopting what Benjamin calls the "negative theology . . . of pure art" in which any social function is denied, but at least to the extent of defining itself in opposition to the grinding imperatives of business, of financial profitability, of "usefulness" in the philistine sense. For most of the last one hundred years, in ways variously adapted to the temper of the times and the fashions of the academy, we have defined ourselves as keepers of the flame, as guardians of values little honored in the marketplace. In fact, we cherish our abnormality, our resistance to the pragmatic demands of the world, our uselessness. And we're not the only ones who have this idea of what we're about: the rest of the world, when it bothers to think of us, largely shares this view, albeit with some difference in valuative emphasis. So when the enlightened mass-market magazines go looking for a humanist commentary on the influx of technology into our culture, it will be the self-marginalizing jeremiad of someone like Birkerts that they will look for and find, whether or not it has any basis in fact, any sense of history, any wisdom—in short, whether or not it has any of the qualities it claims we have lost.

In fact, the most revolutionary aspect of networked communication is not that they deprive us of presence—a presence we lost long ago, if indeed we ever enjoyed it at all—but rather that it makes it possible for us to present ourselves to one another in much more immediate, more elective, and more productive ways. If we were to evaluate the various "sense-extending technologies" according to their economies of communication, we would find that, up until the advent of computer networks, these technologies fell into one of two categories: one-to-one and one-to-many communication. Manuscript writing, speech, the telegraph, and the telephone are all examples of one-to-one communications—granted that in some cases, they might be more accurately called one-to-a-few, still their essential character is person to person. Print, television, movies, and radio—the technologies of broadcasting—are one-to-many technologies: notwithstanding the fact that the content communicated may have been produced by many hands, it emanates from one point and is inherently designed to be received, in a one-way transaction, at many different sites. In contrast to all of these, computer networks offer many-to-many communication, multicasting instead of broadcasting.

The democratization of access and the freedom of examination that Benjamin recognized as a feature of mechanical reproduction are also dramatically increased on the network. While it is true that the penetration of computer technology into our culture is taking place along class lines, it is also true that entry-level equipment costs a tenth of what it did five years ago, in real terms, and the computer is rapidly absorbing other household technologies such as the television, the video deck, the answering machine, and the fax. And finally, it is worth considering that the sole imperative of our economy seems to be that we must have access to information—or, if you prefer, we must be accessible to information—whether we want it or not. Early in his essay, Benjamin quotes Paul Valéry's prediction, circa 1934, that "Just as water, gas, and electricity are brought into our houses from far off to satisfy our needs in response to a minimal effort, so we shall be supplied with visual or auditory images, which will appear and disappear at a simple movement of the hand, hardly more than a sign."[4] It is a matter of some moment, though, whether the hand in this scenario holds a remote control or a mouse. If it is a remote control, then we can expect a sort of Nick at Night future—*Leave It to Beaver* on demand. If it's a mouse, we might hope for something better, and we might hope that the consumer will, *at* will, be able to become a producer. Fiske and the Birmingham school notwithstanding, there is a vast difference between the productiveness of the average television viewer and the productiveness of the average netizen.

This brings me, at last, to the question of electronic scholarship—or rather, at last, to the discussion of its possibilities rather than the refutation of our fears. I think we can expect that, whatever happens in the larger cultural sphere, electronic scholarly editions will alter the course of our profession in significant ways. The disciplines' emphasis on theory over the last two decades will not disappear—after all, electronic forms and practices offer a new field of opportunities for theorizing signification, communication, literature, and culture—but we can expect to see increasing interest in editing (including the theory of editing), in bibliographic and textual scholarship, in history, and in linguistic analysis, since these are areas in which the new technology opens up the possibility of re-creating the basic resources of all our activities and providing us with revolutionary tools for working with those resources. In effect, we have at least a generation's worth of work to do, and probably much more, in reinventing our libraries, preserving physical ephemera, creating new research archives, and revamping our modes of scholarly communication.

Already, scholarly exchange takes place at all levels of the network, from the trivial and ephemeral to the highly filtered and presumably durable. In real-time chat sessions, person-to-person e-mail, networked discussion groups, newsletters, peer-reviewed journals, multimedia databases, and any number of other forms, the network has, for scholars, begun to organize itself into a sort of pyramid: there's a great deal of mostly unfiltered stuff at the base, a smaller amount of more specialized but still fairly conversational discussion in the middle, and an even smaller amount of tightly constructed, highly filtered material at the top. And rather than having to choose one or the other of these levels, most of us participate in all of them at one point or another. Indeed, for many of us, annual conferences are becoming the supplement to our disembodied conversations during the rest of the year—the time when we meet each other, sometimes for the first time—and usually feel a little strange about reconciling the physical presence with the networked one. I venture that each of the scholarly projects discussed in this volume has had its genesis and much of its incubation in the usually informal, collaborative atmosphere of the Internet. As for presence, any participant in a networked discussion group will testify that personality and personal presence are, if anything, amplified in that medium.

But even at its more formal, more filtered levels, electronic scholarly communication still retains the quality of making present that which was hitherto remote, difficult to access, and generally impossible to recontextualize. Each of the projects discussed in this volume, for example, permits the individual scholar, the teacher, the student to have a near-firsthand experience of manuscripts formerly available only to the few, and only to one person at a time. It becomes clear, in this context, that the conservative defense of presence is in fact a defense of exclusivity, especially when one considers that the availability of a digital reproduction does not in any way render the original any less available, to those who seek it.

In addition to making primary materials more accessible to a broader audience, electronic editions have, at least potentially, the disturbing quality of open-endedness, of extensibility, and of collectivity. Because digital presentation makes it possible to add to what exists without continually reproducing the base, electronic editions are very likely to set for themselves a larger scope than one would take on in any print work; in many cases, this will mean that the project must be carried out by many hands, may be deliberately left open to connection with related databases, and probably will continue to grow long after the project's originator has passed on to other things, or has simply passed on. For the purposes of this discussion, the most interesting of those possibilities is the first, especially since the electronic archive has the potential to be added to by its users. To take a concrete and current example, the Civil War archive under construction at the Institute for Advanced Technology in the Humanities, under the direction of Ed Ayers, accepts (and screens, and edits) contributions from the public. Beginning as a research archive, it has developed into a museum installation where interested members of the public may come to browse the archive, but may also bring pertinent materials from their own family collections to contribute to the archive, scanning them in at the museum and then taking the artifact home. In addition, we are currently developing a means for users of the archive to cull information from the archive—on a particular person, date, site, event, or other topic of interest—and to contribute that collection to the archive itself, albeit subject to the scrutiny of the archive's editorial management. The archive is also connected to other relevant projects on the network, such as the Smithsonian's on-line collection of Matthew Brady photographs and, in the near future, to a specially curated digital exhibition of Civil War–era American art, also at the Smithsonian. The significance of this project, then, is not only that it offers a practically infinite lateral connectedness with other archives, but also that it has a kind of vertical porousness that allows the individual user to become a contributor.

Here, then, is a model of interactivity that doesn't fit well into the broadcast architecture, and that implies a role for the user that is far more foreign to the model of broadcast communication than are video on demand or interactive home shopping, the two most frequently cited applications of the emerging national information infrastructure. Video on demand and home shopping not only fit well into the current market system and require no alteration whatsoever in the role of the consumer; they also imply a certain kind of network architecture, with high bandwidth into the home and low bandwidth out of it. And among those who will plan, implement, and finance that information infrastructure, the defense of humanistic values over against the electronification of culture serves the ironic purpose of ensuring that the demand for something more than canned video will not have to be met in the marketplace, but will be safely contained in the university, where mystical presence can be meted out in the traditional quantities of the handmade.

In a fine and intelligent essay called "A Potency of Life: Scholarship in an Electronic Age," Willard McCarty—one of the true pioneers of electronic scholarship—notes that

> what we can observe so far suggests that the assimilation of the computer is following what I take to be a common path for a new technology: first, in the imitative phase, it tends to be used as if it were merely an improvement upon and replacement for what is already known; then, after some time, we begin to see it as genuinely new, and to realize that its newness alters how we think about the world.[5]

Finally, for me, this is the most important point: we have an opportunity to alter how we think about the world—in particular, to alter the relationship between the academy and the marketplace, between the scholar and the public, between the author and the reader. This opportunity is not itself open-ended, by any means, and there are many familiar reasons for not even considering it: we don't imagine ourselves as doing things that interest the public, and we're not sure we want to interest them; on the other hand, we're quite sure that doing so will put us, our publishers, and our standards at some considerable risk. Even if we do produce electronic editions, the very idea of publishing those archives on the network will raise the hackles of those who own the materials we wish to collect and whose permission we must receive. There is no rule, no teleology, that says we must move entirely beyond the imitative phase in our adoption of this technology, nor one that says thinking about the world in a new way must result in a different world. The concerns I've just cited are real issues, real obstacles; however, they are also surmountable, and I do think that some restructuring of our professional and contractual habits is, eventually, inevitable. What's also inevitable, though, is that this restructuring, proceeding as slowly as it has been, will result in little more than a new arrangement of timbers on the existing foundation.

NOTES

1. A portion of *The Gutenberg Elegies,* including the paragraph that sketches out Birkerts's "core fear," was the lead piece in the "Readings" section of the May 1994 issue of *Harper's*—followed by an excerpt from Kevin Kelly's *Out of Control: The Rise of Neo-Biological Civilization.* Kelly is executive editor of *Wired* magazine. In "Readings," the section was titled "The Electronic Hive: Two Views." Letters from Robert Coover, John Perry Barlow, and others followed, in the August 1994 issue of *Harper's.*
2. Sven Birkerts, "The Fate of Reading in an Electronic Age," *New Letters* 60, no. 4 (1994): 111–12. Subsequent references to Birkerts are to this printing of the essay and are given in the text.
3. Walter Benjamin, "The Work of Art in the Age of Mechanical Reproduction," in *Illuminations,* ed. Hannah Arendt, trans. Harry Zohn (New York: Harcourt, Brace and World, 1968), 218.
4. *Pièces sur l'Art,* 226; qtd. in Benjamin, *Illuminations,* 219.
5. Willard McCarty, "A Potency of Life: Scholarship in an Electronic Age," *Serials Librarian* 23, nos. 3–4 (1993): 80–81.

Afterword

A. Walton Litz

When scholars in the humanities first began to use the mainframe and later the personal computer, in the 1970s and 1980s, it was generally assumed that the computer would enable them to perform the conventional scholarly tasks with greater accuracy and far greater speed. Letters of recommendation could be revised without tedious retyping; concordances could be generated quickly and precisely; that staple of traditional Greg/Bowers editing, the textual variant, could be stored and recaptured much more efficiently. Like the photocopying machine, the computer would simply improve traditional methods.

Over the last decade, however, scholars engaged in editing have discovered that electronic resources have profoundly altered many of our conceptions of the editor's function and have changed or reinforced new ideas about authorship, reading, the very nature of the text. The essays in this volume, which represent a stunning variety of problems and approaches, testify to the fluidity of the field and the exciting possibilities that lie ahead.

On first reading, the essays—with their widely different subjects—may appear to be miscellaneous, but there are several major assumptions—sometimes implied, often clearly stated—that bind them together. One common denominator is technical: in such a fast-changing field, any electronic editing project must be independent of particular hardware and word processing programs. The answer for the moment seems to lie in SGML (Standard Generalized Markup Language), which can be adapted to future changes in hardware and software. The electronic text must be able to endure as the classic print editions have endured.

Another common denominator is the growing awareness of what

Jerome McGann calls the "bibliographic code," as opposed to the "linguistic code" that is the language of traditional print editions. Not only can the computer record textual variants and accidentals; it can empower the editor to record layout, physical appearance, and printing history—the stuff from which social history is formed.

At a deeper reach, all these essays take it for granted that electronic editing is tightly bound up with recent developments in literary theory that emphasize the unpredictable productivity of language, the instability of the text, and the ambiguities of authorial intention. It is hard to imagine, for example, a New Critic devoted to organic unity wanting to produce the "continuous manuscript text" that is the foundation of Hans Gabler's synoptic edition of *Ulysses*. Literary theory and editorial practice have intersected over the last few years, and editing has suddenly become an exciting field where theory is tested against the practical demands of presenting a particular work. Rather than using the loaded terms *postmodernism* or *poststructuralism,* I would like to think of contemporary electronic editing as another form of criticism where theory and practice meet and challenge each other.

Since I am not an expert in the use of electronic resources but have done a great deal of editing over the past twenty years, I would like to meditate briefly on how my scholarship and teaching of those years would have been different if I had been able to use some of the methods described in this volume. The most profound impact would have been on the edition *The Collected Poems of William Carlos Williams* that Christopher MacGowan and I produced in the early 1980s. Williams was one of the first of many modern poets to compose on the typewriter (he began around 1916), and this method of composition enabled him to control the visual appearance of the page. Spacing, indentation, and alignment of words could all become part of his poetic. In effect, the typewriter restored to Williams some of the freedoms exercised by the pre-Gutenberg scribes. In recording the many changes that Williams made in reprinting his poems, alterations in format are just as important as verbal revisions. We had to confess in our "Note on the Text" that traditional methods of annotation made it impossible for us to record all the complexities of "variants in lineation and format." Instead we chose to reprint in the notes full versions of the poems that differed significantly in format from the copytext. If we were repeating our work ten years later, we would of course use the wonders of electronic editing to record every change in physical appearance. Williams believed in the "bibliographic code" as part of his poetic;

often there are "rhymes" achieved through visual alignment rather than sound. I cannot think of any modern poet who would profit more from the new powers of electronic editing.

Turning now to both my scholarship and my teaching, hypertext editions of the great modern epics would have been invaluable. Joyce's *Ulysses,* Pound's *Cantos,* Williams' *Paterson:* works such as these are essentially hypertexts in print. Allusions in the first episode of *Ulysses* are sometimes not clear until we have reached much later episodes; obscure references in the early cantos become plain when we encounter a more explicit reference, or even a full translation, later in Pound's great poem "containing history." The same is true of much modern fiction: the first section of Faulkner's *The Sound and the Fury,* Benjy's disjointed interior monologue, can only be fully sorted out when we have reached the end of the novel. What all these writers are demanding is that we read their works both linearly and spatially, that we hold everything in memory so that on second reading, or in retrospect, the book forms a vast pictorial image. In an early review of Cocteau's poetry that has never been reprinted (*Dial,* Jan. 1921), Ezra Pound argued that traditional writing was like a village, a collection of linear narratives; by contrast, modern writing was often like a city, where you can move about in many directions. "In a city the visual impressions succeed each other, overlap, over-cross, they are 'cinematographic,' but they are not a simple linear sequence." Hypertext editions of many modern works would be, in effect, handmaidens to Memory, the mother of all the Muses. They would be of immense value to readers and critics of modern writing.

When I think of my students and their needs, I have more ambiguous feelings about the impact of CD-ROM storage and hypertext programs. I want the students to have access to all the information these methods can provide, but I don't want them to become passive consumers; most of all, I don't want their interpretations of poems and novels to be controlled by the electronic editor, who can so easily do this through the selection and slanting of annotations. The hypertext version of Yeats's "Lapis Lazuli," a token of what we may find in the forthcoming hypertext Yeats, is a case in point. I have seen a demonstration of this poem on hypertext, and the possibilities are spectacular. The student can hear the poem read by an Irish actor; learn about Harry Clifton, to whom it is dedicated; actually see a photograph of the piece of carved lapis lazuli that Clifton gave to Yeats and that provides the imagery for the poem's dramatic close. William H. O'Donnell has chosen his glosses with great tact, but I can easily imagine another editor who might include more interpretative materials, thereby fixing the student's view of the poem and—worse still—leading the student to believe that nothing relevant to "Lapis Lazuli" lies outside the computer screen.

I think the key to making an electronic archive that will be of great use to the student, but not place restrictions on the student's freedom to seek new information or different interpretations, is nonintervention on the part of the editor. The electronic archive should be the equivalent of an extended visit to the relevant special collections of a great research library. I recently saw a demonstration of an electronic F. Scott Fitzgerald archive that allayed all of my worries. It contains all of Fitzgerald's manuscripts and typescripts, many relevant photographs and drawings, and a vast amount of correspondence. In effect the student is given open access to the great Fitzgerald collection in the Princeton University Library, and can use the menu to browse through that collection in any direction. Such an archive exploits all the powers of electronic editing without imposing any particular way of reading on the passive student.

In short, my scholarly life would have been a great deal more productive, and my teaching more effective, if I had been gifted in 1980 with the remarkable variety of realities and possibilities documented in these essays. They provide in convincing detail what Ibsen once called "a history of the future."

Contributors

Phillip E. Doss, doctoral candidate in English, University of Texas at Arlington.

Hoyt N. Duggan, Professor of English, University of Virginia.

Richard J. Finneran, Hodges Chair of Excellence Professor of English, University of Tennessee.

Simon Gatrell, Professor of English, University of Georgia.

Susan Hockey, Director, Center for Electronic Texts in the Humanities, Rutgers and Princeton Universities.

Ian Lancashire, Professor of English and Director, Center for Computing in the Humanities, New College, University of Toronto.

John Lavagnino, Textual Analyst, Women Writers Project, Brown University.

A. Walton Litz, Holmes Professor of Literature, Emeritus, Princeton University.

Jerome McGann, John Stewart Bryan Professor of English, University of Virginia.

William H. O'Donnell, Professor of English, University of Memphis.

Peter M. W. Robinson, Senior Research Fellow, International Institute for Electronic Library Research, De Montfort University.

Charles L. Ross, Professor of English, University of Hartford.

Peter L. Shillingsburg, Professor of English, Mississippi State University.

C. M. Sperberg-McQueen, Senior Research Programmer, Academic Computer Center, University of Illinois at Chicago.

Emily A. Thrush, Associate Professor of English, University of Memphis.

John Unsworth, Associate Professor of English and Director, Institute for Advanced Technology in the Humanities, University of Virginia.